Seeratul Mujtabaa ﷺ

(Selected Chapters from Seeratul Mustafaa)

Biography of the Chosen Messenger of Allah,
Nabi Muhammad Mujtabaa ﷺ

Writings of:
Hadhrat Moulana Muhammad Idrees Kaandhlawi (Rahimahullah)

Title: SEERATUL MUJTABAA

Compiled by:

Jamiatul Ulama (KZN)
Ta'limi Board
4 Third Avenue
P.O.Box 26024
Isipingo Beach
4115
South Africa

Tel: (+27) 31 912 2172
E-mail: info@talimiboardkzn.org
Website: talimiboardkzn.org

First Edition   Shawwaal 1442 / June 2021

Published By:

Islamic Book Store
Gujarat (India)

Contents

Introduction i

Chapter 1 Before Nubuwat 1

Chapter 2 The Mubaarak birth of Rasulullah ﷺ 7

Chapter 3 Prophethood 20

Chapter 4 The First Muslims 24

Chapter 5 The Spread of Islam 33

Chapter 6 Bitter Enemies 39

Chapter 7 Punishing the Poor Muslims 43

Chapter 8 Miracles of Rasulullah ﷺ 49

Chapter 9 First Migration to Abyssinia 51

Chapter 10 Mi'raaj 66

Chapter 11 Invitation to Islam during the days of Haj 75

Chapter 12 Moving to Madinah Munawwarah 83

Chapter 13 Battle of Badr 102

Chapter 14 Battle of Uhud 123

Chapter 15 Incident of Raj'ee 146

Chapter 16 The Story of Bi'r Ma'unah 151

Chapter 17 Battle of Khandaq (Trench) 158

Chapter 18 Hudaybiyyah 167

Chapter 19 Invitation letters to the kings of the world 180

Chapter 20 Battle of Khaybar 191

Chapter 21 Battle of Muta 200

Chapter 22 Conquest of Makkah 206

Chapter 23 Battle of Hunayn 225

Chapter 24 Battle of Tabuk 230

Chapter 25 Hajjatul Wadaa (The Farewell Haj) 236

Chapter 26 Preparation for the Journey to the Aakhirat 239

Chapter 27 The beautiful Features of Rasulullah ﷺ 256

Conclusion 260

INTRODUCTION

Studying the life of Sayyiduna Rasulullah ﷺ is the duty of every Muslim. One who says the kalimah Laailaaha illallah Muhammadur Rasulullah has to believe in Nabi Muhammad ﷺ. Together with believing in him, we also have to love him and one can certainly embed deep rooted love for Rasulullah ﷺ by reading his biography and learning how he lived his noble life.

Among the many books of Seerah, Allah Ta'ala has blessed the book titled "Seeratul Mustafa" ﷺ with great acceptance. This book was written by the great Muhaddith, Hadhrat Moulana Idrees Kaandhlawi (rahimahullah). May Allah Ta'ala reward the author abundantly and fill his grave with noor for having prepared such a masterpiece on the mubaarak life of Rasulullah ﷺ.

There was a need for younger children to also study and learn the mubaarak life of Rasulullah ﷺ. Although there are many books prepared on this topic, but reading it in the words of our pious Ulama has a different effect on the heart. Hence, an effort was made to further simplify this book and bring it onto the level of a child. Thus, it is by the grace of Allah Ta'ala and the duas of our elders that this task has been completed. May Allah Ta'ala accept this humble effort and make it a means of attaining His pleasure as well as the closeness of our beloved Nabi Muhammad ﷺ. *Aameen.*

This book has been titled Seeratul Mujtabaa which also means "The life of the chosen messenger ﷺ".

$$رَبَّنَا تَقَبَّلْ مِنَّا اِنَّكَ اَنْتَ السَّمِيْعُ الْعَلِيْمُ وَتُبْ عَلَيْنَا$$

$$اِنَّكَ اَنْتَ التَّوَّابُ الرَّحِيْمُ$$

CHAPTER 1
BEFORE NUBUWAT

LINEAGE

Allah Ta'ala says in the Qur-aan Shareef:

$$\text{لَقَدْ جَآءَكُمْ رَسُوْلٌ مِّنْ اَنْفُسِكُمْ}$$

"Certainly a messenger has come to you from the best amongst yourselves....."

A prophet of Allah has come to you from amongst your most noble and virtuous families. Rasulullah ﷺ said: "In terms of family lineage, I am the most noble and best of you."

The family of Rasulullah ﷺ is the most noble in the world. This golden lineage is:

Muhammad ﷺ bin (the son of) Abdullah bin Abdul Muttalib bin Haashim bin Abdu Manaaf bin Qusay bin Kilaab bin Murrah bin K'ab bin Luwayy bin Ghaalib bin Fihr bin Maalik bin Nadr bin Kinaanah bin Khuzaimah bin Mudrikah bin Ilyaas bin Mudar bin Nizaar bin Ma'ad bin Adnaan.

Abdul Muttalib, the Grandfather of Rasulullah ﷺ

Before discussing the life of Rasulullah ﷺ, we will first discuss some incidents that took place in the lives of the people before Rasulullah ﷺ.

Nabi ﷺ was an Arab and born from the family of Hadhrat Ismaeel عَلَيْهِ السَّلَام. Many years ago the Banu Jurhum tribe was living in Makkah Mukarramah in the time of Hadhrat Ismaeel عَلَيْهِ السَّلَام. Due to a fight that they had with other tribes living there, they left Makkah Mukarramah. However, as they were leaving, they buried some of the ruins of the K'abah Shareef in the well of Zam Zam, filled sand into it and brought its level to the ground so that no sign of the well could be seen. As time went on, the well was totally forgotten about.

When Makkah Mukarramah was ruled by Abdul Muttalib, the grandfather of Rasulullah ﷺ, Allah Ta'ala decided that the well which had been totally forgotten should now be brought back, Abdul Muttalib was ordered through pious dreams to dig up the area of the well. Clear markings and clues pointing out the area of the well were also shown to him in a dream. Abdul Muttalib himself says: "I was once asleep in the Hateem area when a person came up to me in a dream and instructed me to dig up Zam Zam.' I asked: 'What is Zam Zam?' He replied: 'It is a well whose water does not run dry or decrease in amount and it provides thousands of Haajis with drinking water.' He then went on to point out a few spots showing me where I should dig."

Seeing the dream over and over again convinced Abdul Muttalib that this is a true dream. He told the Quraysh of his dream and told them of his decision to dig up a certain point of the Haram Shareef. The Quraysh opposed him but he was not worried about them. Taking his pick and spade, he set out with his son Haaris and started digging at the spot. Abdul Muttalib would go on digging whilst Haaris would scoop up and remove the sand. On the third day, he found a deep hole. Out of pure joy, he shouted out saying "Allahu Akbar, Allahu Akbar!" He then happily said, "This is the well of Ismaeel"

Abdul Muttalib then built a few ponds close to the well of Zam Zam. He would fill these ponds with Zam Zam water and provide it to the people who came for Haj.

Abdullah, the Honourable Father of Rasulullah ﷺ

Abdullah, the son of Abdul Muttalib was the honourable father of Rasulullah ﷺ. Abdul Muttalib sent a marriage proposal on behalf of his son Abdullah for the hand of a young lady by the name of Aaminah. She was living at that time with her uncle.

Abdul Muttalib left with his son Abdullah for the nikah and got him married to Aamina. After the Nikah, Abdullah stayed with his wife Aamina for three days and then set out on a business journey with a caravan for Syria. While returning he fell ill and was forced to break the journey in Madinah Munawwarah. The moment the caravan arrived in Makkah Mukarramah, Abdul Muttalib asked for Abdullah. The travelers informed him that due to ill health, Abdullah decided to stop over at his mother's family, in Madinah Munawwarah. Without delay, Abdul Muttalib sent his elder son Haaris to Madinah Munawwarah. On reaching Madinah, he discovered that Abdullah had already passed away. He was ill for almost a month and was buried in Madinah Munawwarah. Haaris returned to Makkah Mukarramah informing Abdul Muttalib and his other relatives of this terrible news. This put them all into a state of sadness and sorrow. Rasulullah ﷺ was still in his mother's womb when his father Abdullah passed away. At the time of his death, Abdullah was eighteen years old. He left behind five camels, a few goats and a slave girl by the name of Barakah who was known as Umm-e-Ayman.

Incident of the Elephants

Fifty days before the birth of Rasulullah ﷺ, the incident of the elephants took place. The incident is as follows: Abrahah, the governor of Yemen noticed the Arabs travelling to Makkah Mukarramah to perform Tawaaf of the Ka'bah. He also decided to build a huge building in the name of Christianity so that the Arabs may leave the simple Ka'bah and make tawaaf of his fake Ka'bah instead. He therefore built a beautiful church in the capital city of Sanaa.

When the Arabs heard of this, one person spoilt the building by passing stool in it. He then escaped from there. Some are of the opinion that a few Arab youngsters lit a fire close to the church. A gust of wind carried the fire onto the wooden structure of the church setting it alight and burnning it to ashes. This made Abrahah very angry and he promised that he would not rest until he destroyed the Ka'bah Shareef. With this evil intention, he set out to attack Makkah Shareef. En-route to Makkah Mukarramah, the tribes who tried to stop him were destroyed with the might of his sword. Together with his terrifying army of men, he also took a herd of huge elephants. The camels of the Makkans were grazing just ouside Makkah Mukarramah. Abrahah's army stole all the grazing animals, which also included 200 camels belonging to Rasulullah's ﷺ grandfather, Abdul Muttalib. At that time, Abdul Muttalib was the leader of the Quraysh and in charge of the Ka'bah Shareef. When he came to know of Abrahah's wicked intention, he gathered the Quraysh asking them to remain calm. "Do not worry," he advised, "Leave Makkah, nobody will be able to destroy the Ka'bah. This is the house of Allah Ta'ala and He will protect it."

Together with a few leaders of the Quraysh, Abdul Muttalib set out to meet Abrahah who welcomed Abdul Muttalib politely and walmly. Allah Ta'ala had blessed Abdul Muttalib with lots of beauty and respect that amazed all those who saw him. Abrahah was also amazed when he saw Abdul Muttalib. Therefore he welcomed him with total respect and honour. He even came down from his throne out of respect for Abdul Muttalib. Abdul Muttalib asked Abrahah to return his camels which had been stolen by his army. Shocked by this request, Abrahah said: "It is quite shocking to hear you asking for your camels but I see that you have not mentioned a word about the Ka'bah, which is the main part of the Deen of your forefathers." Abdul Muttalib calmly replied: "I am the owner of the camels whilst the owner of the house (K'abah) is someone else and He will take care of it." In other words, I am the owner of the camels. This is why I have asked for them but the owner of the Ka'bah Shareef is Allah Ta'ala and He will look after it. After a few moments of silence, Abrahah returned all the camels. Abdul Muttalib returned to his people and asked them to leave Makkah Mukarramah. He promised to sacrifice all 200 camels for Allah Ta'ala to protect the K'abah Shareef. He then took a few people to the door of the K'abah Shareef and cried out to Allah Ta'ala making dua in the following words, "O Allah! A man takes care of his house. You take care of Your house. Help Your people against the people of the cross and its worshippers. Their cross and their plans will never overpower Your plans. They brought all their forces and their elephants to capture Your people. Out of ignorance they have come to break Your house with their evil plans but they do not understand Your greatness."

Then, Abdul Muttalib, together with his people, climbed the mountain leaving Makkah Mukarramah empty for Abrahah and his army. As Abrahah moved ahead to destroy the K'abah Shareef, suddenly huge flocks of small birds appeared. Each one of them had pebbles in its beak and claws. Without any warning, with the power of Allah Ta'ala, these pebbles rained down upon this army like bullets. A pebble would strike the head of a soldier pass right through him and come out from his bottom. Whoever was struck by these pebbles would die immediately. This is how Abrahah's army was completely destroyed. Abrahah's whole body was covered with wounds, which left his body rotting with pus and blood dripping. One after the other, his limbs fell off onto the ground. Lastly his chest split open and his heart popped out leaving him dead. When they all died, Allah Ta'ala sent a flood that washed their bodies into the sea.

The following Surah of the Qur-aan explains the incident of the Elephants:

اَلَمْ تَرَ كَيْفَ فَعَلَ رَبُّكَ بِاَصْحٰبِ الْفِيلِ اَلَمْ يَجْعَلْ كَيْدَهُمْ فِيْ تَضْلِيْلٍ وَّ اَرْسَلَ عَلَيْهِمْ طَيْرًا اَبَابِيْلَ تَرْمِيْهِمْ بِحِجَارَةٍ مِّنْ سِجِّيْلٍ فَجَعَلَهُمْ كَعَصْفٍ مَّأْكُوْلٍ

Have you not seen how your Rabb dealt with the people of the elephants? Did He not lay their plans to waste. And send against them flights of birds. Who pelted them with clay pebbles. Making them look like eaten fodder.

Insha Allah, we will now begin the discussion of the mubaarak life of Rasulullah ﷺ.

CHAPTER 2
THE MUBAARAK BIRTH OF RASULULLAH ﷺ

The greatest of humans, the leader of mankind, Muhammadur Rasulullah ﷺ was born fifty days after the incident of the elephants on a Monday in the month of Rabiul-Awwal (April 570 A.D.) in Makkah Mukarramah in the house of Abu Taalib.

A lady by the name of Faatimah bintu Abdullah says: "During the blessed birth of Rasulullah ﷺ, I was with his mother Aaminah. I clearly noticed the whole house shining with Noor (light) and I also saw the stars so low down that I thought they would come crashing down onto me." 'Irbaad bin Saariyah رضي الله عنه says that during the blessed birth, Rasulullah's ﷺ mother saw a Noor (light) that lit up the palaces of Syria.

There was a Jew living in Makkah Mukarramah. On the night Rasulullah ﷺ was born, he asked the Quraysh if a baby boy was born that night. The Quraysh said that they did not hear of a boy being born but he insisted saying: 'At least find out because the Prophet of this Ummah was born tonight. This child has a sign (seal) of prophethood between his shoulder blades. He would not be able to drink any milk for two days because a jinn has placed its finger over his mouth.' The people got up to find out properly. They learnt that a boy was born to Abdullah bin Abdul-Muttalib. The Jew begged to be taken along with them. When he saw the sign (seal) of prophethood between the shoulder blades, he fell down unconscious. When he got up he said: 'Prophethood has disapeared from the

Banu Israa'eel. O people of Quraysh! By Allah! This child will attack you and the news of this attack will quickly spread from the east to the west.'"

The Collapse of Chosroes Palace

On the night that Rasulullah ﷺ was born, an earth-quake struck the palace of Chosroes causing all fourteen towers of the palace to fall down. The fire that was burning for over a thousand years in the Persian fire-temple suddenly went out. Lake Sawah also suddenly dried up. Chosroes was very worried. He organised a meeting by calling all his ministers. During this meeting, he was informed that the "holy fire" has suddenly gone out. This made him even more anxious. When a priest stood up before him and said: "I saw a dream last night in which powerful camels are dragging some Arabian horses. I then saw them crossing over the Tigris River and going to each and every country in the world." This dream showed the coming of Nabi Muhammad ﷺ into this world and also showed that he will rule all these countries.

Aqeeqah and Naming

On the seventh day after Rasulullah's ﷺ birth, Abdul Muttalib performed the Aqeeqah and invited the Quraysh. He then kept the child's name Muhammad. The Quraysh, were shocked by such a strange name and asked: "O Abul Haaris! (This was the title of Abdul Muttalib) Why do you want to keep a name that was certainly not kept by your forefathers or any of your family members?" Abdul Muttalib replied: "I want to name him Muhammad (the praised one) because I want Allah Ta'ala in the sky to praise him and His creation on the earth to also praise him." Whilst Abdul Muttalib was thinking about the name Muhammad, Rasulullah's ﷺ mother, saw a dream in which she was told that she is carrying the holiest of creation and the leader of all the nations. She was instructed to keep his name Muhammad.

Upbringing

For about three or four days after he was born, Rasulullah ﷺ was breastfed by his respected mother. Thereafter, Abu Lahab's slave woman Suwaybah رضى الله عنها, suckled him. When Suwaybah رضى الله عنها gave the good news of Rasulullah's ﷺ birth to Abu Lahab, out of sheer joy, he set her free. Rasulullah ﷺ was very respectful towards Suwaybah رضى الله عنها. After his marriage to Hadhrat Khadijah رضى الله عنها, Suwaybah رضى الله عنها would visit Rasulullah ﷺ. Even after his Hijrah to Madinah Munawwarah, Rasulullah ﷺ would send gifts to her in Makkah Mukarramah. When he conquered Makkah, Rasulullah ﷺ asked about Suwaybah رضى الله عنها and her son. He was told that both of them had passed away. He then asked about her relatives so that he could give them some gifts. However, he was told that none of her relatives were alive.

Halimah Sa'diyyah رضى الله عنها

After Suwaybah رضى الله عنها, Rasulullah ﷺ was breastfed by Halimah Sa'diyyah رضى الله عنها. It was the way of the Arabs to send their babies to the villages to grow up healthy and strong in the clean air of the countryside. Their aim was also to teach the child the pure Arabic language and to learn Arab culture and ways.

Therefore, the women of Banu S'ad would go every year to Makkah Mukarramah to look for suckling babies. Halimah رضى الله عنها says: "A few women from the Banu S'ad and I left for Makkah to look for suckling children. My husband and my young son who was still breastfeeding were with me. We had a very thin donkey and a camel that wouldn't provide a single drop of milk. We were unable to fall asleep all night because of hunger. Our child too was very hungry and cried all night long. I didn't even have enough milk for the child.

Every single one of us was offered to take Rasulullah ﷺ but as soon as we heard that he is an orphan, we all refused. After all, what money can one expect from a child who does not have a father? However, we did not realise that Allah Ta'ala in whose hands lies the treasures of the earth and skies is the guardian of this child. He would give to those who look after this child far more than what they had ever imagined possible."

All the women found at least one child to return home with. Only Halimah رضي الله عنها was left empty-handed. When it was almost time to leave and go back home, Halimah رضي الله عنها found it difficult to return empty-handed. All of a sudden, she felt an urge to go and pick this poor orphan up. She jumped up saying to her husband:

> "By Allah! I will go to this orphan and I will take him with me." Her husband said: "No problem. Who knows, maybe Allah Ta'ala will fill our lives with Barakah because of him."

Halimah رضي الله عنها went and fetched Rasulullah ﷺ. Allah Ta'ala then threw open the doors of Barakah for Halimah رضي الله عنها and her family. The other women of Banu S'ad had their hopes on people whilst Halimah رضي الله عنها had her hopes on Allah Ta'ala alone. Halimah رضي الله عنها says: "I just placed this blessed child to my dried-out chest and they started filling up with milk. I had so much of milk that both he and my son were able to drink to their fill. When we milked our old camel we saw its udders full of milk. My husband and I both filled ourselves with its milk. We passed the night very comfortably." The next morning, her husband said: "Remember, O Halimah! By Allah! You have taken a very blessed child." She replied: "By Allah! I had hoped for nothing but Barakah from Allah Ta'ala."

Now it was time to leave. All the travellers of the caravan climbed onto their animals and set out. Halimah رضي الله عنها also sat on her camel with this blessed child. Her thin camel, which all along was very weak with no energy, was now rushing ahead at top speed. It was, after all carrying the

Chapter Two – The Mubaarak Birth of Rasulullah ﷺ

blessed Nabi of Allah Ta'ala. The other women of the caravan said: "Halimah! Is this the same camel that you came with? By Allah! It now has a totally different behaviour." In this way we arrived back home.

At that time, our area was very badly affected by a drought. However, my goats would return home in the evening with udders full of milk whilst the other goats would return empty without a drop of milk in their udders. On seeing this, the people told their shepherds to graze their goats where Halimah's goats grazed. After doing so, their goats still returned empty whilst Halimah's goats returned at the end of the day with their udders bursting with milk. Halimah رضي الله عنها says: "Allah Ta'ala continued showering His Khair and Barakat (blessings and favours) in this way upon us. It continued like this until I weaned him at the end of two years."

At the end of two years, Halimah رضي الله عنها returned to Makkah Mukarramah to return Nabi ﷺ back to his mother, Aaminah. However, because of the great barakah she had experienced because of Rasulullah ﷺ in her home, Halimah رضي الله عنها asked Hadhrat Aaminah to allow him to continue staying with her. Aaminah gave permission and Halimah رضي الله عنها then returned home with this blessed child. After a few months, he also started grazing the family goats.

The Splitting of the Chest

Once Rasulullah ﷺ was out grazing goats with his milk-brothers when one of them came running back home. Shocked and afraid, he told his parents: "Two white-clothed men laid our Qurayshi brother onto the ground and split open his chest. Now they are busy stitching him up." On hearing this, Halimah رضي الله عنها and her husband were shocked. Both of them rushed across to the grazing field where they saw the young boy standing on one side looking scared. Halimah رضي الله عنها says, "I held him to my chest to comfort him and his foster-father also held him and asked him what happened. He explained that two men split his chest and washed his heart." Halimah رضي الله عنها returned home with him.

Halimah ﷺ became very worried. She returned to Makkah Mukarramah and described to his mother what had happened. Hadhrat Aaminah was not at all surprised. She then mentioned the Barakaat (blessings), Noor and good news she experienced during pregnancy right up to birth. She then said: "This son of mine is going to be a great person. Shaytaan will not be able to trouble him. Calm down. There's nothing to worry about. Nothing will harm him."

Halimah ﷺ then returned home and Rasulullah ﷺ began living with his mother once again. When Rasulullah ﷺ was six years old, his mother decided to travel to Madinah. She took him along with her. Umme Ayman ﷺ also went with them on this trip. She stayed at her parents' home for a month and on the way back to Makkah, she passed away at a place called Abwaa and she was buried there as well.

اِنَّا لِلّٰهِ وَاِنَّا اِلَيْهِ رٰجِعُوْنَ

"To Allah we belong and to Him is our return."

In the Care of Abdul Muttalib (his grandfather)

Umme Ayman ﷺ returned to Makkah Mukarramah with Rasulullah ﷺ and handed him over to Abdul Muttalib. Abdul Muttalib always kept Rasulullah ﷺ with him. Whenever Abdul Muttalib came to Masjidul-Haraam, a special mat would be placed in the shadow of the Baitullah for him. Nobody would dare to even place a foot on this mat. Even Abdul Muttalib's own children would sit on the sides of this mat but Rasulullah ﷺ would sit comfortably right in the centre of the mat. His uncles would try to move him away from this spot but Abdul Muttalib, with love would say: "Leave this son of mine alone. By Allah! This child is going to be a very important person." He would then call him to sit nearby. Whenever Abdul Muttalib would look at Rasulullah ﷺ, he would become very happy.

Death of Abdul Muttalib

Rasulullah ﷺ lived in the loving care of his grandfather Abdul Muttalib for two years. When he turned eight, Abdul Muttalib also passed away. Since Abu Taalib was Abdullah's blood brother, Abdul Muttalib left Rasulullah ﷺ in the care of Abu Taalib. Before passing away he asked Abu Taalib to bring him up with great affection and care and with the greatest of love. Umme Ayman رضى الله عنها says: "When Abdul Muttalib's Janaazah was being carried along, I saw Rasulullah ﷺ running along behind weeping bitterly over his loss."

In the care of Abu Taalib

After the death of Abdul-Muttalib, Rasulullah ﷺ was taken into the care of his uncle Abu Taalib. Rasulullah ﷺ was more beloved to him than his own children. He cared for him more than he cared for his own sons. Right up to his death, Abu Taalib brought him up with much love and affection. Alas! Although he took such loving care of Rasulullah ﷺ, he did not accept Islam. Once there was a severe drought in Makkah. The people begged Abu Taalib to make dua for rain. Abu Taalib took Rasulullah ﷺ to the Masjidul-Haraam and placed him against the K'abah Shareef. He then pointed his finger to the sky. There was not a single cloud in the sky but the moment he pointed to the sky, clouds suddenly appeared all over the place. Within a few moments it started raining so much so that the roads and streets started gushing with water. Abu Taalib said: "He (Rasulullah ﷺ) is such a person because of whom the rain has come from Allah Ta'ala. He is the one who will care for orphans widows."

The First Journey to Syria

When Rasulullah ﷺ turned twelve, his uncle Abu Taalib decided to travel to Syria for business. Because of the difficult and long journey, Abu Taalib did not want to take Rasulullah ﷺ along but when he was about to leave, he saw how sad Rasulullah ﷺ was and decided to take him with. On the way to Syria, they stopped over at a city called Busra where a Christian priest by the name of Bahirah lived. He knew very well the signs of the final Prophet because he had learnt the holy books. As soon as he saw Rasulullah ﷺ, he at once recognised him as the final Prophet. Bahirah held Rasulullah's ﷺ hand and said:

> "This is the leader of the worlds. This is the messenger of the worlds. Allah Ta'ala will send him as a mercy for the people of the world."

The elders of the Quraysh, were amazed and asked: "How do you know this?" He replied: "When you came out from the valley of the mountain, every single boulder and tree went down in sajdah. Trees and boulders don't bow down to anybody but a Prophet. I also recognise him from his seal of prophethood that is similar to an apple and appears just below his shoulder blade." Saying this, the priest left. Because of Rasulullah ﷺ, he prepared a meal for the whole group of travellers. When all of them came to eat, he noticed that Rasulullah ﷺ was not there. When he asked for him, he was told that Rasulullah ﷺ was out looking after the camels. He immediately sent for him. When Rasulullah ﷺ came, a cloud was protecting him from the strong rays of the sun. As he came near to his people, he noticed that they had already taken whatever shade there was under a tree. Since there was no shade available, Rasulullah ﷺ sat down on one side. The moment he sat down, the tree bent in his direction to offer him some shade. The priest said: "Look at this tree, it is bending towards him." The priest then got up and forced the travellers to take an oath not to take the young boy with them to Rome. If the Romans see him they will identify him and kill him.

Bahirah then asked who his guardian was. They pointed towards Abu Taalib. He begged Abu Taalib to send him back to Makkah Mukarramah. Abu Taalib sent him back to Makkah with Abu Bakr and Bilal. The priest also gave them some bread and olive oil as food for the return journey.

The Title of Al-Ameen

Rasulullah ﷺ grew up as the most noble, the most polite, the most kind to his neighbours, the most patient, the most truthful and honest person. He would stay away from fighting, arguing, evil and shameless things. This is why, as a young man, his people gave him the title of Al-Ameen (the trustworthy). Abdullah bin Abi Hamsaa رضى الله عنه says: "Before prophethood, I once did some business with Rasulullah ﷺ. I owed him some money. I promised him that I would return with it shortly but somehow I completely forgot about my promise. Only three days later I remembered my promise to return with the money. The moment I remembered this promise, I rushed out to the meeting place and found him waiting there patiently. All he said was, 'You put me into difficulty. I have been waiting here for you for the last three days.'"

Abdullah bin Saaib رضى الله عنه says: "In the time of ignorance (pre-Islamic days), I was Rasulullah's ﷺ business partner. When I came to Madinah, he asked: "Do you recognise me?" "Surely!" I replied, "Why not? You were my business partner and what an excellent partner you were. You would never delay nor would you argue over anything."

Qays bin Saaib Makhzumi رضى الله عنه says: "I was Rasulullah's ﷺ business partner in the times of ignorance. He was the best of partners. He would neither quarrel nor argue."

Grazing Goats

Just as Rasulullah ﷺ grazed goats in his childhood with his foster brothers whilst living with Hadhrat Halimah رضى الله عنها, similarly, he grazed goats as he grew older. Jaabir bin Abdullah رضى الله عنه says: "We were with Rasulullah ﷺ in a place called Zahraan. When we started picking some fruit off a peelu tree, Rasulullah ﷺ advised us to pick the black ones, as they were more delicious and tastier. We then asked him if he had ever grazed goats in his life (because how would he have known this.)

Rasulullah ﷺ replied: "There is not a single Nabi who did not graze goats."

Second Journey to Syria

Hadhrat Khadijah رضي الله عنها was a very wealthy woman from one of the most noble families of the Arabs. Because of her nobility and her purity, she was known as Taahirah (pure) during the times of ignorance as well as after accepting Islam. When the Quraysh sent their business caravans, Hadhrat Khadijah رضي الله عنها would also send her goods with some honest people in the form of a business partnership. Her goods were equal to all the goods of the Quraysh put together. When Rasulullah ﷺ turned twenty-five and his honesty became famous and when everyone in Makkah called him Al-Ameen, Hadhrat Khadijah رضي الله عنها sent him a message asking him to take her goods to Syria with an offer to double his share of the profits as compared to her other normal business partners. Rasulullah ﷺ accepted the offer and together with Hadhrat Khadijah's slave, Maysarah, he set off for Syria. When Rasulullah ﷺ reached Busra, he sat under the shade of a tree. A priest by the name of Nastoora lived near this tree. When he saw Rasulullah ﷺ under this tree, he came to him and said: "From 'Isa bin Maryam right up till now, besides you no other prophet has sat under this tree." He then said to Maysarah: "He (Rasulullah ﷺ) has this redness in his eyes." Maysarah replied: "Yes, this redness has never left his eyes." The priest said: "Yes, surely this is the Prophet. This is the final Messenger."

Rasulullah ﷺ thereafter continued with his business. During this time, a person once started arguing with Rasulullah ﷺ. The man demanded that Rasulullah ﷺ swear an oath on the idols of Laat and 'Uzza. Rasulullah ﷺ very calmly replied: "I have never taken an oath on Laat and 'Uzza. In fact, even if I somehow come across these idols, I try to stay away from them completely." The man replied: "Definitely, you are right." In other words, you are truthful and honest. The man then said:

"By Allah! This is the man whose description our Ulama find written in their holy books." Maysarah says: "In the severe heat of the afternoon, I would notice two angels offering shade to Rasulullah ﷺ."

As he was returning from Syria whilst the two angels were shading him from the fierce midday sun, Hadhrat Khadijah رضى الله عنها witnessed this wonderful scene as she was sitting in one of the upper floors of her house. She called the women around her to come and see this fantastic sight as well. They were all very surprised. Soon after, Maysarah gave her a full report of the strange happenings of the journey. Rasulullah ﷺ then gave her, her goods and money. Because of the barakah (blessings) of Rasulullah ﷺ, this time, Hadhrat Khadijah رضى الله عنها enjoyed such a huge profit from this business trip that she had never before enjoyed. Hadhrat Khadijah رضى الله عنها paid Rasulullah ﷺ much more than the profit she had promised him at first.

Marriage to Hadhrat Khadijah رضى الله عنها

Hadhrat Khadijah رضى الله عنها, heard Maysarah's story about what the priest said and the angels providing shade, etc. She went to Waraqah bin Nawfal and explained these details to him. Waraqah said: "Khadijah! If what you are telling me is true, then most certainly Muhammad is the final prophet of this Ummah. I know that this Ummah is patiently waiting for a prophet who will be arriving soon. Hadhrat Khadijah رضى الله عنها now wanted to get married to Rasulullah ﷺ. She sent a proposal to Rasulullah ﷺ. After checking with his uncle, Rasulullah ﷺ accepted this proposal. On the date of the Nikah, together with his uncles Abu Taalib and Hamzah and a few other chiefs of the family, Rasulullah ﷺ set out for Hadhrat Khadijah's رضى الله عنها house.

At the time of this Nikah, Rasulullah ﷺ was twenty-five years old whilst Hadhrat Khadijah رضى الله عنها was forty. The Mahr (dowry) was fixed at twenty camels. Some say that the mahr was 500 Dirhams. This was

Rasulullah's ﷺ first Nikah whilst it was Hadhrat Khadijah's رضي الله عنها third nikah.

The Rebuilding of the K'abah Shareef

When Rasulullah ﷺ was thirty-five years old, the Quraysh decided to rebuild the Ka'bah Shareef. The original Ka'bah built by Hadhrat Ibraaheem عليه السلام had no roof and the walls were not very high. Over the years, the building began falling apart. The rain had caused a lot of damage. This is why the Quraysh decided to break down the original Ka'bah and rebuild it. When all the Qurayshi leaders agreed to break down the Ka'bah Shareef and rebuild it, Rasulullah's ﷺ father's uncle, spoke to the Quraysh: "Remember that whatever we spend in the rebuilding of the Ka'bah Shareef must be from Halaal money only. The money which we have from zina, stealing and interest should not be used for this Holy House. Only Halaal wealth should be used in its building. Allah Ta'ala is pure and He only accepts what is pure. In the building of the Ka'bah, use only your purely Halaal wealth." Each and every tribe was given a certain job in the rebuilding.

When it came to the actual moment of the breaking of the Ka'bah, no person had the courage to break the first brick. Eventually, Waleed bin Mughirah, took a spade in his hand and made dua to Allah Ta'ala:

"O Allah! Our intentions are nothing but good." In other words, O Allah we have absolutely no evil intention in breaking the K'abah. Saying this, he started breaking the K'abah Shareef near the Hajr-e-Aswad and Rukn Yamaani. The people of Makkah decided to wait till the next night to see if Waleed is struck by any punishment. If any form of punishment comes to him, we will bring back the house of Allah Ta'ala to how it was, otherwise we will all help Waleed in breaking it down. The next morning they saw Waleed fit and healthy holding a spade and walking into the Haram area. They realised that Allah Ta'ala is happy with the rebuilding of the Ka'bah. All of them then began helping in breaking down the Ka'bah. They continued digging right down until they reached the original foundation built by Hadhrat Ibraaheem عَلَيْهِ السَّلَام. When a Qurayshi delivered a blow to the Ibraaheemi foundation, a terrible explosion rocked the city of Makkah. At once, they stopped digging any more and started their rebuilding on the same original foundation. According to their agreement, each tribe collected their stones and started to rebuild their part of the Ka'bah.

When the building was complete and it was time for placing the Hajr-e-Aswad (black stone), all of them began to argue violently. Swords were taken out and the people were ready to go to war and kill one another for the honour of lifting the stone to its place. After a few days of severe arguing, one of the elders of the Quraysh suggested that the first person that enters the Haram Shareef the next morning will make the decision of the black stone. Everybody happily agreed. The next morning, the first person to enter the Haram was Muhammad Rasulullah صَلَّى اللهُ عَلَيْهِ وَسَلَّم. When they saw him they exclaimed: "This is Muhammad, the trustworthy. We are extremely pleased with him. After all, Muhammad, is trustworthy."

Rasulullah صَلَّى اللهُ عَلَيْهِ وَسَلَّم asked for a sheet and placing the black stone onto it, he instructed: "The chief of each tribe should hold the ends of the sheet so that all the tribes can be included." Thus each leader held a side of the sheet and lifted up the black stone. Rasulullah صَلَّى اللهُ عَلَيْهِ وَسَلَّم then went forward and with his blessed hands raised the stone and placed it in its proper place.

Hatred for Idols

Rasulullah صَلَّى اللهُ عَلَيْهِ وَسَلَّم was once asked if he ever worshiped an idol. He replied, "NO". He was then asked if he ever drank wine. Rasulullah صَلَّى اللهُ عَلَيْهِ وَسَلَّم again replied "NO" and said: "I always thought of those actions to be Kufr even though I had no knowledge of Imaan and the Qur-aan at that stage." Rasulullah صَلَّى اللهُ عَلَيْهِ وَسَلَّم had said to Hadhrat Khadijah رَضِيَ اللهُ عَنْهَا: "By Allah! I will never ever worship Laat. By Allah! I will never ever worship 'Uzza" (names of two idols).

CHAPTER 3
PROPHETHOOD

Rasulullah ﷺ loved being alone and he would often go to the cave of Hira. When Rasulullah ﷺ reached the age of forty, he was in the cave of Hira. Suddenly an angel appeared in the cave. He entered, greeted him with Salaam and said: "Read!" Rasulullah ﷺ replied: "I am unable to read." Rasulullah ﷺ says: "Then the angel hugged me so tight that I was suffering terribly. He then left me saying, 'Read!' Again, I said: 'I am unable to read.' The angel again squeezed me a second and then a third time, left me and asked me to read the following aayaat:

اِقْرَأْ بِاسْمِ رَبِّكَ الَّذِىْ خَلَقَ ۚ خَلَقَ الْاِنْسَانَ مِنْ عَلَقٍ ۚ اِقْرَأْ وَرَبُّكَ الْاَكْرَمُ ۙ الَّذِىْ عَلَّمَ بِالْقَلَمِ ۙ عَلَّمَ الْاِنْسَانَ مَا لَمْ يَعْلَمْ ۙ

"Read in the name of your Rabb Who has created (the entire universe). He has created (above all) man from a clot of blood. Read! And your Rabb is the most gracious Who has taught (knowledge) by the use of the pen. He has taught man that which he did not know."

[Surah 'Alaq verse 1]

Thereafter, Rasulullah ﷺ returned home shivering with worry. The moment he entered, he asked Hadhrat Khadijah رضى الله عنها to wrap him up. When he had calmed down, he explained the whole incident to Hadhrat Khadijah رضى الله عنها saying: "I was terrified of losing my life." Thereafter Jibraa'eel عليه السلام appeared before him giving him the good news of Allah Ta'ala choosing him as His messenger. It was only then that Rasulullah

Chapter Three – Prophethood

ﷺ felt comfortable. He then asked him to read. Rasulullah ﷺ asked: "How must I read?" Jibraa'eel عليه السلام replied: "Read in the name of your Rabb Who created...."up to the aayat "that which he knew not." Rasulullah ﷺ accepted the message of Allah Ta'ala and returned. Every tree and stone he passed on the way to his home greeted him with *"As-Salaamu 'alayka Yaa Rasulallah!"* This is how he returned home and with firm knowledge that Allah Ta'ala had chosen him to be a Nabi."

Hadhrat Khadijah رضي الله عنها consoled him saying: "Congratulations to you! This is really good news. Do not panic! By Allah! He will never disgrace you. You keep good family ties. You always speak the truth. You carry the load of others. You pay the debts of others. You help the poor. You are trustworthy. You return whatever has been kept by you. You always fulfil the rights of the guests. You are always ready to help in good works." Hadhrat Khadijah رضي الله عنها also said: "You have never been close to an evil woman. By Allah in whose absolute control lies Khadijah's life! I definitely believe you to be the messenger of this Ummah."

Hadhrat Khadijah رضي الله عنها then went to her cousin Waraqah bin Nawfal. He was a great aalim of the Torah and he was busy translating the Injeel from Syriac into Arabic. Before Islam, he stayed away from worshipping idols and had accepted Christianity. By this time he was very old and had turned blind. On hearing about what happened from Hadhrat Khadijah رضي الله عنها, Waraqah said: "If you are truthful in whatever you say, certainly this is the same Angel who used to come to 'Isa (عليه السلام)."

Hadhrat Khadijah رضي الله عنها then took Rasulullah ﷺ along with her to Waraqah bin Nawfal. She addressed him saying: "O cousin! Why don't you hear it from your nephew (in his own words)?"

Waraqah then said: "O nephew! Tell me, what did you see? What happened?" Rasulullah ﷺ then explained what had happened. "The moment he heard the details, he became absolutely sure of the truth and he wholeheartedly accepted it."

On listening to these details, Waraqah said: "Yes, this is the same angel that used to come to Musa عَلَيْهِ السَّلَامُ. If only I was strong enough during your prophethood when your people will chase you from your hometown or at least I wish I am alive (to see those times)." Shocked by what he heard, Rasulullah ﷺ asked: "Will they really chase me out?" Waraqah replied: "This is not for you only. All the Prophets were treated very badly by their people. If I live long enough, I will assist you fully." However, not long thereafter, Waraqah passed away.

Whenever Rasulullah ﷺ would think about this, Jibraa'eel عَلَيْهِ السَّلَامُ would come before him and say: "O Muhammad! You are definitely the true Prophet of Allah." After hearing such comforting words, Rasulullah ﷺ would feel much better. Once, Hadhrat Khadijah رَضِيَ اللهُ عَنْهَا asked Rasulullah ﷺ: "When the angel comes to you again, please tell me, if possible." When Jibraa'eel عَلَيْهِ السَّلَامُ came again, Rasulullah ﷺ told her of his arrival. Hadhrat Khadijah رَضِيَ اللهُ عَنْهَا then asked Rasulullah ﷺ to come onto her lap. As he placed his head on her lap, she removed her scarf exposing her head. "Can you still see Jibraa'eel عَلَيْهِ السَّلَامُ now?" she asked. When Rasulullah ﷺ replied that he couldn't, she said: "Good news to you. By Allah Ta'ala! This is an angel, not a shaytaan." Rasulullah ﷺ was exactly forty years old when he was made a prophet.

Salaah - The Main Duty after Imaan

After Imaan, the very first lesson taught to Rasulullah ﷺ was Wudhu and Salaah. Jibraa'eel عَلَيْهِ السَّلَامُ stamped his heel on the ground that caused a spring to gush out. Jibraa'eel عَلَيْهِ السَّلَامُ made wudhu with this water whilst Rasulullah ﷺ watched him carefully. Then Rasulullah ﷺ also performed wudhu in the same way. Then Jibraa'eel عَلَيْهِ السَّلَامُ performed two Rakaats of Salaah with Rasulullah ﷺ who followed him throughout. Then Rasulullah ﷺ returned home and taught this knowledge of salaah to Hadhrat Khadijah رضى الله عنها.

CHAPTER 4
THE FIRST MUSLIMS

The very first person to accept Islam was the beloved wife of Rasulullah ﷺ, Hadhrat Khadijah رضى الله عنها and she was the first person to join him for Salaah. Thereafter Waraqah bin Nawfal accepted Islam followed by Hadhrat Ali رضى الله عنه who who was being looked after by Rasulullah ﷺ. He was ten years old when he accepted Islam. He also joined Rasulullah ﷺ in Salaah. When Hadhrat Ali رضى الله عنه saw Rasulullah ﷺ and Hadhrat Khadijah رضى الله عنها performing Salaah, he asked: "What is this?" Rasulullah ﷺ replied: "This is the Deen of Allah Ta'ala. Every Prophet taught the same Deen to the people of this world. I am also inviting you towards Allah. Worship Him alone and leave (the idols of) Laat and 'Uzza." Hadhrat Ali رضى الله عنه said: "This is something new to me. I haven't heard of anything like this. I need to discuss this with my father, Abu Taalib." Rasulullah ﷺ said: "Ali! If you do not wish to accept Islam, don't mention it to anyone else." Hadhrat Ali رضى الله عنه remained silent. Not even one night passed when Islam was filled into his heart. The next morning he came to Rasulullah ﷺ saying: "What are you inviting us to?" Rasulullah ﷺ replied: "Believe that Allah Ta'ala is one and He has no partner. Leave out Laat and Uzza and dislike idol worship." Hadhrat Ali رضى الله عنه then accepted Islam and for quite a while (possibly a whole year) he kept his Islam a secret from his father Abu Taalib. Then Rasulullah's ﷺ freed slave Hadhrat Zaid bin Haarisah رضى الله عنه accepted Islam and performed Salaah with him.

Islam of Hadhrat Abu Bakr Siddeeq ﷺ

When all his household members accepted Islam, Rasulullah ﷺ invited his close friends to accept Islam. The first person he invited was his best friend, Hadhrat Abu Bakr ﷺ. Without even giving it a second thought, Hadhrat Abu Bakr ﷺ happily accepted Rasulullah's ﷺ invitation to Islam. Rasulullah ﷺ once said: "Whoever I invited to Islam, there was always some hesitation except in the case of Abu Bakr. Without hesitation, he immediately accepted Islam." Hadhrat Abu Bakr ﷺ started inviting others to Islam the moment he accepted Islam. Whenever he met his close friends, he invited them to Islam. Therefore Usmaan bin Affaan, Zubair bin Awwaam, Abdur-Rahmaan bin Awf, Talhah bin Ubaidullah and S'ad bin Abi Waqqaas ﷺ accepted Islam through the invitation of Hadhrat Abu Bakr ﷺ. He brought all of them to Rasulullah ﷺ and they all accepted Islam and joined him for Salaah.

Whenever it was the time of Salaah, Rasulullah ﷺ would secretly perform his Salaah in a quiet valley or mountain pass. Once, Rasulullah ﷺ was performing his Salaah with Hadhrat Ali ﷺ on a mountain pass when all of a sudden Abu Taalib appeared in the distance coming their way. Until that time, Hadhrat Ali ﷺ had kept his Islam a secret from his parents, uncles and other relatives. Abu Taalib asked Rasulullah ﷺ: "Nephew! What religion is this? What kind of worship is this?" Rasulullah ﷺ replied: "Uncle! This is the Deen of Allah Ta'ala, His angels and all His prophets, especially the Deen of our great grandfather, Hadhrat Ibraaheem ﷺ. Allah Ta'ala has chosen me as His messenger to all His people. I invite you towards goodness and guidance from Allah. You should accept this guidance and true religion first and show your support and help towards me."

Abu Taalib replied: "Nephew! I am unable to leave my religion but I give you a guarantee that in my presence nobody will hurt you." He then turned to Hadhrat Ali ﷺ asking: "Son! What is this religion which you have accepted?" Hadhrat Ali رَضِىَ اللّٰهُ عَنْهُ replied: "Father! I believe in Allah and His Rasool صَلَّى اللّٰهُ عَلَيْهِ وَسَلَّم and I believe in whatever he brings to us from Allah. I join him in Salaah and I am his follower." Abu Taalib said: "Very well then! He has definitely invited you to good. Don't ever leave him."

Like this many other people accepted Islam. The names of some of them are; Ja'far bin Abi Taalib رَضِىَ اللّٰهُ عَنْهُ, the brother of Hadhrat Ali رَضِىَ اللّٰهُ عَنْهُ, Talhah رَضِىَ اللّٰهُ عَنْهُ, S'ad bin Abi Waqqaas رَضِىَ اللّٰهُ عَنْهُ and others.

Hadhrat Usmaan رَضِىَ اللّٰهُ عَنْهُ accepts Islam

Hadhrat Usmaan رَضِىَ اللّٰهُ عَنْهُ says: "I once entered my house when I saw my aunty sitting with some family members. She read the following poem to me:

"Usmaan! O Usmaan! O Usmaan! You are a man of beauty and great honour. There is a Prophet who has strong proofs. Allah Ta'ala sent him with the truth. Follow him and do not allow the idols to mislead you."

I said: "Aunty! You say such things which are unheard of in this city. I don't understand." She said:

"Muhammad bin Abdullah is the Rasool of Allah صَلَّى اللّٰهُ عَلَيْهِ وَسَلَّم. He came with the words of Allah inviting everyone to come towards Allah. His words are guidance. His religion is a way of success. He is going to conquer. Fighting him will be useless even if you have many swords and spears."

Saying this, she left but her words affected my heart. I began to think very deeply. Since Hadhrat Abu Bakr رَضِىَ اللّٰهُ عَنْهُ was my friend, I went to him and sat down with him. Seeing my worried face, he asked: "What seems to trouble you?" I told him about my aunt and her poems. Abu Bakr رَضِىَ اللّٰهُ عَنْهُ said: "Usmaan! You are, Masha Allah, intelligent. You are an expert in separating between the truth and falsehood. People like you are not confused between the truth and falsehood. What are these idols that our people are bowing down to? Are these idols not blind and deaf? They can neither hear nor see. Neither can they cause harm nor are they able to help." Hadhrat Usmaan ﷺ replied: "By Allah! You are so right." Abu Bakr ﷺ said: "By Allah! Your aunt spoke the truth. Muhammad bin Abdullah is the messenger of Allah. Allah Ta'ala sent him with His message to the people. Why don't you come for one of his lectures and listen to what he says."

Hadhrat Usmaan ﷺ says: "Whilst we were still talking, Rasulullah ﷺ happened to pass by. Hadhrat Ali ﷺ was with him. On seeing Rasulullah ﷺ, Hadhrat Abu Bakr ﷺ stood up and whispered something into his ear. Rasulullah ﷺ came to us and sat down before us. He then spoke to Hadhrat Usmaan ﷺ saying: "O Usmaan! Allah invites you to Jannah, so accept His invitation. I am the messenger of Allah Ta'ala sent to you and the entire creation."

Hadhrat Usmaan ﷺ says: "By Allah! The moment I heard this, I was unable to stop myself. Without any delay, I accepted Islam saying: 'I bear witness that there is none worthy of worship but Allah, He is alone and has no partner and I bear witness that Nabi Muhammad ﷺ is His slave and messenger.'"

Hadhrat Usmaan ﷺ says: "Shortly thereafter, Rasulullah's ﷺ daughter, Hadhrat Ruqayyaa ﷺ, came into my Nikah."

Muslims gather at Daar-e-Arqam

As the people slowly accepted Islam, a small group of Muslims formed. It was suggested that all of them should gather in the house of Arqam. Hadhrat Arqam ﷺ was one of the earliest Muslims. He was either the 7th or the 10th person to accept Islam. His house was on Mount Safa. Right up to the Islam of Hadhrat 'Umar ﷺ, Rasulullah ﷺ and the Sahaabah ﷺ would gather at Arqam's ﷺ house. After Hadhrat 'Umar ﷺ accepted Islam, the Muslims would gather wherever they liked.

Open Invitation to Islam

Over a period of three years, Rasulullah ﷺ continued inviting people to Islam secretly and the people slowly accepted Islam. After three years, Rasulullah ﷺ was instructed to invite to Islam openly. The following aayaat were revealed:

$$\text{فَاصْدَعْ بِمَا تُؤْمَرُ وَاَعْرِضْ عَنِ الْمُشْرِكِيْنَ}$$

"Clearly announce what (message) you have been commanded with and turn away from the disbelievers." [Surah Hijr verse 94]

Rasulullah ﷺ climbed up Mount Safa and called each of the tribes by name. When they had all gathered around him, he asked them: "If I warn you about an attacking army on the other side of this mountain that is about to attack you, would you believe me?" In one voice they all said: "Surely, why not! We have only known you to be honest and truthful." Rasulullah ﷺ said: "I am warning you about a severe punishment that may come to you (if you do not accept my message from Allah Ta'ala)."

Abu Lahab heard this and said: "Destruction unto you. May you die. Did you gather us here for this reason only?" Upon this the Surah 'Tabbat Yadaa Abi Lahab' (May the hands of Abu Lahab be destroyed.) was revealed.

Invitation to Islam through Meals

Hadhrat Ali رضى الله عنه says: "When the aayat: 'And warn your close relatives' was revealed, Rasulullah ﷺ instructed me to bring some grain, a shoulder of a goat and a bowl of milk. He then asked me to call all the children of Muttalib. I obeyed his instructions. Approximately forty people gathered for this invitation. Amongst them were his uncles; Abu Taalib, Hamzah, Abbaas and Abu Lahab. Rasulullah ﷺ took the meat and shred it (made it into pieces) with his mubaarak teeth. Placing the meat into a bowl, he told the others: 'Take the name of Allah and start eating.'

Everyone ate to their fill from this one small dish of food. In fact, there was a little left over as well. They were well satisfied with this little food whereas it would normally have been enough for one person only. Rasulullah ﷺ then instructed me to bring the bowl of milk and offer it to all of them. All of them drank to their fill from this one bowl whereas one bowl of milk is not really much. Let alone forty people, a bowl of milk is barely enough for just one person. When they finished eating, Rasulullah ﷺ was about to say something when Abu Lahab shouted out: 'People, get up! Muhammad has cast a spell over your food today. We have never seen such magic before this day!' The moment he spoke, people left and Rasulullah ﷺ did not get a chance to speak to them. The following day, Rasulullah ﷺ again instructed Hadhrat Ali ؓ to prepare the same meal. When they finished eating, Rasulullah ﷺ said: 'What I have presented to you, nobody else has presented anything better than that to his people. I have brought to you news about this world as well as the next world (Aakhirat).'"

Hadhrat Abu Bakr ؓ was always leading in his sacrifice and love for Rasulullah ﷺ whilst Abu Lahab was right in the front of kufr, hatred and mockery. May Allah's anger come on him. Because of his hatred for Rasulullah ﷺ, he forced his sons 'Utbah and 'Utaibah (who were married to Rasulullah's ﷺ daughters Ruqayyah ؓ and Umm-e-Kulsoom ؓ before prophethood) to divorce their wives. Abu Lahab wanted to increase the grief of Rasulullah ﷺ as far as he possibly could. However, this divorce proved to be a source of Allah Ta'ala's mercy. One after the other, both these daughters were then married to Hadhrat Usmaan ؓ thereby giving him the title of Zun-Noorain (a man of two lights). As long as Rasulullah ﷺ continued inviting the people secretly to Islam, the Quraysh left him alone but the moment he publicly announced the message of Islam and started to speak against shirk and idol worship, the Quraysh began opposing him. However, Abu Taalib continued supporting Rasulullah ﷺ. Once, a group of the Quraysh came to Abu Taalib and said: "Your nephew speaks bad about our idols, disgraces our religion and says that we are misguided. Either you stop him from doing so or you stop supporting him." Abu Taalib very affectionately continued with his support and Rasulullah ﷺ continued with his invitation towards Imaan and stopping people from shirk and disbelief. Abu Lahab and his friends became even angrier. They sent another group to Abu Taalib saying: "We accept your nobility and goodness amongst us but we will never tolerate anyone speaking bad about our idols and calling our ancestors fools. Either you stop your nephew or we will start a war in which one of us will be destroyed." Saying this, they returned.

Abu Taalib was affected by this. When Rasulullah ﷺ came to him, Abu Taalib said: "Dear nephew! The people of your tribe came to me and this is what they had to say. I beg you to take pity on me and take pity on yourself as well. Please do not ask me to do what I cannot manage.

Rasulullah ﷺ realised that Abu Taalib could not help and support him any more. With tearful eyes, Rasulullah ﷺ said: "O my Uncle! By Allah, if these people place the sun in my right hand and the moon in my left hand and beg me to stop this work, I will never stop it until Allah Ta'ala makes Islam successful or until I die." Saying this, Rasulullah ﷺ burst into tears and stood up to leave. Abu Taalib called for him and said: "My beloved nephew! You do what you want. I will never hand you over to your enemies."

When the Quraysh saw the strong support of Abu Taalib for Rasulullah ﷺ, they came to him now for a third time and said: "Ammaarah bin Waheed is a very handsome and intelligent young man of the Quraysh. Take him instead and give us your nephew who is responsible for causing so many problems amongst our people. We wish to kill him and get rid of him." Abu Taalib replied: "What! How can this ever be possible? How can I allow you to kill the child that I have brought up myself? By Allah! This will never happen!"

When the Quraysh lost all hope on Abu Taalib, they began hurting and harming him (and the Muslims). They started by punishing the weak

Muslims they came across from the other tribes. Abu Taalib invited the Banu Haashim and Banu Muttalib to support and assist Rasulullah ﷺ. All the members of the Banu Haashim and Banu Muttalib families gave their complete support and protection. From the Banu Haashim, only Abu Lahab joined the enemy against Rasulullah ﷺ. One person said: "I saw Rasulullah ﷺ in the market place inviting people towards Islam saying: "O people! Say *Laa Ilaaha Illallahu*, you will be successful." Behind him I saw a squint-eyed man calling out to the people: "This man has turned away from his religion and he is a liar. (Do not believe in what he says.)" When I asked who this man was, I was informed that it is Rasulullah's ﷺ uncle Abu Lahab. Rasulullah ﷺ was inviting the people towards Islam and Jannah whilst Abu Lahab was inviting the people towards kufr and the fire of Jahannam.

Islam of Hamzah رضي الله عنه

Whilst walking near Mt. Safa one day, Rasulullah ﷺ suddenly met Abu Jahal who also happened to be passing that way. The moment he saw Rasulullah ﷺ, he began cursing and swearing Rasulullah ﷺ. However, Rasulullah ﷺ did not reply and calmly departed from there. After all 'Silence is the best answer to a fool'. 'A slave girl witnessed this terrible sight. In the meantime, Hadhrat Hamzah رضي الله عنه, who was just returning from one of his hunting trips, happened to come by that way with his bow and arrows. The moment she saw him, 'the slave girl said: "Abu Ammaarah! If only you were around when Abu Jahal was swearing your nephew."

Hadhrat Hamzah رضي الله عنه became very angry. It was the habit of Hadhrat Hamzah رضي الله عنه that he would first visit the Haram Shareef whenever he returned from hunting. When he came to the Haram Shareef, he saw Abu Jahal sitting with a few other members of the Quraysh tribe. The moment he reached him, Hadhrat Hamzah رضي الله عنه struck him so severely with the bow on his head that he suffered a serious head injury. He then yelled at him: "You have the guts to swear Muhammad (ﷺ). In fact, I am also now a follower of his religion." Some of the people wanted to help Abu Jahal but he stopped them saying: "Yes, I am guilty. Today I swore at his nephew. Leave Hamzah alone." Some of the people said: "Hamzah! Have you also turned Saabi (turned away from your religion)?" Hadhrat Hamzah رضي الله عنه replied: "Muhammad's (ﷺ) truthfulness is known to me. I testify that Muhammad is the messenger of Allah and I believe that whatever he says is absolutely true. I will never leave this belief. Do whatever you can!" Saying this, Hadhrat Hamzah رضي الله عنه returned home. Hamzah رضي الله عنه says: "The next morning, I went to Rasulullah ﷺ and explained to him what had happened. Rasulullah ﷺ made dua for me." Hadhrat Hamzah رضي الله عنه then said:

"I testify that you are definitely truthful. I am a firm believer."

He also said: "O nephew! Practice Islam openly now. By Allah! Even if I am offered the whole world and whatever is contained in it, I would certainly not leave Islam and go back to my family religion."

CHAPTER 5
THE SPREAD OF ISLAM

When the Quraysh realised that Hadhrat Hamzah ﺭﺿﻲﺍﻟﻠﻪﻋﻨﻪ had accepted Islam and that the numbers of the Muslims were increasing, Abu Jahal, 'Utbah, Shaybah, Waleed, Umayyah and other chiefs of the Quraysh had a meeting. According to this meeting, they sent 'Utbah bin Rabi'ah to speak to Rasulullah ﺻﻠﻰﺍﻟﻠﻪﻋﻠﻴﻪﻭﺳﻠﻢ. He was a man who was an expert in magic and poetry. 'Utbah came to Rasulullah ﺻﻠﻰﺍﻟﻠﻪﻋﻠﻴﻪﻭﺳﻠﻢ and said: "O Muhammad! There is no doubt about your special family and position but sadly, you have broken the unity of our nation. You make fun of our idols and call our forefathers fools. This is why I wish to tell you something." Rasulullah ﺻﻠﻰﺍﻟﻠﻪﻋﻠﻴﻪﻭﺳﻠﻢ replied: "Go ahead, Abul-Waleed, I am listening." 'Utbah said: "O Nephew! Why are you doing this? If wealth is what you want, we will gather so much of wealth for you that even the richest man will not be able to compete with you. If you wish to get married, we will get you married to whichever woman you choose and to how many women you want. If leadership is what you are after, we will choose you as our leader. If you are looking for kingdom, we will make you our king. If a jinn has caught you, we will provide the treatment to remove it."

Rasulullah ﺻﻠﻰﺍﻟﻠﻪﻋﻠﻴﻪﻭﺳﻠﻢ replied: "O Abul-Waleed! Are you over with whatever you wanted to say?" When 'Utbah replied that he was, Rasulullah ﺻﻠﻰﺍﻟﻠﻪﻋﻠﻴﻪﻭﺳﻠﻢ said: "Now listen to what I have to say. I don't wish for your riches and wealth and I have no intention of leadership and power. I am the Rasool (messenger) of Allah Ta'ala whom He has sent to you with His message. He has sent a book to me and has ordered me to give His good news of reward and warnings of punishment. I have given His message to you and I have warned you. If you accept this message, it would be a way of success for you in both the worlds. However, if you refuse this message, I will be patient until Allah Ta'ala decides between us."

Saying this Rasulullah ﷺ read some aayaat of Surah Mu'min.

Rasulullah ﷺ continued reading this Surah whilst 'Utbah was sitting leaning with both his hands behind his back listening in amazement to the Qur-aan. When Rasulullah ﷺ reached the aayat, 'and if they turn away', 'Utbah suddenly placed his hand over Rasulullah's ﷺ mouth and said: "By Allah! For Allah's sake, take pity on us."

Actually, 'Utbah was terrified that the punishment of 'Aad and Samood would suddenly land on him. Thereafter, Rasulullah ﷺ continued reading right up to the aayat of Sajdah after which he performed a Sajdah. Rasulullah ﷺ then said to 'Utbah: "Abul-Waleed! You have heard whatever you have heard. The choice is now yours."

Useless Questions of the Makkan disbelievers

After this, the Quraysh made another plan. They told Rasulullah ﷺ: "If you don't accept our first offer, we wish to ask you to do something. You are aware of the poverty of your people. This city of Makkah is also very crowded. We are surrounded by mountains on all sides without any greenery around us. So, ask Allah Ta'ala who sent you as a Nabi to move the mountains of this city somewhere else so that the city becomes more spacious. Also ask Him to create rivers in this city like the cities of Syria and Iraq. Also bring back our forefathers especially Qusayy bin Kilaab so that we may ask him about the truth of what you are saying. If our forefathers agree with what you say and they believe in you, only then would we believe you to be the messenger of Allah." Rasulullah ﷺ replied: "I was not sent as a messenger for this purpose. I have given you the message I was sent with. If you accept the message, it would be for your own good and if you fail to believe in it, I will be patient until such time that Allah Ta'ala decides between us."

The Quraysh said: "If you cannot do what we have asked for, then make dua that Allah Ta'ala sends an angel from the heavens to go with you wherever you go. This angel will confirm whatever you say. Also ask Allah to give you gardens, palaces and treasures of gold and silver, as this will improve your noble position and piety. We see that you also walk about in the market places to earn your money. (We find this to be strange for a Nabi.)" Rasulullah ﷺ replied: "I will never make such duas to Allah Ta'ala. I was not sent for this purpose. I was sent to this world as a Basheer (giver of good news) and as a Nazeer (warner). If you believe in what I say, I guarantee you success in this world as well as the next, and if you fail to believe, I will be patient until Allah Ta'ala decides between us."

The Quraysh replied: "Very well, ask Allah Ta'ala to send His punishment upon us." Rasulullah ﷺ answered: "It is up to Allah Ta'ala to decide. It is His choice to punish you or to leave you for a while."

'Abdullah bin Umayyah jumped up saying: "O Muhammad! Your people have made many requests but you have refused to accept even a single one. O Muhammad! Even if you were to use a ladder and climb up to the sky and return with a written proof of your prophethood and even if four angels return with you confirming your prophethood, then too I will not believe you."

Rasulullah ﷺ returned home very sad. Since Rasulullah ﷺ was sent to this world as Rahmatul-lil 'Aalameen (a mercy to the worlds), the different ways of punishment that had come to the previous Ummahs were not sent to this Ummah because of the barakah (blessing) of Rasulullah ﷺ. Once, the Quraysh asked Rasulullah ﷺ to change the mountain of Safa into gold. Rasulullah ﷺ planned to make dua before Allah Ta'ala but Hadhrat Jibraa'eel عليه السلام came and said: "O Rasulullah ﷺ! Inform them that they will get what they ask for but also warn them that if they fail to believe even after seeing these definite signs, it will not be good for them. They will be destroyed immediately." The Quraysh replied: "We are not in need of this."

The disbelievers trouble Rasulullah ﷺ

When the Quraysh saw that Islam is being practiced openly, they could not tolerate it any more. They became bitter enemies of all the Muslims. They intended to trouble Rasulullah ﷺ so much that he would give up and stop inviting people towards Islam.

One Sahaabi رضي الله عنه says: "I saw Rasulullah ﷺ inviting the people to Islam begging them: 'O people! Say *'Laa Ilaaha Illallah'*, you will be successful.' But alas, I then saw the people abusing him. Some people were spitting at him whilst others were busy throwing sand at him. In this way they continued to abuse him until a young girl carrying water came to Rasulullah ﷺ and washed his face and hands. When I asked who she was, I was told that she is Rasulullah's ﷺ daughter, Zainab رضي الله عنها."

A man of the Banu Kinaanah tribe says that he saw Rasulullah ﷺ in the market of Zul-Majaaz saying: 'O people! Say *'Laa Ilaaha Illallah'*, you will be successful' whilst Abu Jahal was busy throwing sand at Rasulullah ﷺ saying: 'O people! Do not be bluffed by this man. He wants you to break your connection with Laat and 'Uzza'. However, Rasulullah ﷺ calmly continued with his efforts without even looking at Abu Jahal.

Abdullah bin 'Amr bin 'Aas رضي الله عنه says: 'Once, Rasulullah ﷺ was busy in Salaah in the Hateem area when 'Uqbah bin Abi Mu'eet pulled a cloth over Rasulullah's ﷺ neck and tugged it so tightly that he almost strangled him. Abu Bakr رضي الله عنه quickly pushed 'Uqbah aside. He then read the following aayat:

"Are you killing a man who says my Rabb is Allah and he has presented to you strong proofs from your Lord?"

Usmaan bin Affaan ﺭﺿﻲ ﺍﻟﻠﻪ ﻋﻨﻪ says: "I once saw Rasulullah ﷺ performing Tawaaf of the K'abah. 'Uqbah bin Abi Mu'eet, Abu Jahal and Umayyah bin Khalaf were sitting in the Hateem area. The moment Rasulullah ﷺ passed by, they swore Rasulullah ﷺ. The second time round, they again told him something rude. When they swore him on the third round, Rasulullah's ﷺ face changed. He stopped and said: 'By Allah! You will never give up until the punishment of Allah Ta'ala crashes upon you.'" Hadhrat Usmaan ﺭﺿﻲ ﺍﻟﻠﻪ ﻋﻨﻪ says: "There wasn't a single one of them who was not shivering with fear. Saying this, Rasulullah ﷺ returned home with us walking behind him. This is when Rasulullah ﷺ said:

> "Accept good news from me. Allah will make His Deen powerful and He will complete His word and help His Deen. These people whom you are staring at, Allah Ta'ala will slaughter them at your hands. Hadhrat Usmaan ﺭﺿﻲ ﺍﻟﻠﻪ ﻋﻨﻪ says: "By Allah! I saw them all slaughtered at our hands."

'Abdullah bin Mas'ood ﺭﺿﻲ ﺍﻟﻠﻪ ﻋﻨﻪ says: "Rasulullah ﷺ was once performing Salaah in the Haram area. Abu Jahal and his friends were also present. Abu Jahal challenged his friends: "Is there anyone amongst you who has the courage to go and fetch the tripe of a camel and place it on Muhammad's back as he goes into Sajdah?" 'Uqbah bin Abi Mu'eet agreed to take up this challenge. He fetched a load of tripe and threw it on Rasulullah's ﷺ back whilst he was in Sajdah. 'Abdullah bin Mas'ood ﺭﺿﻲ ﺍﻟﻠﻪ ﻋﻨﻪ says: "I was busy watching this whole scene but I could do absolutely nothing. The disbelievers on the other hand, burst out in laughter and were actually falling upon each other in gleeful laughter. In the meantime, Hadhrat Faatimah ﺭﺿﻲ ﺍﻟﻠﻪ ﻋﻨﻬﺎ who was about four or five years old at that time, rushed to the scene and quickly removed the tripe from his back. Rasulullah ﷺ got up from Sajdah and thrice cursed these wicked people. This curse was very frightening for the Quraysh because they firmly believed that duas are readily accepted in this blessed city. Thereafter, Rasulullah ﷺ cursed Abu Jahal, 'Utbah bin Rabi'ah,

Shaybah bin Rabi'ah, Waleed bin 'Utbah, Umayyah bin Khalaf, 'Uqbah bin Abi Mu'eet and 'Amaarah bin Waleed. He cursed each person by name, most of whom were killed in the Battle of Badr.

CHAPTER 6
BITTER ENEMIES

Most of the people of Makkah Mukarramah became Rasulullah's ﷺ enemies but some of them went over the limit. Some of these people were: Abu Jahal, Abu Lahab, Aswad bin 'Abdu-Yaghus, Waleed bin Mughirah, Umayyah bin Khalaf, Ubayy bin Khalaf, 'Aas bin Waa'il, Nadr bin Haaris, 'Uqbah bin Abi Mu'eet and many others.

Most of them were Rasulullah's ﷺ neighbours and they were from the important people of Makkah. They were busy trying to hurt Rasulullah ﷺ. Night and day, they were busy causing pain to Rasulullah ﷺ. Abu Jahal, Abu Lahab and 'Uqbah bin Abi Mu'eet were the three most bitter enemies of the lot.

Abu Jahal bin Hishaam: He was the Firaun of the Ummah of Rasulullah ﷺ. He made every effort in hurting and causing pain to Rasulullah ﷺ. Abu Jahal's name was Abul-Hakam (which means the father of wisdom) but Rasulullah ﷺ changed this to Abu Jahal (the father of ignorance).

Abu Lahab: He was Rasulullah's ﷺ uncle (Rasulullah's ﷺ father's brother). When Rasulullah ﷺ gartherred the Quraysh to invite them to Islam, Abu Lahab was the first person to reject him saying: "Woe unto you! Did you gather us here for this?" Because of this, Surah Lahab was revealed. His wife, Umm-e-Jameel, the sister of Abu Sufyaan, also hated Rasulullah ﷺ. She would often throw sharp thorns on the path of Rasulullah's ﷺ to cause him pain and hurt.

When Umm-e-Jameel learnt that a Surah of the Qur-aan Shareef was revealed about her and her husband, she picked up a stone and rushed out to attack Rasulullah ﷺ. At that moment, Rasulullah ﷺ was sitting with Hadhrat Abu Bakr Siddeeq رضي الله عنه in Masjidul-Haraam. When Umm-e-Jameel reached the Masjid, Allah Ta'ala placed a covering over her eyes. Only Hadhrat Abu Bakr رضي الله عنه was visible. She failed to see Rasulullah ﷺ. Umm-e-Jameel asked Hadhrat Abu Bakr رضي الله عنه: "Where is your friend? I heard that he makes fun of me and mocks me. By Allah! If I see him now, I will smash him with this stone."

Just seven days after the battle of Badr, a boil came up on Abu Lahabs' body and this finally caused him a painful death. Out of fear of infection, his family members refused to even touch his dead body. Therefore, his body remained rotting for three days. Finally, out of fear of disgrace, they hired a few workers to remove his body. They dug a hole and using long wooden poles, they shoved his body and dumped it into the hole. They then quickly covered it up with sand and stones. This was his treatment in this world. What about the disgrace of the hereafter that is still to follow? May Allah Ta'ala protect us from this. Aameen.

Umayyah bin Khalaf: Umayyah bin Khalaf was the master of Hadhrat Bilal رضي الله عنه. He caused lots of pain and hardship to this poor Sahaabi only because he brought Imaan in Allah Ta'ala. Umayyah had an evil habit of openly abusing Rasulullah ﷺ. Whenever he passed Rasulullah ﷺ, he would mockingly wink his eyes. His terrible behaviour caused the revelation of Surah Humazah:

$$\text{وَيْلٌ لِكُلِّ هُمَزَةٍ لُمَزَةٍ ۞ الَّذِىْ جَمَعَ مَالًا وَّ عَدَّدَهُ ۞}$$

"Woe unto every slanderer and backbiter! He, who collects wealth and keeps on counting it.

Umayyah bin Khalaf was killed in the Battle of Badr by Hadhrat Khubaib رضي الله عنه or by Hadhrat Bilal رضي الله عنه.

Chapter Six – Bitter Enemies

Ubayy bin Khalaf: Ubayy bin Khalaf is the brother of Umayyah bin Khalaf. Just like his brother, he caused terrible harm and pain to Rasulullah ﷺ. He was killed in the battle of Uhud at the hands of Rasulullah ﷺ.

Uqbah bin Abi Mu'eet: He was the best friend of Ubayy bin Khalaf. One day, Uqbah sat in the company of Rasulullah ﷺ attentively listening to his words. When Ubayy learnt of this, he hurried over to Uqbah and said: "I heard that you sat in the company of Muhammad ﷺ attentively listening to his words. By Allah! Until you do not go and spit on his face, it is haraam for me to talk to you and even look at your face." Accordingly, the wretched 'Uqbah got up and spat right onto the mubaarak face of Rasulullah ﷺ. Upon this, the following aayaat were revealed:

$$\text{وَ يَوْمَ يَعَضُّ الظَّالِمُ عَلَىٰ يَدَيْهِ يَقُولُ يَٰلَيْتَنِى اتَّخَذْتُ مَعَ الرَّسُولِ سَبِيلًا}$$

$$\text{يَٰوَيْلَتَىٰ لَيْتَنِى لَمْ أَتَّخِذْ فُلَانًا خَلِيلًا}$$

"And the day when the evil-doer will bite his hands (in despair) saying: O! If only I had taken the path of the messenger. Ah! Woe unto me! .... [Surah Furqaan verses 27-31]

Uqbah was captured as a prisoner in the Battle of Badr and was killed in a place called Safra.

Waleed bin Mughirah: He would say: "It is strange that Muhammad (ﷺ) was chosen as a Nabi whilst Abu Mas'ood Saqafi and I were excluded whereas both of us are noble leaders of this city. I am the leader of the Quraysh whilst he is the leader of Saqif."

Nadr bin Haaris: He was also one of the chiefs of the Quraysh. He would often travel to Persia on business. On his travels, he would buy books of stories and history of the non-Arab kings. He would then tell these stories to the Quraysh. He would tell the Quraysh: "Muhammad tells the stories of

'Aad and Samood to you but I will share with you the stories of Rustam, Asfandiyaar and the Persian kings." The people enjoyed listening to these stories (like the novels of today). The people would pay more attention to his fake stories than they paid to the Qur-aan Shareef. He also bought a singing slave girl who could sing very well. Whenever he learnt of anyone being attracted towards Islam, he would take this slave girl to him and ask her to entertain him with food, drink and music. He would then ask him: "Tell me, is this better than what Muhammad invites you to? Is this better than his orders of Salaah, Saum and Jihaad?" He was caught in the Battle of Badr and was killed by Hadhrat Ali رضى الله عنه.

'Aas bin Waa'il: He was the father of Hadhrat 'Amr bin 'Aas رضى الله عنه. He (the father) was also one of the people who was always poking fun and ridiculing Rasulullah ﷺ. All Rasulullah's ﷺ sons passed away when they were very small. In disgracing Rasulullah ﷺ, 'Aas bin Waa'il said: اِنَّ مُحَمَّدًا اَبْتَرُ لَا يَعِيْشُ لَهُ وَلَدٌ - "Certainly Muhammad is an Abtar. None of his sons survive."

The word Abtar refers to an animal with a cut tail. A person who has no sons or a person not remembered by anyone is like an animal with a cut tail. (it is as though the person's name is now cut and finished).

Then, the following aayat was revealed:

"Verily your enemy is an Abtar (cut off from all good in the hereafter)." [Surah Kausar Verse 3]

Rasulullah ﷺ is fondly remembered by millions of people (unlike his enemies). A month after Hijrah, 'Aas was bitten by an animal on his leg. This caused such swelling that his leg turned as thick as a camel's neck. This wound finally caused his death.

CHAPTER 7
PUNISHING THE POOR MUSLIMS

Just as Islam continued spreading and growing in number, the anger and hatred of the kuffaar of Makkah also increased. The kuffaar could not trouble the stronger Muslims too much (those who had the support of their tribes), therefore they began harming and punishing the poor Muslims who had no-one to help them. Some Muslims were beaten terribly whilst others were locked in dark and narrow cages. We will now mention some of the punishments.

Bilal رضي الله عنه (The leader of the Muazzins)

He was an Abyssinian by birth. He was the slave of Umayyah bin Khalaf. In the heat of the afternoon, when the heat was at its strongest and the boulders of the desert turned blazing hot, he (Umayyah, the master) would command his servants to lay Bilal رضي الله عنه down onto the hot stones of the desert and place a boulder onto his chest. He would then shout at him: "You will die like this. If you have any hope of living, then leave Muhammad and start praying to Laat and 'Uzza." Even in these difficult times, nothing but the words, "Ahad, Ahad (He is one, He is one)" would come out from his mouth.

Umayyah would sometimes wrap him in a cow skin or make him wear a suit of armour and force him to sit in the boiling sun. Even in this condition, the words, "Ahad, Ahad" would flow from his tongue. When Umayyah, his master, realised that Bilal رضي الله عنه was really very strong on his Islam, he tied a rope around his neck and told some young boys to continue dragging him around the city but even then too he continued saying the words "Ahad, Ahad". One day, Hadhrat Abu Bakr رضى الله عنه was passing by. Seeing the terrible punishment of Bilal رضى الله عنه, he said to Umayyah, the master: *"Don't you fear Allah? Until when will this torture continue?"*

Umayyah replied: "You are responsible for making him like this. Now you will have to free him." Hadhrat Abu Bakr رضى الله عنه replied: "Very well. I have a slave who is extremely strong and he is very strong on your religion. Take him in exchange of Bilal and give Bilal to me." Umayyah agreed to this offer. Hadhrat Abu Bakr رضى الله عنه then took Bilal رضى الله عنه along with him and set him free. The torture and injuries upon Hadhrat Bilal رضى الله عنه left horrible scars on his back. These scars could be seen whenever his back happened to be open.

Ammaar bin Yaasir رضى الله عنه

Ammaar bin Yaasir رضى الله عنه was the son of Yaasir رضى الله عنه who was originally from Yemen and came to Makkah Mukarramah. Yaasir decided to stay over in Makkah Mukarramah and married a slave woman by the name of Sumayyah. Ammaar was born from this marriage. In the early days of Islam, Yaasir رضى الله عنه, Sumayyah رضى الله عنها, Ammaar رضى الله عنه and his brother 'Abdullah bin Yaasir رضى الله عنه all accepted Islam. Since Ammaar bin Yaasir رضى الله عنه had no family or tribe in Makkah to support him, the Quraysh severely punished him and troubled him with many kinds of torture. In the middle of the boiling midday heat, they would lay him onto the burning hot sand and beat him up so severely that he would fall unconscious. At times they would throw him into (a dam) of water and at times they would force him to lie down on a bed of burning coals. Whenever Rasulullah صلى الله عليه وسلم passed by, he would pass his hands over Ammaar's head and say: "O Fire! Turn cool and safe upon Ammaar as you had become cool for Ibraaheem."

Whenever Rasulullah صلى الله عليه وسلم saw Ammaar رضى الله عنه, his father Yaasir رضى الله عنه or his mother Sumayyah رضى الله عنها in hardship, he would advise them:

"O family of Yaasir! Be patient." Sometimes, he would say: "O Allah! Forgive the family of Yaasir." Sometimes he would say: "Good news upon you! Jannat is waiting for you."

Hadhrat Ali رضي الله عنه says that he heard Rasulullah صلى الله عليه وسلم saying: "From head to toe, Ammaar is filled with Imaan." (He is a perfect Mu'min). Once, Hadhrat Ammaar رضي الله عنه removed his shirt when a few people saw black scars covering his back. When asked about these scars, he replied: "The Quraysh of Makkah would lay me down on the boiling hot stones (of the Makkan desert). These are the scars of those injuries."

The same cruelty was shown to his father Yaasir رضي الله عنه and his mother Sumayyah رضي الله عنها. In the beginning, just seven people openly announced their Islam. They were, Rasulullah صلى الله عليه وسلم, Hadhrat Abu Bakr رضي الله عنه, Bilal رضي الله عنه, Khabbaab رضي الله عنه, Suhaib رضي الله عنه, Ammaar رضي الله عنه and Sumayyah رضي الله عنها. Because of their noble family connections, the kuffaar of Makkah were unable to overpower Rasulullah صلى الله عليه وسلم and Abu Bakr رضي الله عنه. However, the remaining five; Bilal, Khabbaab, Suhaib, Ammaar and Sumayyah رضي الله عنهم were always tortured and punished by the Quraysh. In the middle of the midday heat, they would dress them in metal armour and force them to stand in the boiling heat. One day, Abu Jahal came before them. (In a fit of anger), he poked a spear into Hadhrat Sumayyah's رضي الله عنها private part. This wound caused her to die as a Shaheed. The first martyr in Islam was Hadhrat Sumayyah رضي الله عنها. When Abu Jahal was killed during the Battle of Badr, Rasulullah صلى الله عليه وسلم told Hadhrat Ammaar رضي الله عنه: "Allah has destroyed your mother's killer." Hadhrat Yaasir رضي الله عنه had passed away before Hadhrat Sumayyah رضي الله عنها during those difficult times.

Suhaib رضي الله عنه

Suhaib رضي الله عنه was from Musil. Once, this area came under a fierce attack from the Romans. Suhaib رضي الله عنه was a young boy at that time. During the Roman looting, he was seized by the Romans and taken away to Rome. This is where he grew up and became known as "Suhaib Rumi" (Suhaib, the Roman). A person of the Banu Kalb tribe bought him from the Romans and brought him to Makkah where he was set free. When Rasulullah ﷺ publically invited the people to Islam, Hadhrat Ammaar رضى الله عنه and Hadhrat Suhaib رضى الله عنه both came together in Daar-e-Arqam and accepted Islam. Just as they troubled Hadhrat Ammaar رضى الله عنه, the disbelievers of Makkah also tortured Hadhrat Suhaib رضى الله عنه. When he tried to move away from Makkah Mukarramah, the Quraysh demanded that he may only leave if he gives them all his goods and wealth in Makkah. Hadhrat Suhaib رضى الله عنه agreed to give away all his wealth and property and made hijrat to Madinah Shareef. When he reached Madinah Munawwarah and explained what had happened to Rasulullah ﷺ, who commented:

رَبِحَ صُهَيْبٌ رَبِحَ صُهَيْبٌ

"Suhaib has made a huge profit. Suhaib has made a huge profit."

In other words, by him exchanging his dunya for his aakhirat, he has made a huge profit. The kuffaar of Makkah would trouble Ammaar, Suhaib and 'Aamir bin Fuhayrah رضى الله عنهم so much that they would often fall unconscious.

Khabbaab رضى الله عنه

Hadhrat Khabbab رضى الله عنه was amongst the first group of people to accept Islam. It is said that he was the 6th person to enter Islam. He was honoured with Islam even before entering Daar-e-Arqam. He was a slave and when his master learnt of his accepting Islam she punished him with different types of pain and suffering. Once, Hadhrat Khabbaab رضى الله عنه went to meet Hadhrat 'Umar رضى الله عنه. After seating him with honour, Hadhrat 'Umar رضى الله عنه said: "Nobody is more worthy to this seat than you except Bilal رضى الله عنه." Hadhrat Khabbaab رضى الله عنه said: "O Ameerul-Mumineen! Even Bilal is not more worthy than I am because Bilal had some support from at least a few kuffaar during that time of suffering and torture. Some of them supported and protected him whilst I had absolutely no support from any one of them. I remember one day when the Quraysh laid me flat over burning coals. One of them placed his foot over my chest so that I was unable to move." Hadhrat Khabbaab رَضِيَ اللّٰهُ عَنْهُ then lifted his kurta, showing the terrible scars covering his back.

In short, the Quraysh left no stone unturned in hurting the Muslims. They hung them from the tree-tops and sometimes they tied their feet and dragged them about. They even placed heated iron bars on their backs and stomachs. The kuffaar did all sorts of terrible things to them but not one of them moved away even a little bit from the true Deen. They died tolerating these hardships but they did not turn away from Islam. May Allah Ta'ala be pleased with them and may they be pleased with Him.

There were even those who were noble and people of position but were still not saved from the torture of the kuffaar. Some incidents are as follows:

1. When Hadhrat Usmaan رَضِيَ اللّٰهُ عَنْهُ accepted Islam, his uncle tied him up with a rope and yelled at him: "You have the guts to leave the religion of your forefathers and accept a new religion!" Hadhrat Usmaan رَضِيَ اللّٰهُ عَنْهُ replied: "By Allah! I will never ever leave this Deen." When his uncle realised how strong and sincere he was to this Deen, he left him.

2. When Hadhrat Zubair رَضِيَ اللّٰهُ عَنْهُ accepted Islam, his uncle wrapped him in a sack and smoked him. He tried to force him to return to Kufr but Hadhrat Zubair رَضِيَ اللّٰهُ عَنْهُ would say: "Never! I will certainly not go back to Kufr."

3. When Hadhrat 'Umar's رَضِيَ اللّٰهُ عَنْهُ brother-in-law, who was also his cousin, Sa'eed bin Zaid رَضِيَ اللّٰهُ عَنْهُ accepted Islam, Hadhrat 'Umar رَضِيَ اللّٰهُ عَنْهُ tied him up with ropes.

4. When Khaalid bin Sa'eed bin 'Aas رَضِيَ اللّٰهُ عَنْهُ accepted Islam, his father gave him such a bashing that he suffered serious head injuries. His father also stopped him from all his meals.

5. When Hadhrat Abu Bakr رضي الله عنه and Hadhrat Talhah رضي الله عنه accepted Islam, Nafal bin Khuwaylid – who was known as 'the lion of the Quraysh' – caught both of them and tied them up with one rope. This is why Abu Bakr and Talhah were referred to as Qarnain. (In other words, two people tied together with a single rope.)

6. When Hadhrat Abu Zarr Ghifaari رضي الله عنه accepted Islam and publicly announced his Islam in the middle of the Masjidul-Haraam, the kuffaar gave him such a beating that he fell unconscious to the ground. Hadhrat 'Abbaas رضي الله عنه rescued him from them.

CHAPTER 8
MIRACLES OF RASULULLAH ﷺ

The Splitting of the Moon

About five years before the hijrat to Madinah Munawwarah, the kuffaar of Makkah Mukarramah came to Rasulullah ﷺ. They challenged him to show some sign that would confirm his prophethood. They demanded that he split the moon into two parts. They challenged him at night when the 14th moon was shining brightly. Rasulullah ﷺ replied: "If I show this miracle, would you accept Islam?" "Surely," they replied, "We would certainly believe in you." Rasulullah ﷺ then made dua to Allah Ta'ala and then pointed his mubaarak finger towards the moon. The moment he pointed towards the moon, it split into two; one part towards Mt. Abu Qubais and the other towards Mt. Qayqa'an. For quite a while, people were left amazed staring at this incredible sight. Some of them were so shocked that they wiped their eyes a few times with their clothing and looked again at the moon only to realise that it really was in two parts. Rasulullah ﷺ continued inviting them: "Ish-hadoo! Bear witness: Bear witness!" The moon remained like this for the amount of time equal to the time between 'Asr and Maghrib. It then returned to its original condition. In disgust, the kuffaar of Makkah Mukarramah shouted out: "Nay, Muhammad! You have put magic over all of us. Wait for some travellers coming into Makkah from outside. Ask them about this miracle because it is not possible for Muhammad to do his magic over everybody. If they also saw the moon being split, then Muhammad is genuine and if they say that they did not see the moon in two, then know that it was definitely magic." Many travellers were asked about this. Travellers from every direction said that they had seen the moon split into two. In spite of their witnessing this miracle with their own eyes and listening to the claims of others, these stubborn kuffaar refused to accept Islam saying: "This is just magic."

The miracle of the return of the sun

From the miracles of Rasulullah ﷺ, one of them is the return of the sun, in other words, the coming back of the sun after sunset. Hadhrat Asma bint 'Umais رضي الله عنها says: "Rasulullah ﷺ was in a place called Sahba near Khaybar. He was resting with his head on Hadhrat Ali's رضي الله عنه lap. Hadhrat Ali رضي الله عنه had not as yet performed his 'Asr Salaah when wahi (divine revelation) started coming down. This continued until sunset. Rasulullah ﷺ asked Hadhrat Ali رضي الله عنه if he had performed his 'Asr Salaah. When he replied that he hadn't, Rasulullah ﷺ raised his hands in dua and begged Allah Ta'ala: "O Allah! Ali was serving Your Rasool. I beg You to return the sun so that he may perform his 'Asr Salaah on time." Hadhrat Asma رضي الله عنها continues: "After sunset, the sun came back with its rays falling on the earth and the mountains."

CHAPTER 9
FIRST MIGRATION TO ABYSSINIA

When the kuffaar noticed that day-by-day more and more people are accepting Islam and that Islam is growing larger day by day, they increased their harming of the Muslims. Rasulullah ﷺ then advised the Sahaabah رضي الله عنهم: "Spread out onto the earth. Soon Allah Ta'ala would bring all of you back together." They asked: "Where should we go to?" Rasulullah ﷺ pointed with his hand towards the land of Habshah (Abyssinia). Rasulullah ﷺ also told them that a king, in whose land nobody is oppressed by another, rules this land.

The Sahaabah رضي الله عنهم did not wish to escape but because of the torture, they were forced to do so to protect their Deen and Imaan. Their purpose of hijrat (leaving Makkah and going to Abyssinia) was to worship Allah Ta'ala in peace and safety.

In the month of Rajab in the fifth year of Islam a small group of men and women made the first Hijrah towards Abyssinia. Eleven men and five women secretly escaped from Makkah. Some of them were riding whilst others were on foot. Fortunately, when they reached the port (of Jeddah), two ships were about to leave for Abyssinia. For a fee of just five Dirhams, they took all of them on board. When the kuffaar of Makkah heard of their escape from Makkah, they sent their people to hunt them down. By the time these trackers reached the port, the ships had already left. These Sahaabah got onto the ship from the coast of Jeddah.

They stayed in Abyssinia from Rajab right up to Shawwaal. In Shawwaal they heard that the people of Makkah had accepted Islam, so they all left to go back to Makkah. As they came close to Makkah, they learnt that the information they received was false. This made them all confused. Some of them secretly entered Makkah whilst others entered the city under the protection of someone or the other.

Second Migration to Abyssinia

The Kuffaar started troubling the Muslims even more. This is why Rasulullah ﷺ allowed a second migration towards Abyssinia. When the Quraysh learnt that the Sahaabah رضى الله عنهم were safe in Abyssinia and that they were peacefully practicing Islam, the Quraysh had a meeting. At this meeting they decided to send 'Amr bin Aas and 'Abdullah bin Abi Rabi'ah to Negus, the king of Abyssinia. They took lots of gifts and presents to Negus and his ministers to try and win them over. 'Amr bin 'Aas and 'Abdullah bin Abi Rabi'ah went to Abyssinia. They offered their gifts to Negus' wives and friends. They said: "A few foolish youngsters of our city have left their religion and began living in your city. In fact, they left their religion and have not become Christians, but they have entered a completely new religion. The leaders of our families have sent us to ask the king to hand them over to us. We beg you to speak to the king to hand them over to us without any problems." After giving their gifts and begging the ministers, they received their full support. 'Amr bin 'Aas and 'Abdullah bin Abi Rabi'ah did not want the king to call the Sahaabah رضى الله عنهم and speak to them. They did not want the king to listen to what the Sahaabah رضى الله عنهم had to say.

The king became very angry. He made it clear to them that he will not hand them over without proper investigation and without first speaking to the Sahaabah رضى الله عنهم. He said: "How can I hand them over to their enemies without first investigating properly?" He then sent one of his messengers to call the Sahaabah رضى الله عنهم. When the messenger called them, a Sahaabi became worried and asked: "What would you say when you are in front of the king?" (In other words, the king is a Christian whilst we are Muslims. We do not agree on many beliefs.) Another Sahaabi said: "We will say whatever our Nabi ﷺ has taught us and we will do as he had coached us. We will not break his instructions."

Nonetheless, when they came to the court, they made Salaam only and did not bow down before the king. The the ministers became very upset at the Muslims. They asked the Muslims: "Why didn't you bow down before the king?"

Hadhrat Ja'far رضي الله عنه replied: "We do not bow before anyone besides Allah. Allah Ta'ala has sent a prophet to us and he instructed us not to bow down to anyone but Allah." The other Muslims said: "We Muslims greet Rasulullah ﷺ also in this way with Salaam only. Our Prophet ﷺ also informed us that the people of Jannah would greet each other with Salaam. As for bowing down before anyone, may Allah Ta'ala save us, how can we bow down before you and make you equal with Allah?"

Negus then asked: "Which religion have you accepted?"

Hadhrat Ja'far رضي الله عنه delivers a sermon

Hadhrat Ja'far رضي الله عنه stood up to speak on behalf of the Sahaabah رضي الله عنهم.

"O king! We were ignorant. We worshipped idols and ate dead animals. We were involved in many sins. We would cut off family relationships and treated our neighbours very badly. The powerful from us would oppress the weak. Whilst we were in this terrible condition, Allah Ta'ala sent to us His Rasool whose noble lineage, truthfulness, honesty and purity we all knew. He ordered us to worship Allah Ta'ala and believe in Him alone. He instructed us to leave the idols we and our forefathers used to respect. He commanded us to speak the truth, be honest, keep good family relations, be good to the neighbours and to stay away from killing and other evils. He also stopped us from shameless actions, lies, stealing the wealth of orphans and from falsely accusing a pure woman. He commanded us to worship Allah Ta'ala alone without believing in any partners to Him. He commanded us to perform Salaah, pay Zakaat and to fast. In short, we should be ready to sacrifice our lives and our wealth in the path of Allah Ta'ala."

Hadhrat Ja'far ﷺ continued: "So we believe in him and we have faith in him. We have followed whatever he has brought to us from Allah Ta'ala. We worship Allah Ta'ala alone and we do not make any partner to Him. We do what is Halaal and we stay away from Haraam. Because of this, our people have started to trouble us. They have tortured us to force us to leave the worship of Allah Ta'ala and to go back to our old days of shamelessness. When we could not manage their punishments any longer and worshipping Allah Ta'ala became difficult, we decided to move away with the hope that you would not oppress us. We chose to be your neighbour."

Negus asked: "Do you remember any part of the message which your Nabi has brought from Allah Ta'ala?" When Hadhrat Ja'far replied that he did, Negus asked him to read some of it. Hadhrat Ja'far ﷺ started reading from the beginning of Surah Maryam. The king and all his people were unable to control themselves. They started crying so much so that the king's beard was wet with tears. (It appears that the king had a beard and this is also the way of all the Ambiyaa. Not a single Nabi ever shaved his beard. Keeping a beard is an important Sunnah of all the Ambiyaa ﷺ.)

When Hadhrat Ja'far ﷺ stopped reading, the king said: "These words and the words brought by 'Isa ﷺ are the same." He then said to the two men of the Quraysh: "I will never hand over these people to you."

When 'Amr ibnul 'Aas and 'Abdullah bin Abi Rabi'ah left the court in failure, 'Amr ibnul 'Aas said: "Tomorrow I will once more speak to the king in such a way that he will kill them all." 'Abdullah bin Abi Rabi'ah pleaded: "Don't do something that would put their lives in danger. They are, after all, our own flesh and blood. These are our relatives even though we follow different religions." 'Amr bin 'Aas did not listen. He was not bothered about 'Abdullah's plea. The next day, 'Amr bin 'Aas came again to the king and said: "O King! These people say terrible things about 'Isa عَلَيْهِ السَّلَام." The king called the Sahaabah رَضِيَ اللّٰهُ عَنْهُ again. The Sahaabah رَضِيَ اللّٰهُ عَنْهُ were shocked to be called again. When one of the Sahaabah رَضِيَ اللّٰهُ عَنْهُ asked what they would say about 'Isa عَلَيْهِ السَّلَام, all of them agreed that they will say exactly what Allah Ta'ala and His Rasool صَلَّى اللّٰهُ عَلَيْهِ وَسَلَّم said. They would not say anything diffrent.

When they reached the king's court, the king asked the Muslims: "What do you say about 'Isa عَلَيْهِ السَّلَام? Hadhrat Ja'far رَضِيَ اللّٰهُ عَنْهُ replied: "Hadhrat 'Isa عَلَيْهِ السَّلَام was a servant and a Nabi of Allah. He was the Ruh (soul) and Kalimah (word) of Allah." After hearing this, king Negus picked up a stick from the ground and raising it said: "By Allah! Whatever the Muslims have said, 'Isa عَلَيْهِ السَّلَام is nothing more than that, not even to the amount of this stick."

This announcement upset all the people of the king. All of them began to frown but King Negus was not worried in the least. He told them clearly that you may frown as much as you like but this is the truth. He then said to the Muslims: "You may live here in peace. I would not want to trouble you even if your enemies give me a mountain of gold." He then commanded his people to return the gifts of the Quraysh saying: "I have no need for their gifts. By Allah! Allah had blessed me with power and kingdom without any bribery. So I will definitely not accept any bribery and hand the Muslims over to you." The Muslims left the court very happy whilst the two Qurayshis left in shame and failure.

After this, the Muhaajireen (emigrants) settled down in Abyssinia with ease and lived peacefully. When Rasulullah صَلَّى اللّٰهُ عَلَيْهِ وَسَلَّم moved to Madinah Munawwarah, most of them left Abyssinia and also moved to Madinah. Twenty four of them took part in the Battle of Badr. The other Muhaajireen left Abyssinia for Madinah with Hadhrat Ja'far ﷺ in the 7th year of Hijrah around the time of the conquest of Khaybar.

When Hadhrat Ja'far ﷺ and his people decided to leave Abyssinia for Madinah, king Negus paid for all their travel costs and gave them provisions (food, etc) for the journey as well. He also gave them many gifts and sent a messenger along with them saying: "Kindly inform Rasulullah ﷺ about my behaviour with you. Also tell him that I believe that there is none worthy of worship besides Allah and I also believe that you are His Rasool. I also beg you to ask for forgiveness from Allah Ta'ala for me."

Hadhrat Ja'far ﷺ says: "We left Abyssinia and went to live in Madinah. When we reached Madinah, Rasulullah ﷺ hugged me and said: 'I wonder if the conquest of Khaybar has brought me more joy or the arrival of Ja'far.'

Rasulullah ﷺ then sat down. The messenger of Negus, who had accompanied the Sahaabah ﷺ, stood up and said: '(O Prophet of Allah Ta'ala!) Here Ja'far is right before you. Ask him how our king had treated him.' Hadhrat Ja'far replied: 'Negus gave us a warm welcome. He treated us very well. In fact, when we decided to leave Abyssinia, he provided us with transport and provisions for the journey. He offered us his complete help. He also believes that there is none worthy of worship besides Allah and he believes that you are the Rasool of Allah. He also requests that you make dua of forgiveness for him.'"

Rasulullah ﷺ stood up, performed wudhu and read the following dua thrice:

"O Allah! Forgive Najaashi (Negus)."

The Muslims said Aameen to this dua.

Hadhrat Ja'far ؓ says: "I asked the king's messenger to describe whatever he has saw about Rasulullah ﷺ to his king after returning to Abyssinia."

Boycott of Banu Haashim and the Oppressive Ruling

The Qurayshi messengers returned as failures from Abyssinia and the kuffaar heard about King Negus' admiration for Hadhrat Ja'far ؓ and the Muslims. In Makkah, Hadhrat Hamzah ؓ and Hadhrat 'Umar ؓ accepted Islam, which also decreased the power of the kuffaar. The Muslims seemed to be growing day by day and when no other plan was working, all the Qurayshi tribes agreed to make an agreement that would stop all dealings with Muhammad ﷺ and the Banu Haashim. They decided not to marry anyone from the Banu Haashim tribe or to be friendly with them until the Banu Haashim handed over Muhammad's ﷺ life to the Quraysh.

They wrote an agreement with all the details and stuck it onto the inside wall of the K'abah Shareef. Mansoor bin Ikramah, the writer of this agreement, was immediately punished by Allah Ta'ala. His fingers became paralysed and he was unable to use his fingers to write again.

Due to these difficult rules, Abu Taalib, together with other members of his family, moved to the valley of Abu Taalib. The Banu Haashim and the Banu-Muttalib – Muslims and non-Muslims – both gave him their full support. The Muslims gave their support because of Islam whilst the kuffaar gave their support because of family relationship. From the Banu Haashim, only Abu Lahab chose to remain with the Quraysh.

For three long years, the Muslims lived alone and in a terrible condition. The crying of babies out of hunger could be heard right outside the valley where the Quraysh would hear the crying and celebrate in happiness. However, some kind people from them did not like this type of behaviour and said said: "Don't you see how Allah has punished Mansoor bin 'Ikramah?"

During these terrible times, the Muslims lived on leaves and somehow managed to survive. S'ad bin Abi Waqqaas رضي الله عنه says: "I was very hungry and would remain starving. One night, I stepped onto something wet. I immediately picked it up and swallowed it. Up until now I have absolutely no idea what it was."

He also says: "One night I was on my way to relieve myself when I saw a dried out camel skin. I picked it up, washed it and burnt it. I crushed it into a powder, which I then swallowed with water. I survived on this for three days."

The problems of the Muslims were increased when Abu Lahab instructed the business caravans not to sell goods to the Muslims at normal prices but at very high prices. In fact, Abu Lahab even agreed to pay the businessmen for lost business. The Sahaabah رضي الله عنهم would come to buy from the business caravans but because of the high prices, they would return without buying anything.

Some of the kuffaar could not see their family members suffering so much and would secretly send some food for them. One day Hakeem bin Hizaam, together with his slave, was taking some provisions for his aunt (father's sister) Hadhrat Khadijah رضي الله عنها when Abu Jahal spotted him. He screamed angrily: "You are taking food to the Banu Haashim! I will never allow you to take any food for them. I will disgrace you in front of everyone." At that time Abul-Bakhtari was passing by. When he saw what happened, he said to Abu Jahal: "The man is sending some food to his aunt. Why do you have to interfere?" This really made him angrier and he beagn screaming and swearing. Abul-Bakhtari picked up a camel bone and hit Abu Jahal so hard on the head that his head was badly wounded. What hurt Abu Jahal more was that Hadhrat Hamzah رضي الله عنه was watching this whole scene from the valley of Abu Taalib.

Due to these terrible hardships, some of the kuffaar thought about disobeying this horrible ruling. The first person who decided this was Hishaam bin Amr. He kept on thinking that the Quraysh are eating and drinking to their fill whilst their close relatives are passing their days in

Chapter Nine – First Migration to Abyssinia

starvation and are wishing for just a few grains of food. So every night he would leave a camel-load of grain at the entrance of the valley of Abu Taalib.

One day, Hishaam bin Amr spoke to Zuhair bin Umayyah. He was the grandson of 'Abdul-Muttalib and the son of 'Aatikah bint 'Abdul-Muttalib. In other words, he was Rasulullah's ﷺ cousin – his father's sister's son. Hishaam went up to Zuhair saying: "O Zuhair! Are you pleased to eat, drink, dress well and get married whilst your mother's brother wishes for a few grains of food? By Allah! If Abu Jahal's uncle and relatives were to suffer such hardships, he would never have bothered about this ruling." Zuhair replied: "Alas! I am alone. What can I do on my own? If only I can get another person to help me I will stand up against this cruel rule." Hishaam bin 'Amr then went to Mut'im bin 'Adi and spoke to him as well. Mut'im bin 'Adi then spoke to someone else to go against this ruling. From here, Hishaam went to Abul-Bakhtari and then to Zam'ah bin Aswad for more support.

When these five people together wanted to challenge this terrible rule, they agreed to speak about it when all the other people gather. Zuhair took up the courage to do the speaking. The next morning, when the people had gathered in the Masjid, Zuhair stood up saying: "O people of Makkah! It is a shame that we eat, drink, marry and dress ourselves whilst the Banu Haashim are dying with starvation. By Allah! I will not sit comfortable until this horrible agreement is torn up." Abu Jahal replied: "This holy decision of Allah can never be torn."

Zam'ah bin Aswad answered him: "By Allah! It will certainly be torn. Even when this agreement was written, we were not happy about it." Abul-Bakhtari said: "Yes, Zam'ah is speaking the truth. We were not pleased with the ruling." Mut'im added: "Certainly, both of them are true in what they say." Hishaam bin 'Urwah also confirmed what he said. Looking at what was happening around him, Abu Jahal was shocked and said: "It seems like a decision was already made last night."

In the meantime, Rasulullah ﷺ informed his uncle that besides the names of Allah Ta'ala, ants had eaten up the written agreement. Besides the sentence *Bismika Allahumma* which was usually written at the beginning of every document, the rest of the words had been eaten up by ants.

Abu Taalib explained this to the Quraysh and said: "This is what my nephew says and up to this day, my nephew has never spoke a lie. Come, let us make a decision; if what Muhammad says is true, you will stop this cruelty and if what he says is false, I am prepared to hand over Muhammad to you. You may then kill him or set him free." The people said: "Surely, Abu Taalib! You have been very fair."

The written agreement was then sent for. When they saw it, they were shocked to see that besides the names of Allah Ta'ala, ants had eaten up the rest of the document. All of them lowered their heads in shame and embarrassment.

In this way the cruel rule came to an end. In the tenth year of prohethood, Abu Taalib and all his companions came out from this lonely valley. Abu Taalib then went to the Haram Shareef and holding onto the curtain of the K'abah, he and his companions made the following dua: "O Allah! Those who oppressed us, those who broke our family ties and those who put us through such dishonour, O Allah! We beg of You to take revenge on our behalf."

Death of Hadhrat Khadija رضي الله عنها and Abu Taalib

A few days after coming out from the valley of Abu Taalib, in the month of Ramadhaan or Shawwaal in the tenth year of prophethood, Abu Taalib passed away and just three or five days after this, Hadhrat Khadijah رضي الله عنها also passed away.

When Abu Taalib was about to breathe his last, Rasulullah ﷺ came close to him. Abu Jahal and 'Abdullah bin Umayyah were also present at his bedside. Rasulullah ﷺ begged him: "O uncle! Say *Laa Ilaaha Illallah* once only so that I may beg for your forgiveness before Allah Ta'ala." Abu Jahal and 'Abdullah bin Umayyah who thought that perhaps Abu Taalib may read the kalimah said: "O Abu Taalib! Do you wish to leave the religion of 'Abdul Muttalib?"

Abu Taalib refused to say *Laa Ilaaha Illallah* and the very last words to leave his tongue were, "'*Alaa Millati 'Abdil Muttalib*. I am on the religion of 'Abdul Muttalib."

Abu Taalib died saying this but Rasulullah ﷺ said, "I will continue to make dua of forgiveness for Him as long as Allah Ta'ala does not stop me." Then the following aayat was revealed:

$$\text{مَا كَانَ لِلنَّبِيِّ وَالَّذِيْنَ اٰمَنُوْٓا اَنْ يَّسْتَغْفِرُوْا لِلْمُشْرِكِيْنَ وَلَوْ كَانُوْٓا اُولِيْ قُرْبٰى مِنْۢ بَعْدِ مَا تَبَيَّنَ لَهُمْ اَنَّهُمْ اَصْحٰبُ الْجَحِيْمِ ۝}$$

"It is not permissible for the Nabi and the Muslims to ask for forgiveness for the Kuffaar even if they are relatives when it is clear to them that they are the people of Jahannam. (In other words, they died in kufr.)" [Surah Taubah verse 113]

The following aayat was also revealed:

$$\text{اِنَّكَ لَا تَهْدِيْ مَنْ اَحْبَبْتَ وَلٰكِنَّ اللّٰهَ يَهْدِيْ مَنْ يَّشَآءُ}$$

"You are unable to guide whom you wish but Allah guides whomsoever He chooses to." [Surah Qasas verse 56]

Hadhrat 'Abbaas ؓ says: "I asked Rasulullah ﷺ, 'Of what help were you to your uncle? After all, he was your supporter and he helped you very much.' Rasulullah ﷺ replied: 'He is up to his ankles in the fire. If I did not beg Allah for his forgiveness, he would have been in the middle of the fire of Jahannam.'"

Hadhrat Ali ﷺ says: "When Abu Taalib died, I informed Rasulullah ﷺ: 'O Nabi of Allah! Your kaafir uncle has died.' Rasulullah ﷺ replied: 'Go and bury him.' I said: 'He died a Mushrik.' Rasulullah ﷺ said: 'Still too, go and bury him.'" When Hadhrat Ali ﷺ returned to Rasulullah ﷺ after burying Abu Taalib, Rasulullah ﷺ commanded him to take a bath. This is why 'Ulama say that it is better to take a bath after doing the Ghusl and burial of a kaafir.

Journey to Taaif for Inviting to Islam

After Abu Taalib passed away, Rasulullah ﷺ was left with no supporter and after the death of Hadhrat Khadijah ﷺ, he was left with no one to comfort him. This is why, at the end of Shawwaal in the tenth year of prophethood, Rasulullah ﷺ decided to go to Taaif. Perhaps, he thought, these people would accept the Deen of Allah Ta'ala and turn out to be his main supporters. Together with Zaid Bin Haarisah ﷺ, Rasulullah ﷺ set out for Taaif.

Rasulullah ﷺ invited three brothers who were the chiefs of that area to Islam. Instead of listening to the words of truth, they replied very rudely. One of them said: "Did Allah Ta'ala send you as a prophet to tear the curtains of the K'abah?" Another mockingly said: "Could Allah Ta'ala not choose someone else for His prophethood?" The third brother shouted: "By Allah! I absolutely refuse to speak to you! If you are really a Nabi, it is very dangerous to refuse you. (This foolish man did not understand that poking fun at a prophet is even more dangerous than that.) If you are not the Prophet of Allah, then you I don't need to listen you."

He then encouraged the hobos and other youngsters to throw stones at him and poke fun at him. They threw so many stones upon his blessed body that they wounded him badly. Whenever Rasulullah ﷺ was forced by his injuries to sit down, these terrible people would grab him by the arm

Chapter Nine – First Migration to Abyssinia

and force him to stand up again for another round of stone throwing and mockery.

Zaid bin Haarisah ﷺ bravely tried to protect Rasulullah ﷺ by placing his body infront of Rasulullah ﷺ. This left him with serious head injuries whilst Rasulullah ﷺ suffered serious injuries to his (body and) legs so much so that blood flowed down his legs (into his shoes).

After coming out from Taaif, Rasulullah ﷺ decided to take a rest under a tree in the garden of 'Utbah bin Rabi'ah and Shaybah bin Rabi'ah. As he sat down, he humbly expressed his helplessness to Allah Ta'ala by making the following dua:

اَللّٰهُمَّ اِلَيْكَ اَشْكُوْ ضُعْفَ قُوَّتِيْ وَقِلَّةَ حِيْلَتِيْ وَهَوَانِيْ عَلَى النَّاسِ يَا اَرْحَمَ الرَّاحِمِيْنَ اَنْتَ رَبُّ الْمُسْتَضْعَفِيْنَ اِلٰى مَنْ تَكِلُنِيْ اِلٰى عَدُوٍّ بَعِيْدٍ يَتَجَهَّمُنِيْ اَمْ اِلٰى صَدِيْقٍ قَرِيْبٍ مَلَّكْتَهُ اَمْرِيْ اِنْ لَمْ تَكُنْ غَضْبَانًا عَلَىَّ فَلَا اُبَالِيْ غَيْرَ اَنَّ عَافِيَتَكَ اَوْسَعُ لِيْ اَعُوْذُ بِنُوْرِ وَجْهِكَ الَّذِيْ اَشْرَقَتْ لَهُ الظُّلُمَاتُ وَصَلُحَ عَلَيْهِ اَمْرُ الدُّنْيَا وَالْاٰخِرَةِ مِنْ اَنْ تُنْزِلَ بِيْ غَضْبَكَ اَوْ يَحِلَّ بِيْ سَخْطُكَ وَلَكَ الْعُتْبٰى حَتّٰى تَرْضٰى وَلَا حَوْلَ وَلَا قُوَّةَ اِلَّا بِكَ

"O Allah! Only to You do I complain of my weakness, my lack of plans and of my humiliation before the people. O most merciful of the merciful! You are the Rabb of the weak and helpless. To whom do You entrust me? Would You entrust me to an impolite enemy who will frown at me or would You entrust me to a close friend whom You would put incharge of my affairs? If You are not angry with me, I am not worried in the least but Your protection and safety is more accommodating and pleasant to me. I seek refuge with the Noor (brightness) of Your being that has brightened the darkness and the light upon which the affairs of this world and the aakhirat depend, through this noor I seek Your refuge, O Allah, from Your anger coming down upon me or from Your anger overpowering me. And

only to You (do I complain) until You are pleased. There is no power (to chase away evil) nor strength (to do good) but only that which You have decided."

You can very well imagine the duas of a person like Nabi Muhammad ﷺ who besides being a Rasool of Allah is also opressed, a traveller and is far away from his family. Such a dua hardly left his lips when the doors of acceptance were thrown open.

The same 'Utbah and Shaybah, whose hearts were harder than stone, turned soft when they saw Rasulullah's ﷺ sad and terrible condition. They ordered their slave 'Addaas to fill a tray with grapes and take it to the man sitting in the garden. They ordered him to ask the man to eat. 'Addaas brought the tray to Rasulullah ﷺ and placed it before him. Rasulullah ﷺ read *Bismillah* and started eating. 'Addaas said: "By Allah! Nobody in my city has ever used such words." Rasulullah ﷺ asked: "Where are you from and what religion do you follow?" 'Addaas replied: "I am from the city of Nenwaa and I am a Christian." Rasulullah ﷺ asked: "Is this the same Nenwaa where the Nabi Allah, Yunus bin Matta lived?" Shocked, 'Addaas replied: "What do you know about Yunus bin Matta?" Rasulullah ﷺ replied: "He was my brother, a Nabi and I am also a Nabi." 'Addaas kissed Rasulullah ﷺ on his forehead, hands and legs and said: "I believe that you are the slave and Nabi of Allah." When 'Addaas returned to 'Utbah and Shaybah, they scolded him for kissing Rasulullah ﷺ on his hands and feet. They also warned him: "Make sure this man does not move you from your religion. Your religion is far better than his religion."

Hadhrat 'Aa'ishah رضى الله عنها says: "I once asked Rasulullah ﷺ if he ever experienced a day more severe than the day of Uhud. Rasulullah ﷺ replied: "Well, the difficulties I suffered at the hands of your people, were difficulties that I had somehow managed, but the most punishing day to me was the day at Taaif. I returned from them very disappointed. I recovered a bit as I reached a place called Qarn Al-Sa'aalib when all of a sudden I lifted my head and saw a cloud covering me. Jibraa'eel ﻋَﻠَﻴْﻪِﭐﻟﺴَّﻼَﻡ who was also in the cloud called out to me: "Allah knows about the behaviour of your people. Allah has sent to you Malakul-Jibaal (the angel of the mountains). You may command him to do as you wish." The angel in charge of the mountains greeted me with Salaam and said: "O Muhammad! Allah has sent me to you. I am Malakul-Jibaal (the angel in charge of the mountains). The mountains are in my control. You may command me to do as you wish. If you command me, I will drop these two mountains (on either side of Makkah and Taaif) and crush everyone within them." Rasulullah ﺻَﻠَّﻰﭐﻟﻠَّﻪُﻋَﻠَﻴْﻪِﻭَﺳَﻠَّﻢ replied: "No, I have hope that Allah Ta'ala will create from their children, people who will worship Him alone without joining any partners to Him."

CHAPTER 10
MI'RAAJ

After his return from Taaif, Allah Ta'ala took Rasulullah ﷺ for Mi'raaj from Masjidul-Haraam to Masjidul-Aqsa and from there to the seven heavens all in one night with his physical body and soul whilst he was awake. This journey is known as Mi'raaj or Israa. It took place on the 27th night of Rajab. Ten years of prophethood had gone by and Rasulullah ﷺ had suffered many difficulties in the path of Allah Ta'ala. Allah Ta'ala then honoured Rasulullah ﷺ by taking him for mi'raj and lifted him to such a high level that even the greatest of angels were left behind. He was taken right up to the throne of Allah Ta'ala after which there is no higher rank.

Mi'raaj in Detail

One night Rasulullah ﷺ was lying down in the house of Umme Haani رضى الله عنها. He had just dozed off when the roof of the house suddenly split open. Through this gap, Hadhrat Jibraa'eel عليه السلام and other angels came to Rasulullah ﷺ. They woke him up and took him to Masjidul-Haraam. When he reached there, he went into the Hateem area and fell asleep. Jibraa'eel عليه السلام and Mikaa'eel عليه السلام woke him up again and took him to the well of Zam Zam. There they laid him down and split his chest open. They removed his blessed heart and rinsed it with the water of Zam Zam. A tray full of Imaan and wisdom was then brought to him. After placing this Imaan and wisdom into his blessed heart, they put back the heart in its position and closed up his chest. They then stamped the seal of prophethood between his shoulder blades. (This was a clear sign of Rasulullah ﷺ being the last of all the Ambiyaa عَلَيْهِمُ السَّلَام.)

The Buraaq was then brought before him. Buraaq is an animal like a small horse. It was white in colour and was so fast that one step would fall as far as the eye could see. When Rasulullah ﷺ sat on this animal, it started jumping around. Jibraa'eel عَلَيْهِ السَّلَام scolded: "O Buraaq! What is this? To this day, not a single servant of Allah more honourable than Muhammad (ﷺ) has sat on you." The Buraaq almost fell over in shame. It then left with Rasulullah ﷺ. Jibraa'eel عَلَيْهِ السَّلَام and Mikaa'eel عَلَيْهِ السَّلَام also joined Rasulullah ﷺ on this animal.

Rasulullah ﷺ said: "On the way we saw a land with many date-trees. Jibraa'eel عَلَيْهِ السَّلَام asked me to get off and perform Nafl Salaah. I got down and performed Salaah. Jibraa'eel عَلَيْهِ السَّلَام then asked: 'Do you have any idea where you performed Salaah?' I replied: 'I have absolutely no idea.' Jibraa'eel عَلَيْهِ السَّلَام said: 'You performed Salaah in Yasrib (Madinah Tayyibah) where you are going to migrate.' We then left once again when we passed another area. Jibraa'eel عَلَيْهِ السَّلَام asked me to get down and perform Salaah here as well. I got down and performed Salaah. Jibraa'eel عَلَيْهِ السَّلَام informed me: 'You performed Salaah in the valley of Seenaa near the tree of Musa عَلَيْهِ السَّلَام where Allah Ta'ala spoke to Musa عَلَيْهِ السَّلَام.' We then passed another area where I was again asked to perform Salaah. I got down once again and performed Salaah. Jibraa'eel عَلَيْهِ السَّلَام informed me that I had just performed Salaah in Madyan (the land of Shu'aib عَلَيْهِ السَّلَام). We set off once again until we came to another area where Jibraa'eel عَلَيْهِ السَّلَام asked me to get down and perform Salaah. I got down from the animal and performed Salaah. Jibraa'eel عَلَيْهِ السَّلَام informed me that this place is called Baitul-Lahm (Bethlehem) where 'Isa عَلَيْهِ السَّلَام was born."

The wonders of this journey

Whilst Rasulullah ﷺ was on this journey, he passed by an old woman who called out to him. Jibraa'eel عَلَيْهِ السَّلَامُ advised Rasulullah ﷺ to move ahead without paying any attention to her in the least. As he went on, he came to an old man who also called out to him. Hadhrat Jibraa'eel عَلَيْهِ السَّلَامُ again advised Rasulullah ﷺ to move on. As he went further, Rasulullah ﷺ saw a group of people who greeted him thus:

اَلسَّلَامُ عَلَيْكَ يَا اَوَّلُ اَلسَّلَامُ عَلَيْكَ يَا اٰخِرُ اَلسَّلَامُ عَلَيْكَ يَا حَاشِرُ

"Assalaamu 'Alayka Yaa Awwal, Assalaamu 'Alayka Yaa Aakhir, Assalaamu 'Alayka Yaa Haashir."

Jibraa'eel عَلَيْهِ السَّلَامُ asked Rasulullah ﷺ to reply to their Salaam. He then explained to him, "The old woman you saw at the roadside is actually the dunya (the world). The remaining age of this world is according to the remaining life of this old woman. The old man you saw was actually shaytaan. Both of them tried to bring you close towards them. The group that greeted you with Salaam were Hadhrat Ibraaheem عَلَيْهِ السَّلَامُ, Hadhrat Musa عَلَيْهِ السَّلَامُ and Hadhrat 'Isa عَلَيْهِ السَّلَامُ."

Rasulullah ﷺ said: "On the night of Mi'raaj I passed Musa عَلَيْهِ السَّلَامُ who was standing busy in Salaah in his grave."

Rasulullah ﷺ said: "On the night of Mi'raaj, I saw Musa عَلَيْهِ السَّلَامُ, Dajjaal and the gatekeeper of Jahannam whose name is Maalik."

Rasulullah ﷺ also saw a group of people with copper fingernails. They were busy scraping the skin off their faces and chests with these copper fingernails. When asked about these people, Jibraa'eel عَلَيْهِ السَّلَامُ replied: "These are the people who eat the flesh of others." In other words, they backbite and speak bad about others.

Rasulullah ﷺ also saw a person swimming in a river. He was busy eating pieces of stones. When Rasulullah ﷺ asked about this man, Jibraa'eel عليه السلام replied: "This man takes ribaa (interest)."

Rasulullah ﷺ also saw a group of people who, during just one day, could plant their crops and harvest it. The field would then change back to its original condition. When Rasulullah ﷺ asked about this, Jibraa'eel عليه السلام replied: "These are people who go for Jihaad in the path of Allah. Their good deeds are multiplied seven hundred times. Whatever they spend, Allah Ta'ala replaces them with a far better replacement."

Rasulullah ﷺ then passed a group of people whose heads were being crushed by boulders. Each time the heads were crushed, they would come back to their normal shape. This continued again and again. When Rasulullah ﷺ asked about these people, Jibraa'eel عليه السلام replied: "These are people who are not worried about their Fardh Salaah."

He then passed by a group of people whose private parts were wrapped in rags and they were grazing like camels and oxen. Rasulullah ﷺ asked who they were. Jibraa'eel عليه السلام replied: "These are people who do not pay Zakaat on their wealth."

Rasulullah ﷺ then saw a group of people in front of whom were two huge pots. One contained cooked meat and the other had raw and rotten meat. These people were eating the rotten meat without eating any of the healthy cooked meat. Rasulullah ﷺ asked: "Who are these people?" Jibraa'eel عليه السلام replied: "These are the men of your Ummah who, in spite of having Halaal and pure women available to them, spend the entire night with Haraam women of bad character, and this group is also made up of women who leave their Halaal and pure husbands to pass the night with Haraam and dirty men."

He then came to a group of people whose tongues and lips were being cut by iron scissors. As soon as their lips and tongues were cut off, they came back to their original condition. This continued without stopping. When Rasulullah ﷺ asked about this, Jibraa'eel عليه السلام said: "These are the preachers of your Ummah (who as the aayat says 'they preach what they do not do')," in other words, they preach to others but do not practise themselves.

Thereafter Rasulullah ﷺ passed an area with lovely fragrances (smells) and cool breezes. Jibraa'eel عليه السلام informed him that this was the fragrance of Jannah (paradise). They then passed an area stinking of disgusting smells. Jibraa'eel عليه السلام said that this was the stink of Jahannam (hell).

Baitul-Muqaddas

Rasulullah ﷺ arrived at Baitul-Muqaddas and got down from the Buraaq. Rasulullah ﷺ tied the animal to the iron ring on which all the previous Ambiyaa عليهم السلام had tied their animals. Thereafter, Rasulullah ﷺ entered Masjidul-Aqsa and read two Rakaats (of Tahiyyatul-Masjid). The other Ambiyaa عليهم السلام were already waiting for him in the Masjid. Hadhrat Ibraaheem عليه السلام and Hadhrat Musa عليه السلام were also from those who were waiting for Rasulullah ﷺ. After a short while, many people gathered in Masjidul-Aqsa. A Muazzin called out the Azaan and then the Iqaamah. Everybody was waiting to see who would be the Imaam for the salaah? Jibraa'eel عليه السلام held Rasulullah ﷺ by the hand and took him forward. Rasulullah ﷺ says: "I led all of them in Salaah. When I completed the Salaah, Jibraa'eel عليه السلام asked me if I knew who had read Salaah behind me. When I replied that I did not, he said: 'All the Ambiyaa who were sent before you, every single one of them read Salaah behind you.'" According to another narration, even the angels came down from the skies and also read salaah behind Rasulullah ﷺ.

When Rasulullah ﷺ came out from the Masjid, three cups were placed before him. One had water, the other milk and the third contained wine. Rasulullah ﷺ chose the cup of milk. Upon this Jibraa'eel علیہ السلام then said: "You have chosen Deenul-Fitrah (the pure Deen). Had you chosen wine, your Ummah would have gone astray and had you chosen the cup with the water, your Ummah would have drowned." According to some narrations, a cup of honey was also presented to him. He had a bit of this as well.

Going up to the Heavens

After this, Rasulullah ﷺ, together with Jibraa'eel علیہ السلام and other noble angels climbed up to the heavens. According to some narrations, Rasulullah ﷺ climbed the skies whilst sitting on the Buraaq animal and, according to other narrations, Rasulullah ﷺ climbed the skies with the help of a ladder decorated with gems and emeralds with the group of angels on either side of him.

Meeting the Ambiyaa علیہم السلام

In this wonderful manner, Rasulullah ﷺ reached the first heaven. Jibraa'eel علیہ السلام asked to enter. The gatekeeper of the first heaven asked: "Who is with you?" "Muhammad Rasulullah ﷺ is with me," he replied. "Was he invited over here?" he asked. When Jibraa'eel علیہ السلام replied that he was, the angels warmly welcomed him and opened the door for him. Rasulullah ﷺ entered the entrance of the first heaven where he saw an elderly man. Jibraa'eel علیہ السلام explained: "This is your father Aadam علیہ السلام. Go and make Salaam to him." Rasulullah ﷺ made Salaam to him. He affectionately responded to the Salaam warmly and said: "Marhabaa! Welcome to a pious son and a pious Prophet." He then made dua for Rasulullah ﷺ. Whilst meeting him, Rasulullah's ﷺ saw some people on Hadhrat Aadam's علیہ السلام right and some on his left. When Aadam علیہ السلام saw those on his right, he would smile in happiness and when he saw those on his left, he would weep in sadness.

Jibraa'eel عَلَيْهِ السَّلَام explained: "Those on his right are his pious children, who will go to Jannah. When he looks at them he is pleased. Those on his left are his evil children, who will be thrown into Jahannam. He weeps in sorrow when he sees them."

Then Rasulullah ﷺ climbed to the second heaven. Again Jibraa'eel عَلَيْهِ السَّلَام asked to be allowed in. When the gatekeeper asked who was with him, Jibraa'eel عَلَيْهِ السَّلَام replied: "Muhammad Rasulullah ﷺ is with me." "Was he invited?" he asked. When Jibraa'eel عَلَيْهِ السَّلَام replied that he was, the gatekeeper said: "Welcome! Welcome to such a wonderful guest." Here, Rasulullah ﷺ saw Hadhrat Yahya عَلَيْهِ السَّلَام and Hadhrat 'Isa عَلَيْهِ السَّلَام. Jibraa'eel عَلَيْهِ السَّلَام introduced them saying: "Here, this is Yahya عَلَيْهِ السَّلَام and that is 'Isa عَلَيْهِ السَّلَام. Go and make Salaam to them." Rasulullah ﷺ went to them and made Salaam to both of them. They replied to his Salaam and said: "Welcome to a pious brother and a pious Prophet."

Then Rasulullah ﷺ climbed to the third heaven and here again Jibraa'eel عَلَيْهِ السَّلَام asked to enter. Here Rasulullah ﷺ met Yusuf عَلَيْهِ السَّلَام and greeted him with salaam. Rasulullah ﷺ said: "Yusuf عَلَيْهِ السَّلَام was extremely handsome."

Then Rasulullah ﷺ visited the fourth heaven where he met Hadhrat Idrees عَلَيْهِ السَّلَام. He then went to the fifth heaven where he met Hadhrat Haroon عَلَيْهِ السَّلَام. From there, he climbed to the sixth heaven where he met Hadhrat Musa عَلَيْهِ السَّلَام, then to the seventh heaven where he met Hadhrat Ibraaheem عَلَيْهِ السَّلَام. Jibraa'eel عَلَيْهِ السَّلَام told Rasulullah ﷺ that this is his father and he should make Salaam with him. Rasulullah ﷺ went ahead and made Salaam with him. Ibraaheem عَلَيْهِ السَّلَام replied to the Salaam and said: "Welcome to a pious son and to a pious Prophet."

In the Presence of Allah Ta'ala

Finally Rasulullah ﷺ arrived in the sacred presence of Allah Ta'ala. When Rasulullah ﷺ reached this area of 'closeness', he went into Sajdah. Here he saw the noor of Allah Ta'ala and he was allowed to talk directly with Allah Ta'ala. Rasulullah ﷺ said: "I saw the greatest of all noors. Then Allah Ta'ala spoke whatever He wished to speak to me." Rasulullah ﷺ was blessed with seeing Allah Ta'ala and speaking with Him directly without any person between them. Allah Ta'ala spoke with Rasulullah ﷺ and blessed him with three gifts on this great occasion; the first gift was made up of the five daily Salaah; the second gift was the last few aayaat of Surah Baqarah, which includes the mercy, love, ease and forgiveness of Allah Ta'ala upon this Ummah and it speaks about the victory and help to the Muslims against the Kuffaar. The third gift given to Rasulullah ﷺ on this night was that Allah Ta'ala would forgive the major (big) sins of any Ummati who does not believe in any partners to Him. Any person whose heart has even an iota (spec) of Imaan will, one day be removed from Jahannam.

In short, Allah Ta'ala gave Rasulullah ﷺ many gifts and blessed him with many glad tidings and gifted him with the fifty daily Salaah. Accepting all these commands and orders most happily, Rasulullah ﷺ turned back to return to this earth. On his return journey, he met Hadhrat Ibraaheem عليه السلام. He did not say anything about these commands of Salaah, etc. "Then I passed Musa عليه السلام who asked me what I was commanded with. I replied: 'During the day and night, fifty Salaahs have been commanded.' Musa عليه السلام said: 'I have a lot of experience with the Bani Israa'eel. Your Ummah is much weaker. They will not manage with this command. So return to your Rabb and ask Him to make it less.'" Rasulullah ﷺ returned to Allah Ta'ala and asked Him to lessen the number of Salaahs. Allah Ta'ala lessened it by five. When Rasulullah ﷺ passed Musa عليه السلام again, he asked the same question. Once more he asked Rasulullah ﷺ to ask for less Salaah. This going up and down happened many times until just five daily Salaah remained. Even then, Musa عَلَيْهِ ٱلسَّلَامْ begged Rasulullah ﷺ to return to Allah Ta'ala and ask for even less. Rasulullah ﷺ replied: "I have asked so many times already. Now I am embarrassed to ask Allah Ta'ala to make it less." Saying this Rasulullah ﷺ continued with his journey. A voice from the unseen then called out: "These are five (salaah) but are equal to fifty." That is, these are just five Salaah but the reward of these five Salaah is equal to fifty Salaah. "My rule will not be changed. These five Salaah were already decided in My knowledge."

CHAPTER 11
INVITATION TO ISLAM DURING THE DAYS OF HAJ

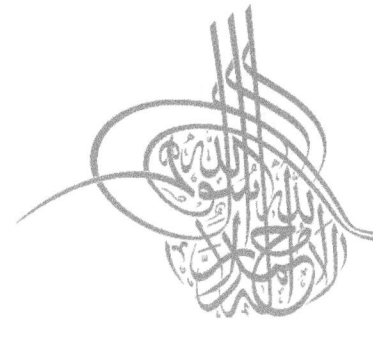

When Rasulullah ﷺ realised that the Quraysh are continuing with their evil ways, he would go to the camps of the Hajis who would come to Makkah during the days of Haj and there he would invite them towards Islam. He would advise them to support the true religion. He would invite the people towards tauheed, truth and sincerity. However, his uncle Abu Lahab would leave all his other work and, walking behind Rasulullah ﷺ, he would say: "People! This man wants you to leave Laat and 'Uzza. He is calling you towards misguidance. Don't ever believe what he says."

Nonetheless, Rasulullah ﷺ invited many tribes to Islam. Some of them listened to him whilst others refused.

"What do you invite to?" some of them would ask. Rasulullah ﷺ read the following aayaat in reply:

> *That you do not join any partners to Him, keep good relationship with parents, and that you do not kill your children out (of fear) of poverty. We sustain you as well as them."* [Al-An'aam verse 151]

After listening to his reading they would say: "By Allah! This is definitely not the word of a human."

Rasulullah ﷺ would also read the following aayaat:

"Verily Allah commands you to be just, and Ihsaan (doing good) and giving to the relatives and He stops you from shameless things, evil deeds and injustice. He advises you so that you may be warned."

[Surah Nahl verse 90]

Islam in Madinah Munawwarah - 11th Year of Prophethood

Most of the people of Madinah were part of the Aws and Khazraj tribes who were idol worshippers. There were also some Jews living in Madinah. Since the Jews were few in number in Madinah, whenever they had a problem with the Aws or Khazraj, the Jews would say: "Very soon the final Nabi is going to be sent to this earth. We will follow him. After joinning with him, we will destroy you like the people of 'Aad and Iram."

During the days of Haj six people of the Khazraj tribe came to Makkah Mukarramah. This was the 11th year of prophethood. Rasulullah ﷺ came to them inviting them towards Islam. He also read to them a few aayaat of the Qur-aan Shareef. As soon as they saw him, they recognised him and said to one another: "By Allah! This is the very same Prophet whom the Jews talk about. Listen, do not let the Jews beat you to this good fortune and virtue."

In this meeting, they all accepted Islam before getting up from their places. They said: "O Prophet of Allah! We have accepted Islam and we believe in you. The Jews and us are always having problems with one another. If you allow, may we return and invite them to this religion of Islam as well? If they accept Islam and both of us live peacfully, nobody will be dearer to us than you." (Rasulullah ﷺ allowed them to invite them to Islam.)

These six people took permission from Rasulullah ﷺ and returned to Madinah Munawwarah. Whomsoever they met, they had to speak about Rasulullah ﷺ.

The First Pledge of the Ansaar - 12th Year of Prophethood

The next year, which was the 12th year of prophethood, twelve people came to Makkah Mukarramah to meet Rasulullah ﷺ. Five of them were part of the orignal six whilst another seven joined them. These twelve people came to Rasulullah ﷺ and at night in Mina they took bay'at (took a promise) at the hands of Rasulullah ﷺ near a place called 'Aqabah. Therefore this bay'at (promise) is known as, Bay'atul-'Aqabah. They promised not to believe in any partners to Allah, to stay away from stealing, zina, burying their daughters alive, false accusation and slander. This was the first promise of the Ansaar, which is known as Bay'atul-'Aqabah Al-Ulaa (the first promise at 'Aqabah).

When this group was returning to Madinah Munawwarah after taking bay'at, Rasulullah ﷺ sent 'Abdullah bin Ummu Maktoom رضي الله عنه and Mus'ab bin 'Umair رضي الله عنه with them to teach the people of Madinah the Qur-aan Shareef and the rules of Islam. When they reached Madinah Munawwarah, they lived in the house of As'ad bin Zuraarah رضي الله عنه.

Mus'ab bin 'Umair رضي الله عنه would invite the people towards Islam and lead them in Salaah. He was their Imaam. One day, as he was giving a talk about the beauty of Islam in front of a huge crowd of people, Usaid bin Hudhair, with a sword in his hand, appeared before him and asked: "What have you come here for? Why are you misleading our women and children? It would be better if you left this place!"

Mus'ab bin 'Umair رضي الله عنه replied: "Is it possible for you to sit down for a little while and listen to what I have to say? If it pleases you, well and good otherwise you may choose to go back." Usaid replied: "Very well, this seems quite fair." He then took a seat. Mus'ab bin 'Umair رضي الله عنه explained the beauty of Islam and read some aayaat of the Qur-aan Shareef before him. After hearing this, Usaid said: "How beautiful and excellent are these words."

He then asked about how to accept Islam. Mus'ab bin 'Umair رضى الله عنه replied: "Firstly, you should clean your body and clothing. Take a bath. Read the Kalimah Shahaadah and perform Salaah." Usaid stood up right away, cleaned his clothing, took a bath, read the Kalimah Shahaadah and read two Rakaats of Salaah. He then said: "There is another man – meaning S'ad bin Mu'aaz, the leader of the Aws tribe – who, if he accepts Islam, then every single member of the Aws tribe will also accept Islam. Let me go and I will send him to you now." When S'ad bin Mu'aaz saw Usaid bin Hudhair رضى الله عنه comming, he said: "The Usaid returning does not seem like the same Usaid who left from here earlier on." As he came closer, S'ad asked Usaid: "What happened?" Usaid replied: "I did not find anything wrong in his (Mus'ab's) words."

S'ad bin Mu'aaz became very angry. He took his sword and went to the home of As'ad bin Zuraarah's (the host of Mus'ab رضى الله عنه).

When he reached, S'ad shouted: "If it was not because of your family relationship with me, if you were not my cousin I would have finished you off with this sword. Have you brought this man (Mus'ab) here to bluff the people?"

Mus'ab replied: "S'ad, is it possible for you to sit and listen to me for a few moments? If you like what you hear you may accept it otherwise you are free to do as you please." "Okay," replied S'ad, "what you say is fair." Saying this, he sat down. Mus'ab رضى الله عنه explained the beauty of Islam to him and read a few aayaat of the Qur-aan Shareef to him. When he heard the aayaat of the Qur-aan, his colour changed. He asked: "How do I enter this religion?"

Mus'ab رضى الله عنه replied: "Firstly, you should clean your clothing and take a bath. Read the Kalimah Shahaadah and perform two Rakaats of Salaah."

Without delay, S'ad got up, took a bath, read the Kalimah Shahaadah and performed two Rakaats of Salaah.

Then he went towards his people. When his people saw him coming from a distance, they realised that there was something different about him. When he reached them, Sʿad said: "What do you think of me?" In one voice they all agreed: "You are our leader. As far as your understanding and advice is concerned, you are the best from us." Sʿad said: "By Allah! I will never speak to you until and unless each one of you believes in Allah and His Rasool ﷺ." The entire tribe then accepted Islam.

Islam of Rifaʾah ؓ

Rifaʾah ؓ says: "Even before those six Ansaaris could come to Makkah, my cousin (my mother's sister's son) Muʿaaz bin ʿAfraa and I came to Makkah. We met with Rasulullah ﷺ and he explained the beauty of Islam to us.

He asked me: "O Rifaʾah! Tell me, who created the earth, skies and the mountains?" We replied: "Allah created them." He then asked: "Who is more worthy of being worshipped; the Creator or the created?" We replied: "The Creator." Rasulullah ﷺ then said: "So you are supposed to be worshipped by these idols whilst you are supposed to worship Allah because you created these idols whilst you were created by Allah. I am inviting you to the worship of just one Allah. Believe in the oneness of Allah and do not believe in any partners with him and believe me to be the Rasool and Nabi of Allah. Be good with your family and stay away from oppression and harming others." To this I replied: "You have certainly invited us towards beautiful character and wonderful qualities." I then got up from there and went towards the Haram Shareef where I loudly shouted out: "I believe that there is none worthy of worship besides Allah and that Muhammad ﷺ is His messenger."

Jumuʿah in Madinah

Asʿad bin Zuraarah ؓ saw that the Jews and Christians have a special day of the week in which they gather; the Jews on Saturday and the

Christians on Sunday. He felt that the Muslims should also have a day of the week in which they gather to remember Allah, to show their Shukr (appreciation) before him, to read Salaah and to worship Him. As'ad bin Zuraarah ﷺ suggested the day of Friday as this special day for the Muslims, and on this day he led everyone in Salaah. In short, the Sahaabah ﷺ started off the performance of Jumu'ah and suggested that the name of that holy day should be the day of Jumu'ah. A few days later, Rasulullah's ﷺ letter addressed to Mus'ab bin 'Umair ﷺ reached the people of Madinah wherein he instructed them to gather and perform two Rakaats of Salaah after midday on a Friday.

Second Promise of the Ansaar – 13th Year of Prophethood

The next year, which was the 13th year of prophet-hood, Mus'ab bin 'Umair ﷺ, with a group of Muslims, left for Makkah Mukarramah with the intention of performing Haj. With these Muslims there were many kuffaar from the Aws and Khazraj tribes who had not yet accepted Islam. Most of the group, which numbered more than 400, was of these people. Hadhrat Jaabir ﷺ says: "For ten long years Rasulullah ﷺ would go to meet the people in their houses, in the market places and at their functions. He would invite them towards Islam begging them: 'Who will help me? Who will support me? Who will help me in explaining the message of my Rabb? For him I guarantee Jannah.' But alas, he would return without any support or help.

This continued till Allah Ta'ala sent us from Yasrib (Madinah) to Rasulullah ﷺ. We trusted him and offered him our help. Everyone of us who came to him returned as a Muslim. When Islam reached almost every home in Madinah, we had a meeting in which we discussed Rasulullah ﷺ. We thought, for how long more are we going to leave Rasulullah ﷺ in this condition? For how long more will we see him worriedly walking about on the mountains of Makkah?

Chapter Eleven – Invitation to Islam During the Days of Haj

When they reached Makkah, they secretly sent a message to Rasulullah ﷺ telling him that they wished to meet him. Rasulullah ﷺ promised to meet them during the days of Haj in the same valley in Mina where the other people of Madinah had taken bay'at last year.

Together with his uncle, Hadhrat 'Abbaas رضى الله عنه, Rasulullah ﷺ met them as promised in the valley of Mina. Although Hadhrat 'Abbaas رضى الله عنه had not as yet accepted Islam, he was a good supporter of Rasulullah ﷺ. When he sat down Hadhrat 'Abbaas رضى الله عنه spoke to the Ansaar saying: "Muhammad (ﷺ) is a very noble man in Makkah. We are his supporters and loyal protectors. He wishes to come over to you. If you are able to give your loyal support and total protection and you sincerely believe you would do so right till your death, well and good, otherwise give me an honest answer now."

The Ansaar replied: "Okay, we understand what you are worried about."

Speaking to Rasulullah ﷺ, they then said: "O Nabi of Allah! Whatever you want from us, we are ready to obey. Whatever you and Allah demand, we are totally ready and you may even take a promise from us."

Rasulullah ﷺ replied: "I am inviting you towards Allah." He then spoke to them about Islam and read a few aayaat of the Qur-aan Shareef. He then said: "For Allah, I beg you to worship Him Alone and stop believing in any partner to Him. For my friends, I request you to give us a place of safety, offer us your protection just as you would protect your own wives and children, and that you will obey me in good times and in bad times, in comfort and in difficulties, in wealth and in poverty. In every condition you will listen and follow my instructions."

"What will we get in return?" asked the Ansaar." Rasulullah ﷺ replied: "Jannah!" (In other words, the everlasting gifts of the aakhirat.) The Ansaar replied: "We accept all your conditions. Come, stretch out your blessed hand, we wish to take bay'at."

Abul-Haysam bin Tayhaan رضي الله عنه asked: "O Nabi of Allah! I am a bit worried about something. We have a good relationship with the Jews. Since we are now with you, the Jews are going to break this good relationship. Let it not be such that when Allah Ta'ala makes you victorious and provides you with help, you return to Makkah leaving us alone here in Madinah." Rasulullah ﷺ smiled and said: "Never! Your life is my life. You are mine and I am yours. Your enemies are my enemies and your friends are my friends."

After this, all of them happily stretched out their hands for bay'at.

Hadhrat Abbaas رضي الله عنه replied: "The first person to take bay'at at the blessed hands of Rasulullah ﷺ was As'ad bin Zuraarah." (who was the most fortunate).

CHAPTER 12
MOVING TO MADINAH MUNAWWARAH

Rasulullah ﷺ saw some dreams about the place where he should move to but he was not shown the name of the place. He was shown that he will move to a place full of date trees. Allah Ta'ala then commanded him to move to Madinah Munawwarah as the place of migration. Rasulullah ﷺ then commanded his Sahaabah رضى الله عنهم to move to Madinah Munawwarah.

The first person to prepare himself for this Hijrah was Rasulullah's ﷺ milk-brother Abu Salmah رضى الله عنه with his wife and son. However, Hijrah was not something so easy. Whoever wanted to move would have to first pass through the Quraysh. They would do their best in stopping them from Hijrah.

Nonetheless, Abu Salmah رضى الله عنه, with his wife and child, got ready to leave for Madinah Shareef. His carriage was put over his camel and his wife and child were already sitting on the camel. He was about to leave when the people heard about it. His wife Umme Salmah's رضى الله عنها family, rushed up to him and said: "You can do whatever you want with your life but you can't take our daughter away." Saying this, they grabbed her hand and pulled her away. Then Abu Salmah's رضى الله عنه family came to him saying: "This child belongs to our family and nobody has the right to take him away." They then snatched the child from her lap and took him away. The father, mother and child all were seperated in this way. Abu Salmah رضى الله عنه finally left all alone for Madinah Munawwarah.

Umme Salmah ﷺ says: "I would go to Abtah every morning and cry my heart out. A whole year passed like this before one of my cousins felt sorry for me and scolded my people saying: "Don't you have any pity for this poor woman?" Thus, they allowed me to move to Madinah. My son was also returned to me. I took the child on my lap, sat on the camel and left for Madinah all alone.

When I reached Tan'eem (just outside Makkah), I saw 'Usmaan bin Talhah ﷺ who asked me where I was going. I replied: "I am on my way to Madinah to meet my husband." He asked: "Is there anybody with you?" I replied: "No, nobody but Allah and this young son of mine." After hearing this, 'Usmaan ﷺ was about to weep. He took hold of the reins of the camel and started walking ahead of us. Whenever we stopped, he would make the camel sit and move away. When I would get off, he would take the camel a distance away, tie it to a tree and lie down under its shade. When we had to continue on our journey, he would bring the camel and move aside saying: "Go on, sit on the camel." When I was seated, he would take its reins and walk ahead. Whenever we stopped, he would behave like this (full of shame) until we reached Madinah. When we saw the buildings of Quba from a distance, he said: "Your husband lives in this village. Enter this village with the Barakah (blessings) of Allah Ta'ala." Thereafter, he returned to Makkah.

Utbah and Abu Jahal were both silently watching the Muslims leaving Makkah one by one. The houses of Makkah were slowly becoming empty, 'Utbah took a deep breath and cried: "Every house is becoming a house of sadness."

He then said: "This is all because of our nephew. He has caused such division in our society." In Makkah it was only Rasulullah ﷺ, Hadhrat Abu Bakr ﷺ and Hadhrat Ali ﷺ who remained. Yes, a few helpless and weak Muslims trapped by the kuffaar still remained behind in Makkah.

The Quraysh plan to kill Rasulullah ﷺ

When the Quraysh realised that almost all the Sahaabah رضي الله عنهم had moved to Madinah Munawwarah and that Rasulullah's ﷺ would also leave soon, their leaders gathered in Daarun-Nadwah for a meeting. Some of them were: 'Utbah bin Rabi'ah, Shaybah bin Rabi'ah, Abu Sufyaan bin Harb, Jubair bin Mut'im, Haaris bin 'Aamir, Abul-Bakhtari bin Hishaam, Zam'ah bin Aswad, Hakeem bin Hizaam, Abu Jahal bin Hishaam and Umayyah bin Khalaf. Shaytaan was also in this gathering in the form of an old man. When he came to the door, people asked him who he was. He replied: "I am a Shaikh from Najd. I wish to listen to your discussion and if possible, I would help you by giving you my opinion."

The people allowed him to enter and the meeting began. One of them suggested that Rasulullah ﷺ should be imprisoned. The 'Najdi Shaikh' said: "No, this is not the answer because if his Sahaabah hear of his imprisonment, they would overpower you and free him." Someone else wanted to chase him from Makkah altogether. To this the 'Najdi Shaikh' said: "No! This too is not acceptable. His way of speaking is very sweet. If you chase him out of here, the people of another city would listen to his sweet words and believe in him. Then all of them may get together and suddenly attack us."

Abu Jahal said: "I think that neither should we imprison him nor should we throw him out of the city. Rather we should choose a young man from each tribe and all of them should kill Muhammad together. In this way, Muhammad's (ﷺ) killing will be shared by all the tribes and his tribe, Banu Abdu Manaaf, would not be able to fight all the tribes. They will be forced to accept the blood money."

The 'Najdi Shaikh' became very happy and said: "By Allah! This seems like the best plan." Everybody else also accepted this idea. It was also agreed in this meeting that this evil plan be carried out that very night.

They had just left when Hadhrat Jibraa'eel عَلَيْهِ السَّلَامُ came to Rasulullah ﷺ with wahi informing him about their evil plot in the following aayaat:

$$\text{وَاِذْ يَمْكُرُ بِكَ الَّذِيْنَ كَفَرُوْا لِيُثْبِتُوْكَ اَوْ يَقْتُلُوْكَ اَوْ يُخْرِجُوْكَ ۚ وَيَمْكُرُوْنَ وَيَمْكُرُ اللّٰهُ ۚ وَاللّٰهُ خَيْرُ الْمٰكِرِيْنَ}$$

"And remember when the kuffaar were planning against you either to imprison, kill or chase you out. They were plotting and Allah was plotting but Allah Ta'ala is the best of plotters." [Surah Anfaal verse 30]

Thus, he knew about this evil plot of the kuffaar and he was commanded by Allah to move to Madinah Munawwarah. Rasulullah ﷺ was also advised to read the following dua:

$$\text{وَقُلْ رَّبِّ اَدْخِلْنِيْ مُدْخَلَ صِدْقٍ وَّاَخْرِجْنِيْ مُخْرَجَ صِدْقٍ وَّاجْعَلْ لِّيْ مِنْ لَّدُنْكَ سُلْطٰنًا نَّصِيْرًا}$$

"And say: 'My Rabb Let my entry (into Madinah) be good and (similarly) let my leaving (from Makkah) be good. And give me from Your side a rule and help." [Surah Israa verse 80]

The Hijrat (Migration)

Rasulullah ﷺ asked Jibraa'eel عَلَيْهِ السَّلَامُ who would join him in the hijrat. Jibraa'eel عَلَيْهِ السَّلَامُ replied: "Abu Bakr رَضِيَ اللّٰهُ عَنْهُ will travel with you."

Hadhrat 'Aa'ishah رَضِيَ اللّٰهُ عَنْهَا says: "At midday, Rasulullah ﷺ came to Abu Bakr's رَضِيَ اللّٰهُ عَنْهُ house and told him that his hijrat to Madinah had been decided by Allah Ta'ala. Full of excitement, Hadhrat Abu Bakr رَضِيَ اللّٰهُ عَنْهُ asked: "May my parents be sacrificed for you, O Nabi of Allah! Will this unworthy man get the honour of travelling with you?" Rasulullah ﷺ replied: "Yes, surely."

After hearing this happy news, Hadhrat Abu Bakr رضي الله عنه burst into tears. Hadhrat 'Aa'ishah رضي الله عنها says: "Before this, I never knew that anyone could cry out of happiness and joy. Long before this, Hadhrat Abu Bakr رضي الله عنه, had kept aside two camels, which he was feeding with acacia leaves for the last four months. He offered one of these camels to Rasulullah ﷺ saying: "O Nabi of Allah! May my parents be sacrificed for you! Please choose one of these camels; it is a gift for you." Rasulullah ﷺ replied: "No, I would not accept it without paying for it." Hadhrat Abu Bakr رضي الله عنه replied: "Okay, if you want to pay for it, well and good. You may pay for it."

That night when it became dark, the Quraysh, according to their plan, surrounded Rasulullah's ﷺ house planning to attack him later that night. Rasulullah ﷺ asked Hadhrat Ali رضي الله عنه to wear his green sheet and lie down on his (Rasulullah's ﷺ) bed. He also told him: "Do not panic. Nothing will happen to you."

Although the Quraysh were his nasty enemies, they still regarded him as trustworthy and honest. They would leave their valuables in his care. Rasulullah ﷺ gave these items to Hadhrat Ali رضي الله عنه asking him to return them to their rightful owners.

Abu Jahal, was standing outside and while laughing he was mockingly telling his friends: "Muhammad believes that if you follow him you will become the rulers of the Arabs and non-Arabs and you will enter Jannah forever after your death and if you do not follow him, you will be killed by his Sahaabah and thereafter you will burn in the fire of Jahannam.

Whilst he was mockingly saying this, Rasulullah ﷺ came out from the door. Taking a handful of sand, he said: "Yes, this is what I guarantee you would happen. You are also one of those who are going to die at the hands of my Sahaabah and you are going to burn in the fire of Jahannam."

Rasulullah ﷺ then read the beginning aayaat of Surah Yaaseen until the aayat *"Fa Aghshaynaahum Fa Hum Laa Yubsiroon"* (and We have covered them so they cannot see) and threw this sand over their heads. Allah Ta'ala placed a covering over their eyes. He passed right before their very eyes without them seeing him.

Rasulullah ﷺ then went to Hadhrat Abu Bakr's رضي الله عنه house. Together they left home and took the road leading to Mount Saur. They climbed the mountain and hid in one of its caves. During this time, a man passed Rasulullah's ﷺ house and saw many of the Quraysh moving about. When he asked what they were waiting for, they replied: "We are waiting for Muhammad to come out. The moment he takes one foot out of his house, we will kill him." The man said: "May Allah Ta'ala make your efforts go to waste. Muhammad (ﷺ) has threw sand over your heads and passed by."

The next morning, when they saw Hadhrat Ali رضي الله عنه getting up from Rasulullah's ﷺ bed, they said: "By Allah! That man was right." Very dissapointed, they asked: "Where is Muhammad?" Hadhrat Ali رضي الله عنه replied: "I have no idea."

Rasulullah ﷺ continued his journey. As he was leaving Makkah, he climbed a hill and said to Makkah sadly saying: "By Allah! You are the best of lands. You are the most dear to Allah. If I was not chased from you, I would never have left you. What a pure land you are. You are very much dear to me. If my people did not chase me from you, I would not live anywhere else."

Hadhrat Abu Bakr's رضي الله عنه daughter Hadhrat Asma رضي الله عنها, prepared their food for the road. Because she was in a hurry, instead of using a string, she tore out her waist band and used it as a string to tie the food. From that day, she was known as Zaatun-Nitaaqayn (a woman with a double waist band). She used one part of it to tie the food and the other to tie the mouth of the water-skin.

'Abdullah, the son of Abu Bakr ﷺ, who was a still a young man, would spend the day in Makkah and in the evenings he would come to his father in the cave and give a report about what the Quraysh were doing. 'Aamir bin Fuhayrah, who was the freed slave of Hadhrat Abu Bakr ﷺ would graze goats all day long and at Isha time he would come to the cave and feed Rasulullah ﷺ and Abu Bakr ﷺ with goat's milk.

Abdullah bin Urayqeet was hired as a guide to take them along the unknown road to Madinah. Although the guide was a kaafir, Rasulullah ﷺ and Hadhrat Abu Bakr ﷺ still trusted him and relied on his knowledge. They left the camels with the guide asking him to meet them on the third day at Mount Saur from where they would leave for Madinah.

The Cave of Saur

When Rasulullah ﷺ began moving towards the cave, Hadhrat Abu Bakr ﷺ became very restless. Sometimes he would walk behind Rasulullah ﷺ and sometimes in front of him. At times he would walk on his right and sometimes to his left. Rasulullah ﷺ asked: "What is the matter Abu Bakr? Sometimes you walk infront of me and sometimes behind me?" Hadhrat Abu Bakr ﷺ replied: "O Rasulullah ﷺ! When I fear someone hunting for you from the back, I quickly move behind you. When I think that someone is waiting infront for you, I move quickly to get infront of you." Rasulullah ﷺ asked: "Abu Bakr! You are doing this to sacrifice your life for me?" Hadhrat Abu Bakr ﷺ replied: "Yes, O Nabi of Allah! I swear by the Being who has sent you with the truth, I wish to sacrifice my life for yours." When they reached the cave, Hadhrat Abu Bakr ﷺ said: "O Nabi of Allah! Just wait a bit. I will enter the cave first and clean it for you."

Hadhrat Abu Bakr ﷺ entered the cave first and after a little while Rasulullah ﷺ followed him. Soon thereafter, with the mercy of Allah Ta'ala, a spider spun its web over the mouth of the cave.

The Quraysh surrounded Rasulullah's ﷺ house all night long. The next morning, they were shocked to see Hadhrat Ali رضى الله عنه waking up from Rasulullah's ﷺ bed. When they asked Hadhrat Ali رضى الله عنه about Rasulullah ﷺ, he replied: "I have no idea." They ran off in all directions hunting for him until they reached the cave. When they saw the web on the mouth of the cave, they said: "This web would not have been here if he had entered the cave."

When Rasulullah ﷺ hid in the cave of Saur, with the command of Allah Ta'ala, a tree miraculously grew infront of him. A pair of wild doves then laid their eggs in the nests that were on the tree. Whilst the kuffaar were hunting for Rasulullah ﷺ, they reached the cave but when they saw the nests covering the tree, they moved away. Rasulullah ﷺ says: "Allah Ta'ala saved us from their (evils)." Hadhrat Abu Bakr رضى الله عنه says: "When Rasulullah ﷺ and I were in the cave whilst the Quraysh were searching for us and they somehow reached the cave, I worriedly said: 'O Nabi of Allah! If one of them has to look down, he will definitely see us.' Rasulullah ﷺ replied: 'What do you think, O Abu Bakr, of those two people of whom the third is Allah.' (In other words), we are not alone. Allah Ta'ala is with us and He will save us from their evil." When Rasulullah ﷺ saw Hadhrat Abu Bakr رضى الله عنه looking worried, he said:

Chapter Twelve – Moving to Madinah Munawwarah

لَا تَحْزَنْ إِنَّ اللهَ مَعَنَا

"Don't be worried. Certainly Allah is with us."

He also made a special dua for Hadhrat Abu Bakr رضى الله عنه after which, Hadhrat Abu Bakr رضى الله عنه became very calm and relaxed.

For three long days, Rasulullah صلى الله عليه وسلم remained hidden in the cave. 'Abdullah, the son of Abu Bakr رضى الله عنه would spend the day in Makkah gathering information about the kuffaar and in the evenings, he would give them a detailed report what was happening in Makkah and quickly leave as early as possible. 'Aamir bin Fuhayrah رضى الله عنه (the slave of Abu Bakr رضى الله عنه) would come daily to the cave after 'Isha when it was dark. He would come with a few she-goats so that Rasulullah صلى الله عليه وسلم and Abu Bakr رضى الله عنه could drink whatever milk they needed. This is how they passed three nights in the cave.

On the fourth morning, 'Abdullah bin Urayqeet (who was appointed as their guide to Madinah), came to the cave with two she-camels. He took them on the unknown coastal road to Madinah Munawwarah.

Rasulullah صلى الله عليه وسلم sat on one camel whilst Hadhrat Abu Bakr رضى الله عنه sat on the other. In order to serve them, Abu Bakr رضى الله عنه also took his freed slave, 'Aamir bin Fuhayrah, with him and made him sit behind him on the same camel. 'Abdullah bin Urayqeet sat on his own camel and since he was the guide, he would ride slightly in front of them.

Abdullah bin Urayqeet took Rasulullah صلى الله عليه وسلم and Hadhrat Abu Bakr رضى الله عنه towards the lower parts of Makkah along the coastal road. From here they moved to the lower parts of 'Asfaan travelling slowly until they reached Quba (on the outskirts of Madinah).

Asma bint Abi Bakr رضى الله عنها says: "After Rasulullah صلى الله عليه وسلم left, some people came to my father's house asking for Abu Bakr رضى الله عنه. Amongst them was Abu Jahal. When he asked me about my father, I said: 'By Allah! I have no idea at all.' Abu Jahal gave me such a terrible slap that my ear-ring fell off."

Story of Umm-e-Ma'bad

As Rasulullah ﷺ left the cave and began moving towards Madinah Munawwarah, he passed the tent of Umm-e-Ma'bad. She was a noble and hospitable woman. She would often sit in the front of her tent. They asked her to sell to them some dates and meat but she had nothing to offer. Rasulullah ﷺ saw a young goat in the corner of the tent. When he asked about it, Umm-e-Ma'bad replied: "This goat is thin and weak. This is why it cannot graze with the rest of the goats in the fields." Rasulullah ﷺ asked: "Does she have any milk?" She replied: "How can she have milk in this condition?" Rasulullah ﷺ asked: "Do I have your permission to milk her?" She replied: "May my parents be sacrificed for you. If there is any milk in them, you are more than welcome to help yourself." Reciting Bismillah, Rasulullah ﷺ placed his blessed hand over its udders, which miraculously started filling up with milk. Rasulullah ﷺ then began milking the goat. A huge container, which was enough for about eight to ten people, filled up with its milk. Rasulullah ﷺ offered the milk to Umm-e-Ma'bad first. She drank to her fill. He then offered the container to his companions and then he drank right at the end. He once again milked the goat until the container was full with milk again. He then handed the container over to her and after accepting her in Bay'at (pledge of allegiance), he continued on his journey once more. In the evening, when Abu Ma'bad returned home after grazing the goats, he noticed a huge container of milk lying there. He asked: "Where did this milk come from, Umm-e-Ma'bad? This goat had not a drop of milk." She replied: "Today a very blessed man passed by. By Allah! This is due to his Barakah (blessings)." She then explained what happened. Abu Ma'bad said: "Tell me a bit more about this man." Umm-e-Ma'bad described Rasulullah's ﷺ face, his nobility and his execellent ways.

Abu Ma'bad said: "Yes! Now I know who you are talking about. This is the same man from the Quraysh tribe. I will go to him as well."

The story of Suraaqah bin Maalik

The Quraysh offered a reward of 100 camels each for the person who kills or catches either Muhammad (ﷺ) or Abu Bakr (رضي الله عنه).

Suraaqah bin Maalik says: "I was sitting in my usual place when a man came up to me saying that he saw a few people secretly leaving towards the coastal route. He also said that he thinks that these people were Muhammad and his companions."

Suraaqah continues: "I was sure that these people were really Muhammad and his friends but out of fear of this man receiving the prize of 100 camels instead of myself, I somehow managed to convince him that it was someone else and not Muhammad."

Suraaqah continues: "A little while later, I got up from my place and asked my slave girl to take the horse to a certain hill and wait for me there. I grabbed my spear and quietly came out of the back of the house. I reached the horse and with lightning speed I jumped onto it and began to gallop."

After some time, Hadhrat Abu Bakr رضي الله عنه noticed someone riding fast in their direction. Hadhrat Abu Bakr رضي الله عنه worriedly said: "O Rasulullah ﷺ! Now we will really be caught. This man is coming in search of us." Rasulullah ﷺ replied: "Don't worry! Certainly Allah is with us."

Rasulullah ﷺ then cursed Suraaqah. Immediately thereafter, Suraaqah's horse sunk into the rocky ground right up to its knees. Suraaqah said: "I am certain that this happened because of your curse. I beg both of you to please make dua for me. By Allah! I swear that I will chase away whoever is hunting for you."

Rasulullah ﷺ made dua for him and Suraaqah's horse came out of the ground. Suraaqah says: "From this I understood that Allah Ta'ala was going to give Rasulullah ﷺ success. I informed him about the Quraysh's evil plan to kill him and I also told him of the reward of 100 camels offered by them. I then offered him whatever food provisions I had on me but he did not accept it. However, he asked me not to tell anyone about him.

Whenever I saw anyone searching for Rasulullah ﷺ, I would turn him back saying: "There is no need for you to go this way. I have already searched this area."

The story of Buraidah Aslami

As they continued ahead, Buraidah Aslami, was also hunting for Rasulullah ﷺ with seventy other people. He also hoped to receive the one hundred-camel-reward offered by the Quraysh. As he came closer, Rasulullah ﷺ asked him: "Who are you?" "I am Buraidah," he replied: "Who are you?" Rasulullah ﷺ replied: "I am Muhammad, the son of 'Abdullah and the Rasool of Allah."

To this Buraidah said:

اَشْهَدُ اَنْ لَّا اِلٰهَ اِلَّا اللهُ وَاَنَّ مُحَمَّدًا عَبْدُهُ وَ رَسُوْلُهُ

"I bear witness (believe) that there is none worthy of worship besides Allah and certainly Muhammad is His servant and messenger."

Buraidah, together with the seventy others with him all accepted Islam. Buraidah then advised Rasulullah ﷺ saying: "You should carry a flag in front of you as you are entering Madinah." Rasulullah ﷺ removed his 'Imaamah (turban) and fixed it onto a spear. He offered it to Buraidah ؓ. When Rasulullah ﷺ finally entered Madinah Munawwarah, Buraidah was walking in front of him carrying this flag. The wonderful news of Rasulullah's ﷺ having left Makkah and his coming towards Madinah Munawwarah had already reached the people of

Madinah. Every single person of Madinah would come and wait for him at a place called Harrah (on the outskirts of Madinah). This was their daily practice. One day, as they were leaving without having seen him, a Jew who was on top of one of the hills of Madinah, exitedly shouted out:

يَا بَنِيْ قِيْلَةَ هٰذَا جَدُّكُمْ

"O children of Qilah! Here comes your source of good fortune and blessings."

The moment the Ansaar heard this announcement, they were overjoyed and rushed to welcome him shouting out the Takbeer.

After Rasulullah ﷺ left from Makkah Mukarramah, Hadhrat Ali ؓ stayed over in Makkah for another three days. Once he returned to the people all their trusts which were given to him by Rasulullah ﷺ just before he left for Hijrah, Hadhrat Ali ؓ also left Makkah. He joined Rasulullah ﷺ in Quba and he also stayed with Rasulullah ﷺ at the house of Kulsoom bin Hadam.

The Building of Masjidut Taqwa

Before entering Madinah Munawwarah, Rasulullah ﷺ stopped over at a place called Quba. The first thing that Rasulullah ﷺ did in Quba was the laying of the foundation of a Masjid. He brought a stone with his own mubaarak hands and placed it in the direction of the Qiblah. Hadhrat Abu Bakr ؓ and then Hadhrat Umar ؓ also placed a stone each in the same direction. After them, the other Sahaabah ؓ fetched a stone each and then the actual building of the Masjid started. Rasulullah ﷺ would also carry heavy boulders. At times, to hold it more firmly, he would hold it close to his blessed stomach. The Sahaabah ؓ would ask him to leave it but Rasulullah ﷺ would not listen to them. About this Masjid, the following aayat was revealed:

$$\text{لَمَسْجِدٌ أُسِّسَ عَلَى التَّقْوَىٰ مِنْ أَوَّلِ يَوْمٍ أَحَقُّ أَنْ تَقُومَ فِيهِ ۚ فِيهِ رِجَالٌ يُحِبُّونَ أَنْ يَتَطَهَّرُوا ۚ وَاللَّهُ يُحِبُّ الْمُطَّهِّرِينَ}$$

"Surely the Masjid that was founded upon Taqwa (Allah-consciousness) from the first day is more rightful that you stand (for Salaah) within it. In it are men who love (physical and spiritual) cleanliness. And Allah loves those who clean themselves."

[Surah Taubah verse 108]

When this aayat was revealed, Rasulullah ﷺ asked 'Amr bin 'Awf: "On what type of Tahaarat (purity) did Allah Ta'ala praise you?"

The people replied: "O Rasulullah ﷺ! After using pieces of sand, we make Istinjaa with water as well. Perhaps this type of double tahaarat (purity) pleases Allah Ta'ala, therefore he has praised us in the Qur-aan." Rasulullah ﷺ said: "Yes, this is the practice which has attracted Allah's praise. You should stick firmly to this and remain attached to it."

Rasulullah ﷺ would visit Masjid-e-Quba every Saturday. Sometimes he would go on foot and at times he would go riding on an animal. He would read two Rakaats Salaah in this Masjid." Rasulullah ﷺ said: 'He who performs wudhu at home and performs two Rakaat Salaah in Masjid-e-Quba will receive the Sawaab of an Umrah'."

Rasulullah ﷺ then left Quba and set off for Madinah Munawwarah. He performed the Jumuah Salaah on the way and gave a beautiful khutbah to all those who were present. After Jumu'ah, Rasulullah ﷺ got onto his camel and began moving towards Madinah Shareef. He seated Hadhrat Abu Bakr ؓ directly behind him on the camel. A large number of Ansaar, with their weapons, were walking to his right, to his left and behind him. Every single resident of Madinah wished to host Rasulullah ﷺ in his home. From every corner, the people invited Rasulullah ﷺ. Each one begged him to come to his house. Rasulullah ﷺ would make dua for them and reply: "This camel is commanded by Allah. Wherever she sits down with the order of Allah, I will stay there." Rasulullah ﷺ left the reins absolutely loose. He would not move the animal in any direction. The ladies climbed onto the roofs of their houses singing:

$$طَلَعَ الْبَدْرُ عَلَيْنَا مِنْ ثَنِيَّاتِ الْوَدَاعِ$$

"The full moon has risen upon us from the valley of Wad'aa.

$$وَجَبَ الشُّكْرُ عَلَيْنَا مَا دَعَا لِلَّهِ دَاعٍ$$

Giving thanks towards Allah is necessary upon us as long as there remains a caller to Allah.

$$اَيُّهَا الْمَبْعُوْثُ فِيْنَا جِئْتَ بِالْاَمْرِ الْمُطَاعِ$$

O you who has been sent to us! You have come to us with something that has to be obeyed."

Baraa bin Aazib ؓ says: "I have not seen the people of Madinah as overjoyed as they were on the day Rasulullah ﷺ came to Madinah."

Hadhrat Anas ؓ says: "When Rasulullah ﷺ came to Madinah, every single atom shorn brightly and the day he passed away, everything was looking dark and gloomy."

Some of the Sahaabah ؓ tried to grab the reins of the camel but Rasulullah ﷺ would gently advise them:

$$دَعُوْهَا فَاِنَّهَا مَأْمُوْرَةٌ$$

"Leave her alone as she is commanded (by Allah Ta'ala)."

Finally the camel came to the area of the Banu Najjaar (Rasulullah's ﷺ mother's relatives) where she stopped right at the spot where the door of Masjidun-Nabawi would be. However, Rasulullah ﷺ did not get off. The camel then got up and sat down at Hadhrat Abu Ayyub Ansaari's ﷺ door. A little while later, she got up and sat at the first spot where she lowered her head onto the ground. At this moment, Rasulullah ﷺ jumped off from his camel and Hadhrat Abu Ayyub ﷺ carried his goods into the house. Hadhrat Abu Ayyub Ansaari ﷺ wanted Rasulullah ﷺ to stay upstairs whilst he and his family would stay downstairs. However, Rasulullah ﷺ felt that since he would be getting lots of visitors all the time, it would be incorrect for Hadhrat Abu Ayyub ﷺ and his family to stay downstairs. This is why Rasulullah ﷺ did not agree to stay upstairs. Hadhrat Abu Ayyub ﷺ says: "Daily we would prepare meals for Rasulullah ﷺ and send it down to him. He would send the leftover back to us. As a form of getting his Tabarruk (blessings), Umme Ayyub and I would look for the spot he ate from and we would also eat from there. One day we added a bit of garlic and onions to the food. When he sent it back to us, we were shocked to find that he had not eaten any of the food. Full of worry, I went to Rasulullah ﷺ and said: "O Rasulullah! You sent the food back to us without eating. Umm-e-Ayyub and I always eat from the spot that your blessed fingers had touched." Rasulullah ﷺ replied: "I could smell garlic and onions in the food. You may go ahead and eat it. Since I speak to the angels, I stay away from such foods." Abu Ayyub ﷺ says: "From that day on, we did not add onions and garlic to his food."

Building of Masjid-e-Nabawi

The first spot the camel chose to sit on was an area where they would dry dates. Rasulullah ﷺ was told that the plot of land belongs to two orphans; Sahal and Suhail. Rasulullah ﷺ called both of them to buy this plot of land to build a Masjid. Rasulullah ﷺ also spoke to their uncle, in whose care these orphans were, about buying the land. Both of them wished to donate the land to Rasulullah ﷺ without any price hoping for great rewards from Allah Ta'ala alone. However, Rasulullah

ﷺ did not accept it without any payment. He paid them for the land. Rasulullah ﷺ instructed Hadhrat Abu Bakr ؓ to pay for the plot of land. He paid ten Dinaars (gold coins) for the land.

Thereafter, Rasulullah ﷺ commanded the Sahaabah ؓ to chop down the date trees and level the graves of some kuffaar that were on the land. He then instructed them to make some bricks and he himself joined the Muhaajireen and Ansaar in the making of these bricks.

Rasulullah ﷺ would also carry these bricks and read: "O Allah! The actual reward is the reward of the aakhirat. So shower Your mercy upon the Muhaajireen and the Ansaar (who are hoping for the reward of the aakhirat only)."

The Sahaabah ؓ, in the meantime were singing: "If we sit down whilst the messenger of Allah works, this action of ours (this sitting) would be extremely disliked."

Talq bin Ali ؓ says: "Rasulullah ﷺ told me to mix the cement. I got up to mix the cement with a spade." He says: "I asked, O Rasulullah ﷺ! Should I carry the bricks as well?" Rasulullah ﷺ replied: "No, you should only mix the cement, as you are an expert in that."

This Masjid was very simple. The walls were made of unbaked bricks. The pillars were made from the trunks of date trees. The roof was prepared from the leaves and branches of date trees. Whenever it rained, water would drip into the Masjid. Later on, the roof was plastered with cement.

When Rasulullah ﷺ planned to extend the Masjid, he came to the Ansaari owner of the plot of land next to the masjid and said: "Give us this land in exchange of a palace in Jannah." The Ansaari, who was very poor with a large family, was unable to offer the land for free. This is why Hadhrat Usmaan ؓ bought this plot for 10 000 Dirhams from this Ansaari. He then came to Rasulullah ﷺ and said: "O Rasulullah ﷺ! Please accept this land from me (in exchange of a palace in

Jannah)." Rasulullah ﷺ accepted this plot from Hadhrat 'Usmaan رضي الله عنه in exchange of a palace in Jannah and joined this plot of land into the Masjid. Rasulullah ﷺ placed the first brick with his own blessed hand and, according to his instructions, the next brick was placed by Hadhrat Abu Bakr رضي الله عنه, then by Hadhrat Umar رضي الله عنه, followed by Hadhrat Usmaan رضي الله عنه and then by Hadhrat Ali رضي الله عنه.

Brotherhood between the Muhaajireen and Ansaar

When the Muhaajireen shifted from Makkah Mukarramah, leaving behind their children, family, homes and property and arrived in Madinah Munawwarah, Rasulullah ﷺ made brothers between the Muhaajireen and Ansaar so that their difficulty and hardships may be replaced by the love and friendship of the Ansaar. At times of need, they may help one another and comfort one another at times of sadness. The weak may gain strength from the strong and all of them may hold firmly together onto the rope of Allah Ta'ala. This Ummah should be completely safe from the fighting and hatred that caused the destruction of the Banu Israa'eel.

The brotherhood that the the Ansaar showed and their sincere sacrifices for Deen is absolutely amazing. Their generosity with the Muhaajireen with their wealth, lands and property was really wonderful but even more than that they offered their wives to the Muhaajireen. An Ansaari who had two wives would offer his Muhaajir brother one of his two wives saying: "Choose whichever one you wish. I will divorce her and you may marry her (after the 'Iddah period)."

Hadhrat Anas رضي الله عنه says: "None of the Ansaar would ever regard anyone more rightful to his wealth than his Muhaajir brother."

When the Muhaajireen saw this compassion and love shown by the Ansaar, they asked: "O Rasulullah ﷺ! We have not seen anyone more compassionate, sincere and more devoted than the Ansaar. We fear that they will take all the rewards whilst we will be left with nothing."

Rasulullah ﷺ replied: "No, as long as you continue making dua for them."

CHAPTER 13
BATTLE OF BADR

The battle of Badr took place in the year 2 A.H. This battle was the greatest battle in the history of Islam because this battle showed the honour and strength of Islam. It marked the beginning of the fall and disgrace of kufr (disbelief). Through the divine mercy of Allah Ta'ala, the Deen of Islam was strengthened from the unseen whilst a powerful blow was given to the forces of kufr. Perhaps no other battle can be equal with the battle of Badr.

Before the Battle

During the early part of the month of Ramadhaan, Rasulullah ﷺ heard that Abu Sufyaan was returning to Makkah with a business caravan full of goods.

Rasulullah ﷺ gathered the Sahaabah رضي الله عنهم and told them: "This is a fully loaded business caravan of the Quraysh. Let us confiscate this caravan. It would not surprise me if Allah Ta'ala decides to give this caravan to you as 'the spoils of war'."

Since they did not expect a battle, they left without any war preparations. Abu Sufyaan, on the other hand, was expecting an attack from the Muslims and he kept on asking every traveler on his journey for some news about Rasulullah ﷺ. One traveler told him that Rasulullah ﷺ had commanded his companions to confiscate the caravan.

Abu Sufyaan immediately paid Damdam Ghifaari an amount of money and sent him off to the Quraysh of Makkah with the message: "As quick as you can, protect your caravan and save your money because Muhammad and his companions have already left to confiscate this caravan."

Departure

On the 12th of Ramadhaan, Rasulullah ﷺ left from Madinah Munawwarah. 313 Mujaahideen joined him on this journey. They were so unprepared that the entire group had just two horses and seventy camels. One horse belonged to Hadhrat Zubair bin 'Awwaam رضي الله عنه and the other to Hadhrat Miqdaad رضي الله عنه. Each camel was being shared by two or three people. Hadhrat 'Abdullah bin Mas'ood رضي الله عنه says: "In the battle of Badr, one camel was being shared by three people, which they would take turns in riding. Abu Lubaabah رضي الله عنه and Ali رضي الله عنه were joined with Rasulullah ﷺ. When it was Rasulullah's ﷺ turn to walk, Abu Lubaabah رضي الله عنه and Ali رضي الله عنه would plead: "O Rasulullah ﷺ! You continue riding, we will walk for you." Rasulullah ﷺ would reply: "You are neither stronger than I am nor am I independent of sawaab and reward of walking than you are."

When they reached about a mile out of Madinah, Rasulullah ﷺ gathered all of them for an inspection. Youngsters, who wanted to take part in this battle, were sent back home. When he reached a place called Rawhaa, he chose Abu Lubaabah رضي الله عنه as his deputy in Madinah and sent him back home.

There were three battle flags in this army. One was held by Hadhrat Ali رضي الله عنه, the second one was held by Hadhrat Mus'ab bin 'Umair رضي الله عنه and the third by an Ansaari Sahaabi رضي الله عنه.

When they came close to a place called Safraa, Rasulullah ﷺ sent two Sahaabah to spy on Abu Sufyaan's caravan.

In the meantime, Damdam Ghifaari came to Makkah Mukarramah with Abu Sufyaan's message warning the people of Makkah that their caravan was in danger of attack. "Hurry", he told the people of Makkah, "run and save your wealth."

The moment this news reached the people of Makkah, the whole city was up in arms because everybody in Makkah had some wealth in this caravan. Worried about loosing their wealth, the people of Makkah became afraid. They immediately prepared an army of 1000 fully armed men. Abu Jahal was the leader of this army.

Fully loaded with musical instrumenets of fun and amusement and together with singing women, drums and tambourines, the Quraysh puffed up with pride, came out from Makkah, as Allah Ta'ala says:

> "Do not be like those who came out from their homes full of pride and showing off (their power) before the people." [Surah Anfaal verse 47]

Almost all the leaders of the Quraysh took part in this battle. Only Abu Lahab, for some reason, was unable to join the battle. He sent Abu Jahal's brother, 'Aas bin Hishaam in his place instead.

'Aas bin Hishaam was owing Abu Lahab 4000 Dirhams. He was unable to repay this debt. Because of this debt, he agreed to go to battle for Abu Lahab.

Similarly, Umayyah bin Khalaf refused to take part in Badr but with the order and threat of Abu Jahal, he finally accepted and joined them. When Abu Jahal heard that he was not going to take part, he said to him: "You are one of the leaders. If you do not take part in this battle, the others will also follow and they too will not join us." Anyway, Abu Jahal carried on forcing Umayyah. He finally told him: "O Abu Safwaan! I will buy a fast horse especially for you. (The moment you feel afraid you can climb onto it and return home.)" This finally changed his mind and he agreed to go along. He then went home and asked his wife to make his preparations for this journey. His wife begged him: "O Abu Safwaan! Do you remember the warning of your Yasribi (Madani) brother?" He replied: "Yes, I will travel just a bit out of Makkah and return home." Umayyah came out with this intention and wherever the army stopped, he would keep his camel close by but he could not find a chance to escape. He somehow landed in Badr and was killed at the hands of the Sahaabah ﷺ.

In short, Umayyah was convinced of his death but because he was forced by Abu Jahal, he unhappily agreed to join them. Abu Jahal destroyed himself and destroyed others as well. "They made their people live in the place of destruction; Hell, in which they will burn and what a dreadful place it is."

Mashwarah with the Sahaabah ﷺ

As Rasulullah ﷺ left Rawhaa and reached Safraa, The two spies returned with news that the Quraysh were on their way. Rasulullah ﷺ gathered all the Muhaajireen and Ansaar for mashwarah (a meeting). Rasulullah ﷺ informed them about the comming of the well-equipped army of the Quraysh. The moment Hadhrat Abu Bakr ﷺ heard this, he quickly got to his feet and happily showed his support to Rasulullah ﷺ. He understood the message of Rasulullah ﷺ with all his heart and pushed himself to obey the wishes of Rasulullah ﷺ. Thereafter, Hadhrat Umar ﷺ stood up and he too showed his willingness to sacrifice his life for Islam.

Speech of Miqdaad bin Aswad ﷺ

Thereafter, Miqdaad bin Aswad ﷺ stood up and said:

> "O Rasulullah ﷺ! Go ahead and do what you have been ordered to do. We are with you all the way. By Allah! We will never be like the Jews who told Musa عَلَيْهِ ٱلسَّلَام: 'You and your Rabb go and fight the enemy whilst we will remain seated here.' (We instead are promising you): 'You and your Rabb go and fight the enemy and we will fight side by side with you.'"

Hadhrat 'Abdullah bin Mas'ood ﷺ says: "(After this promise) I noticed Rasulullah's ﷺ mubaarak face shinning in happiness." Rasulullah ﷺ made a special dua for Hadhrat Miqdaad ﷺ.

After all these promises, Rasulullah ﷺ once again, for a third time, asked the Sahaabah ﷺ:

اَشِيْرُوْا عَلَىَّ اَيُّهَا النَّاسُ

"O people! What is your opinion? Give me your Mashwarah."

The leader of the Ansaar S'ad bin Mu'aaz ﷺ understood what Rasulullah ﷺ, was trying to say. He immediately said: "O Rasulullah ﷺ! Perhaps you are referring to the Ansaar?" Rasulullah ﷺ replied that he was.

The valiant speech of S'ad bin Mu'aaz ﷺ

Upon this, Hadhrat S'ad bin Mu'aaz ﷺ powerfully said:

> "O Rasulullah ﷺ! We confirm our belief in you, we believe in you, we sincerely believe that whatever you came with is the truth and we had promised to obey you competely. O Rasulullah ﷺ! Perhaps you left from Madinah for a certain reason but Allah has brought about something else. So do as you like. You may be good with whom you wish and you may cut off ties with whomsoever you wish. You may enter into a peace agreement with whom you wish and you may wage war with whom you wish. We are with you all the way. You may take from our wealth whatever you please and you may give us whatever you please. Whatever you take from our wealth would be dearer to us than what you would leave behind, and whatever you command us to do we will do it without question. If you instruct us to set off for Barkul-Ghamaad with you, we will definitely join you. I swear by the Being Who has sent you with the truth, if you command

> us to jump into the ocean we would throw ourselves into it and not one of us would be left behind. We are not scared to fight the enemy. Yes, during the heat of battle we are tolerant and we are ready to face the enemy. We hope that Allah Ta'ala will show you something of ours that would make you happy. So, in the name of Allah, take us along with you."

Listening to the words of these Sahaabah ﷺ brought great joy to Rasulullah ﷺ. He announced: "Come! Let us go in the name of Allah and many glad tidings for you. Allah Ta'ala had promised me that He would grant me victory over one of the two groups; either the group of Abu Jahal or the group of Abu Sufyaan."

He also said: "I was also shown the places of where the kuffaar will be killed. I was shown that this is where so and so will fall killed and this is where so and so will die."

After changing the direction of the caravan, Abu Sufyaan travelled along the coastal road until he safely reached Makkah unnoticed by the Muslims.

As he reached Makkah, he sent a message to the Quraysh advising them: "You came out with the intention of saving your property, wealth and the lives of the travellers. Allah has saved your property and lives. So why do you not return to Makkah?"

Abu Jahal replied: "Until and unless we go to Badr to eat, drink and celebrate for three days, we will never return to Makkah."

By the time Rasulullah ﷺ and the Sahaabah ﷺ reached Badr, the kuffaar had already taken control of the water springs. They also took control of the better areas of Badr. The Muslims had no water and no suitable areas. Their area was made up of rough ground where it was very difficult to walk. Their feet would sink into the ground.

Allah Ta'ala sent down rain. The soft sand turned to hard ground and the Muslims dug up a few small ponds for Ghusal and Wudhu purposes.

Although this water rained down for the Muslims, out of His mercy, Rasulullah ﷺ, who was full of compassion, allowed his enemies also to drink from the water.

Two slaves of the Quraysh were caught and brought to Rasulullah ﷺ. He asked them: "Where are the Quraysh?" "By Allah", they replied: "they are at the foot of Muqanqas mountain." "What is the total number of people?" asked Rasulullah ﷺ.

They replied: "They are quite a few in number."

"How many in number are they?" he asked. The slaves replied that they had no idea what their numbers were. Rasulullah ﷺ asked: "Okay, tell me, how many camels do they slaughter daily?" They replied: "One day nine and one day ten." To this Rasulullah ﷺ pointed out: "They are between nine-hundred to a thousand."

After this, Rasulullah ﷺ asked them which of the Quraysh leaders were there. They replied: "Utbah bin Rabi'ah, Shaybah bin Rabi'ah, Abul-Bakhtari bin Hishaam, Hakeem bin Hizaam, Nawfal bin Khuwaylid, Haaris bin 'Aamir, T'amiyyah bin 'Adi, Nadr bin Haaris, Zam'ah bin Aswad, Abu Jahal bin Hishaam, Umayyah bin Khalaf, Nubayh bin Hajaaj, Munabbih bin Hajaaj, Suhail bin 'Amr and 'Amr bin 'Abdwud."

When Rasulullah ﷺ heard of this 'large number' of the leaders, he turned to his Sahaabah and said: "Today Makkah has sent its best people to you." In short, this was how Rasulullah ﷺ gathered information from these slaves.

Preparation for War

Hadhrat Umar رضي الله عنه says: On the night before the Battle of Badr, Rasulullah ﷺ took us with him to the battlefield so that we may see for ourselves the places of those who would be killed in the battle. As we reached the battleground, he continued pointing out to us with his blessed hand: "This is the spot so and so would collapse and this is the spot so and so would fall, in the morning Insha Allah." Pointing with his hand, he proceeded to reveal the exact location of where each person would be slain."

Hadhrat Anas رضي الله عنه says: "I swear by the Being Who has sent Rasulullah ﷺ with the truth, not one of them had fallen even the amount of a hair past the spot that was pointed out by Rasulullah ﷺ."

Thereafter, Rasulullah ﷺ entered his hut and read two Rakaats of Salaah. Hadhrat Abu Bakr رضي الله عنه was with him. Meanwhile, S'ad bin Mu'aaz رضي الله عنه stood guard at the door, holding a sword.

Hadhrat Ali رضي الله عنه says: "On the night before the battle of Badr, there was not a single one of us who stayed awake except Rasulullah ﷺ. He spent the whole night in Salaah and sincere dua right until the morning."

At the time of Fajr, Rasulullah ﷺ announced: "As-Salaah! O people! The time for Salaah has arrived." As soon as the people heard this announcement, they quickly gathered for Salaah. Rasulullah ﷺ led them in Salaah whilst standing near a tree. After Salaah, Rasulullah ﷺ encouraged the Sahaabah رضي الله عنهم to fight the enemy with bravery and without fear.

Thereafter, Rasulullah ﷺ straightened the lines of the Mujaahideen for battle whilst the lines of the kuffaar had already been arranged for battle. It was a Friday the 17th of Ramadhaan. On one side of the battlefield was the group of Haq, whilst on the other end of the battlefield was the forces of baatil (falsehood).

When Rasulullah ﷺ saw the well-equipped Qurayshi army moving ahead with all their pride, he made dua to Allah Ta'ala;

"O Allah! Here are the Quraysh marching full of pride and pomp. They have come to challenge You and falsify Your Rasool. O Allah! I

> *beg of You Your victory and help over them as promised by You. O Allah! Destroy them (these forces of baatil)."*

As the Quraysh settled down, before the actuall battle, they decided to send 'Umair bin Wahab Jumahi to work out the numbers of the Muslims. After looking at the Muslims, he got on his horse, 'returned and said: "The Muslims only number about three hundred but give me a chance and I will check if they have any other armies hiding and waiting for us." Once again he climbed his horse and rode far and wide checking for secret armies. He returned to the Quraysh and said: "I've checked but I could not find any other army. However, O People of the Quraysh! I see these Madani camels carrying red death (killers) on their backs. These people have no support besides their own swords. By Allah! As long as these people do not kill their enemy, they themselves will not be killed. So even if from our army 300 men are killed, what joy will we have? (with over three hundred of our people dead)? Think about what I am saying and let us decide on what to do."

Hakeem bin Hizaam says: "I went to Abu Jahal, with this message. He was busy putting on his armour at that time. I said: 'Utbah sent me with this message.' I then gave 'Utbah's message to him.

The moment he heard the message, he exploded with anger and shouted: '(This is not the only reason 'Utbah is escaping from war). 'Utbah does not want to fight the Muslims because his son Abu Huzaifah is with the Muslims. No harm should come to him. I swear by Allah! We will never go back until Allah makes a final decision between Muhammad and us.'

Abu Jahal then called 'Amr bin Hadrami's brother, Aamir bin Hadrami, and said to him: 'Your friend, 'Utbah wishes to take everyone back with him without fighting the enemy whereas the blood of your brother is right before your eyes!' On hearing this, Aamir cried out: 'O 'Amr! O 'Amr! How terrible!' His cries of sorrow encouraged them and once again, they decided to fight the Muslims."

The War Begins

Abu Jahal's plan had such a great effect on the Quraysh that even 'Utbah wore his armour and got ready for battle.

In fact, from the kuffaar, 'Utbah, his brother Shaybah bin Rabi'ah and his son Waleed were the first fighters to come out of the lines of the kuffaar onto the battlefield. They challenged the Muslims for someone to fight them.

From the rows of the Muslims, three warriors from the Ansaar stepped forward. "Who are you?" shouted 'Utbah. They replied: "We are a group of the Ansaar." 'Utbah replied: "We have no need to fight you. We wish to fight with our own people." Saying this, he shouted: "O Muhammad! Why don't you send us equal fighters from our own tribe!"

Rasulullah ﷺ then instructed the Ansaar to go back to their lines and called for Hadhrat Ali ؓ, Hadhrat Hamzah ؓ and Hadhrat 'Ubaidah bin Haaris ؓ. He called each of them by name and encouraged them to go out and fight.

The three of them came out from their lines. Since their faces were covered by protective masks, 'Utbah asked them who they were. "I am 'Ubaidah," said Hadhrat 'Ubaidah bin Haaris ؓ. Hadhrat Hamzah ؓ answered: "I am Hamzah." Hadhrat Ali ؓ replied: "I am 'Ali." 'Utbah said: "Yes! Now these are noble and equal fighters."

Rasulullah ﷺ said: "Rise O children of Haashim, with the truth with which Allah Ta'ala has sent your Nabi. Fight this falsehood with which they have come in order to put out the light of Allah."

Killing of 'Utbah, Shaybah and Waleed

The fighters faced one another. 'Ubaidah ؓ fought with 'Utbah. Hamzah ؓ challenged Shaybah and Ali ؓ was challenged by Waleed.

Hadhrat Ali رضي الله عنه and Hadhrat Hamzah رضي الله عنه killed their enemies with a single stroke of the sword. Meanwhile, 'Ubaidah رضي الله عنه, who was fighting with 'Utbah, was seriously injured. Both fighters suffered injuries but continued fighting. Eventually, 'Utbah gave such a severe blow with his sword that 'Ubaidah رضي الله عنه suffered a serious injury to his leg. In the mean time, Hadhrat Hamzah رضي الله عنه and Hadhrat Ali رضي الله عنه quickly went to help 'Ubaidah رضي الله عنه. They then sent 'Utbah to his death. Thereafter, they carried 'Ubaidah رضي الله عنه and brought him to Rasulullah صلى الله عليه وسلم. He was bleeding heavily from his shin area. 'Ubaidah رضي الله عنه hopefully asked: "O Rasulullah صلى الله عليه وسلم! Am I a martyr?" When Rasulullah صلى الله عليه وسلم replied that he was, 'Ubaidah رضي الله عنه said: "If only Abu Taalib was alive he would have known that most definitely, we are more deserving of his poem than he ever was:

$$\text{وَنُسْلِمَ حَتَّى نُصَرَّعَ حَوْلَهُ} \quad \text{وَنَذْهَلَ عَنْ اَبْنَائِنَا وَالْحَلَائِلِ}$$

"We will give up Muhammad to the enemy only when all of us around him are killed and when we are absolutely unaware of even our own wives and children."

Rasulullah's صلى الله عليه وسلم Dua for Victory

After the deaths of 'Utbah and Shaybah, the battle between the two groups began raging. Rasulullah صلى الله عليه وسلم came out from his hut and laid out the positions of the Sahaabah رضي الله عنهم and then with Abu Bakr رضي الله عنه, he returned to his hut. Holding a sword, Hadhrat S'ad bin Mu'aaz رضي الله عنه stood guard at the door.

When Rasulullah صلى الله عليه وسلم saw his Sahaabah's' small numbers and their lack of equipment against the well-equipped army of the kuffaar, he got to his feet and performed two Rakaats of Salaah. He then busied himself in dua. He begged Allah Ta'ala: "O Allah! I beg you to honour Your word (of victory over the enemy). O Allah! If You wish, You may not be worshipped (after this day)."

Rasulullah ﷺ was overcome with a condition of extreme humility. Sometimes he would humbly bow down in Sajdah before Allah Ta'ala and at times he would helplessly spread his hands out in dua and beg Allah Ta'ala for His help and victory. He was so busy in this state of humility that his shawl kept on falling off his shoulders.

Hadhrat Ali ؓ says: "On the day of Badr, I fought the enemy for a little while and then I hurried to check on Rasulullah ﷺ. I found him in sajdah before Allah Ta'ala helplessly begging Allah Ta'ala repeatedly with the words 'Yaa Hayyu Yaa Qayyum!' I returned and busied myself with fighting. I went to check on him a second and then a third time but still found him in sajdah. However, when I went to check on him the fourth time, by then Allah Ta'ala had blessed him with victory."

Allah Ta'ala revealed the following aayat:

$$\text{اِذْ تَسْتَغِيْثُوْنَ رَبَّكُمْ فَاسْتَجَابَ لَكُمْ اَنِّيْ مُمِدُّكُمْ بِاَلْفٍ مِّنَ الْمَلٰٓئِكَةِ مُرْدِفِيْنَ ۝ وَمَا جَعَلَهُ اللّٰهُ اِلَّا بُشْرٰى وَلِتَطْمَئِنَّ بِهٖ قُلُوْبُكُمْ ۚ وَمَا النَّصْرُ اِلَّا مِنْ عِنْدِ اللّٰهِ ؕ اِنَّ اللّٰهَ عَزِيْزٌ حَكِيْمٌ ۝}$$

"Remember the time when you asked for help from your Rabb and He answered you (saying): 'I will help you with a thousand Angels one behind the other. Allah made this (his help) only as glad tidings and so that your hearts are comforted with it. There is no help (of victory) except from Allah. Verily Allah is the All-mighty, the All-wise."

[Surah Anfaal verses 9-10]

After the revelation of this aayat, Rasulullah ﷺ came out from his hut reading the following aayat on his tongue:

$$\text{سَيُهْزَمُ الْجَمْعُ وَ يُوَلُّونَ الدُّبُرَ}$$

"Their army will be defeated and they will turn on their backs and escape." [Surah Qamar verse 45]

Whilst Rasulullah ﷺ was making dua to Allah Ta'ala, he dozed off. When he awakened, he said to Hadhrat Abu Bakr رضي الله عنه: "O Abu Bakr! Glad tidings to you. Allah's help has come. Here is Jibraa'eel عليه السلام holding the reins of his horse and riding it along. It has dust on its teeth."

Angels come to help the Muslims

Allah Ta'ala sent down a thousand angels, then three thousand and finally five thousand angels to help the Muslims.

Note: Since Iblees (shaytaan) and his friends were all ready to help the kuffaar in this battle, Allah Ta'ala sent down a group of angels under Jibraa'eel عليه السلام, Mikaa'eel عليه السلام and Israafeel عليه السلام to help the Muslims. Since shaytaan came in the shape of Suraaqah bin Maalik and his friends came in the form of men, the angels also came in the form of normal men as mentioned.

One Sahaabi says: "On the day of the battle of Badr, the angels came down from the skies wearing yellow turbans. The ends of their turbans were hanging between their shoulders. Hadhrat Zubair رضي الله عنه was also wearing a yellow turban on the day of this battle." According to some kitaabs, the colour of the turbans of the angels was black and according to others, they had white turbans on their heads.

Another Sahaabi says: "On the day of Badr, those killed by humans could easily be made out from those killed by the angels. Those killed by the angels had dark fire-burns on their necks and fingertips." A Muslim would run behind an escaping kaafir when suddenly he heard the crack of a whip and a voice: 'Hayzum! Go on! Charge!' The moment he saw the kaafir, he found him lying flat on the ground. His face, especially his nose, was bruised green with the lash of a whip. When this Sahaabi explained this to Rasulullah ﷺ, he said: "You have spoken the truth. This is Allah's help from the third heaven."

Rasulullah ﷺ came out from his hut and after encouraging the Sahaabah رضى الله عنهم to fight the enemy, he said: "I swear by the Allah in whose absolute control lies Muhammad's life, today whosoever is brave and fights the enemy with patience and sincerity and he is then martyred, Allah Ta'ala will certainly enter him into Jannah." Whilst Rasulullah ﷺ was making this announcement, 'Umair bin Hamaam رضى الله عنه had a few dates in his hand, which he was busy eating. The moment he heard these words, he jumped up in happiness and said: "Bakh! Bakh! (Hooray! Bravo!) The only barrier between me and my entry into Jannah is my martyrdom at these people's hands." Saying this, he threw away those dates and grabbing a sword he jumped into the thick of battle and fought bravely until he was martyred. May Allah Ta'ala shower His mercy upon him. Aameen.

Killing of Umayyah bin Khalaf and his Son

Umayyah bin Khalaf was one of the most bitter enemies of Rasulullah ﷺ. He had already heard the warning of his killing from the mouth of S'ad bin Mu'aaz رضى الله عنه in Makkah long before the battle of Badr. This is why he did not want to take part in this battle.

Umayyah was the same person who put Hadhrat Bilal رضى الله عنه through so much of punishments. He would make Hadhrat Bilal رضى الله عنه lie on the boiling hot boulders of Makkah. When Umayyah came to the battlefield of Badr and Hadhrat Bilal رضى الله عنه saw him, he shouted out a challenge to the Ansaar. "Chop off the head of the kaafir Umayyah! I am not safe if Umayyah is saved."

As soon as the Ansaar heard this cry, they rushed over and attacked him with their swords and killed him.

Killing of Abu Jahal – The Firaun of this Ummah

Hadhrat 'Abdur-Rahmaan bin 'Awf رَضِيَ اللَّهُ عَنْهُ says: "I was standing on the battle lines of Badr when suddenly I saw two youngsters to my left and right. I was a bit worried (perhaps the enemy, spotting me between two youngsters, would try to attack me). I was thinking about this when one of them came up to me and whispered: 'Uncle! Would you point out Abu Jahal to me?'

"What would you want to do with Abu Jahal?" I asked in amazement.

This young man replied: "I have made a vow to Allah Ta'ala that when I see Abu Jahal I will surely kill him or I will be killed. I heard that he says terrible things about Rasulullah صَلَّى اللَّهُ عَلَيْهِ وَسَلَّمَ. By Allah in Whose complete control lies my life! As soon as I see Abu Jahal, I will make sure that my shadow does not leave his shadow until one of us is killed.'

When I heard these words, I did not wish to be between two strong men instead of these two boys.

When I pointed out Abu Jahal to these young men, they rushed over to him like an eagle attacking its prey. They pounced on him and finished him off."

These two youngsters were Mu'aaz and Mu'awwiz, the sons of 'Afraa.

Mu'aaz bin 'Amr bin Jamooh رَضِيَ اللَّهُ عَنْهُ says: "I was looking for Abu Jahal. When I saw him, I pounced on him with my sword and gave him such a powerful blow that cut his leg off."

Abu Jahal's son 'Ikrimah (who accepted Islam at the conquest of Makkah), struck Mu'aaz bin 'Amr bin Jamooh with such force that left his arm hanging by its skin. However, this injury did not stop Mu'aaz from continuing to fight bravely right until the evening. When fighting with this loose hand became extremely painful, he placed the hand under his foot and ripped off the hand completely. He lived until the Khilaafat of Hadhrat 'Usmaan رَضِيَ اللَّهُ عَنْهُ."

Chapter Thirteen – Battle of Badr 2 AH

After finishing off with Abu Jahal, Mu'awwiz bin 'Afraa, however, continued fighting until he was martyred. We belong to Allah and to Him shall we return.

Although Abu Jahal was very badly injured, he still had some life left in him. Hadhrat Anas رضي الله عنه says: "On the day of Badr, Rasulullah ﷺ instructed the Sahaabah رضي الله عنهم: 'Is there anyone who can tell me about Abu Jahal?' 'Abdullah bin Mas'ood رضي الله عنه went to look for him amongst the dead bodies. When he found him, he realised that he still had a bit of life in him." Ibn Mas'ood رضي الله عنه planted his foot on Abu Jahal's neck and said: "O enemy of Allah! Allah has disgraced you." Saying this, he cut off his head from his body. He then carried the head and brought it before Rasulullah ﷺ saying: "This is the head of Abu Jahal, the enemy of Allah."

Rasulullah ﷺ asked, "Really? By Allah, besides Whom there is no other god! Is this really the head of Abu Jahal?"

He replied: "By Allah besides whom there is no other god! This is really the head of Abu Jahal."

Rasulullah ﷺ made shukr to Allah Ta'ala thrice and said: "All praise is due to Allah Who has honoured Islam and its people." Rasulullah ﷺ performed two Rakaat Salaah out of shukr (gratitude) before Allah Ta'ala.

'Abdullah bin Mas'ood رضي الله عنه says: "I climbed onto Abu Jahal's chest and sat on him. Abu Jahal opened his eyes and said: "O sheep herder! You have parked yourself on a very honourable place."

I replied: "All praise is due to Allah Who has allowed me to do so." He then asked me: "Who won and who lost?" I replied: "Allah and His Rasool ﷺ have won."

"What is your intention now?" he asked. I replied: "I wish to cut off your head." He said: "Very well. Here, this is my sword. It is extremely sharp. It would help you. But listen, be sure to cut off my head closer to my shoulders as this would cause more fear for those who will see me. Also, when you return to Muhammad, give him this message that I have more hatred for him today than I did yesterday."

Ibn Mas'ood ﷺ says: "I then chopped his head off and brought it to Rasulullah ﷺ saying: "O Rasulullah! This is the head of the enemy of Allah, Abu Jahal." I then gave his message to Rasulullah ﷺ. Rasulullah ﷺ praised Allah and said: "This man was the Firaun to me and my Ummah. His evil was worse than the evil of the Firaun of Musa (alayhis salaam). At least the Firaun of Musa (alayhis salaam) tried to read the Kalimah at his death but the Firaun of this Ummah spoke words of pride and kufr even at the time of his death." Rasulullah ﷺ then gave Abu Jahal's sword to 'Abdullah bin Mas'ood ﷺ.

Hadhrat Zubair's ﷺ bravery

In the battle of Badr, 'Ubaidah bin Sa'eed bin 'Aas - one of the kuffaar – was fully covered in body armour. Nothing but his eyes could be seen. Not afraid by this, Hadhrat Zubair ﷺ aimed for this tiny hole in his armour. He threw a spear with such force and accuracy that it went all the way through his head. He died immediately. Hadhrat Zubair ﷺ says: "Only when I placed my foot on his head and pulled with all my strength did the spear come out but its edges were slightly bent."

The Prisoners of Badr

Alhamdulillah, after a complete defeat of the kuffaar, the battle came to an end. Seventy of the Quraysh were killed and seventy were taken as prisoners. Rasulullah ﷺ ordered that the bodies of the kuffaar be dumped into the well of Badr. However, the dead body of Umayyah bin Khalaf was so badly swollen that when they tried to remove his armour, his body started breaking into pieces. This is why his body was buried into the ground there and then.

Chapter Thirteen – Battle of Badr 2 AH

As 'Utbah bin Rabi'ah's body was being thrown into the well, Rasulullah ﷺ noticed 'Utbah's son Abu Huzaifah رضى الله عنه, very sad. Rasulullah ﷺ asked him: "O Abu Huzaifah! Looking at your father in this disgraceful condition causes your heart to pain?" He replied: "O Rasulullah ﷺ! By Allah, I am not upset by this but the only thing that really worries me is that my father was an intelligent and patient man. That is why I had expected his intelligence to guide him towards Islam. However, when I realised that he died with kufr (disbelief), I was really disappointed."

Rasulullah ﷺ then made dua for Abu Huzaifah رضى الله عنه.

Throwing the dead bodies in the well of Badr

On the day of Badr, Rasulullah ﷺ instructed that twenty-four bodies of the Qurayshi leaders be thrown into an extremely dirty, filthy and stinking well. All those who were thrown into the well were the leaders of the kuffaar. The remaining dead bodies were dumped somewhere else.

Whenever Rasulullah ﷺ won any battle, it was his noble habit to spend another three days at that place. As was his noble habit, on the third day, Rasulullah ﷺ ordered his animal to be saddled and he set out. The Sahaabah رضى الله عنهم followed, guessing that Rasulullah ﷺ was perhaps going for some important work. They followed until Rasulullah ﷺ reached the edge of that well and he called out each one of them by name. He called out: "O 'Utbah! O Shaybah! O Umayyah! O Abu Jahal! You did not find obedience to Allah and His Rasool very pleasing. Verily, whatever our Rabb has promised us; we found it to be true. Did you also find the promise of your Lord to be true?"

Rasulullah ﷺ then spoke to them saying:

"O people of the pit! You were an extremely evil tribe for your Prophet. You did not believe in me whilst others believed in me. You threw me out whilst others protected me. You fought against me whilst others helped me. You called a trustworthy person as dishonest. You called a truthful person to be a liar. May Allah severely punish you."

Hadhrat 'Umar رضى الله عنه said: "O Rasulullah صلى الله عليه وسلم! You are speaking to lifeless dead bodies?" Rasulullah صلى الله عليه وسلم replied: "Yes! I swear by Him in whose total control lays my life! You are not more understanding of my words than they are. The only difference is that they cannot answer."

Dividing of the War prisoners amongst the Muslims

When Rasulullah صلى الله عليه وسلم reached Madinah Munawwarah, he divided the prisoners amongst the Muslims (to guard them) and warned them:

$$\text{اِسْتَوْصُوْا بِالْاُسَارٰى خَيْرًا}$$

"Treat the prisoners kindly."

Therefore, those Sahaabah رضى الله عنهم who had prisoners to look after would first feed the prisoners and then feed themselves if there was anything left over, otherwise they would eat only dates.

Mus'ab bin 'Umair's رضى الله عنه blood brother Abu Aziz bin 'Umair was also one of the prisoners of war. Abu Aziz says: "The family members of the Ansaari household were such kind people that whatever little bread they baked in the morning and in the evening, they would feed it to me whilst they lived on dates. I was very embarrassed by this and I would always insist that they eat the bread but they would not listen. They would say: 'Rasulullah صلى الله عليه وسلم instructed us to treat the prisoners well.'"

Rasulullah صلى الله عليه وسلم was a mercy to mankind. Thus he commanded the Sahaabah to free the prisoners if they paid a ransom."

Back in Makkah

When the news of the Quraysh's disgraceful defeat reached Makkah, the whole city began to panic. The first person to reach Makkah was

Haysamaan Khuzaa'i. When the people asked him about the news of the war, he cried out: "'Utbah bin Rabi'ah has been killed, Shaybah bin Rabi'ah has been killed, Abul-Hakam bin Hishaam (Abu Jahal) has been killed, Umayyah bin Khalaf has been killed, Zam'ah bin Aswad has been killed, Nabihah bin Hajjaaj has been killed, Munabbihah bin Hajaaj has been killed, so and so has been killed." He then went on to mention a few more leaders who were killed in the battle.

Safwaan bin Umayyah, who was sitting in the Hateem area listening to this news said: "I cannot understand. Is this man perhaps gone mad! Why do you people not test him and ask him where is Safwaan bin Umayyah?" When asked, Haysamaan replied: "Here is Safwaan bin Umayyah sitting in the Hateem. With my own eyes, I saw his father and brother being killed."

About a week after Badr, Abu Lahab beagn suffering with horrible boils on his whole body and he died. The stink given off by his dead body was so terrible that nobody could come close. After three days, his sons got a hole dug and with the help of long poles, roughly pushed him into it.

Virtues of the Badriyeen (those Sahaabah who took part in the Battle of Badr)

Rasulullah ﷺ said to Hadhrat 'Umar ﷺ:

لَعَلَّ اللهَ اِطَّلَعَ اِلٰى اَهْلِ بَدْرٍ فَقَالَ اِعْمَلُوْا مَاشِئْتُمْ فَقَدْ وَجَبَتْ لَكُمُ الْجَنَّةُ

"Verily Allah Ta'ala looked carefully at those who took part in Badr and said: "Do whatever you wish, for Jannah has become compulsory for you."

Hadhrat Jaabir ﷺ says that Rasulullah ﷺ said:

لَنْ يَدْخُلَ النَّارَ اَحَدٌ شَهِدَ بَدْرًا

"Anyone who took part in Badr will never enter the fire of Jahannam."

Once Jibraa'eel ﷺ came to Rasulullah ﷺ and asked: "What do you think of the Badri Sahaabah ﷺ?" Rasulullah ﷺ replied: "They are the best of people." Jibraa'eel ﷺ said: "Yes, even, the angels who took part in the battle of Badr are regarded as the best of angels."

The total number of the Badri Sahaabah ﷺ were 313. There were eight people who, for some reason or the other, were unable to take part in the battle of Badr but they are counted as Badri Sahaabah ﷺ and Rasulullah ﷺ also gave them a share of the spoils.

CHAPTER 14
BATTLE OF UHUD

When the Quraysh returned to Makkah Mukarramah, they discovered that the business caravan which Abu Sufyaan managed to save by escaping through the coastal route, was kept safely in Daarun-Nadwah. They suffered a disgraceful loss at Badr. Those who lost their fathers, brothers, nephews and other close relatives in Badr were waiting to take revenge.

Eventually, Abu Sufyaan and other leaders of the Quraysh had a special meeting in which they suggested that the entire profit from the business caravan be used in preparation for war against Muhammad (ﷺ). In this way they felt that they would be able to take revenge from the Muslims who killed their fathers, brothers, relatives and leaders in Badr. In one voice, all of those who took part in this meeting happily accepted this suggestion. After this, the profits of this caravan, which added up to about 50 000 Dinaars (gold coins) were kept aside for this purpose.

Quraysh Take the Women along

The Quraysh made proper preparations for this battle. They also decided to take some women along to sing poems to increase the courage of the warriors and to embarrass those who turn away.

The Quraysh sent messengers to the diffrent tribes inviting them to show their bravery. In this way, they gathered an army of 3000 people including 700 well-armoured warriors. They had 200 horses, 3000 camels and fifteen women with them. This well equipped army left from Makkah under the command of Abu Sufyaan on the 5th of Shawwaal 3 A.H.

Hadhrat 'Abbaas رضى الله عنه wrote down this news and sent it to Rasulullah ﷺ with a high-speed messenger. He asked him to make sure that he gets this message to Rasulullah ﷺ somehow or the other within three days.

Rasulullah ﷺ meets with the Sahaabah رضى الله عنهم

When Rasulullah ﷺ received this news, he sent Anas رضى الله عنه and Munis رضى الله عنه to get more information about the Quraysh. They returned and informed Rasulullah ﷺ that the Qurayshi army was almost reaching Madinah. Thereafter, Rasulullah ﷺ sent Habbaab bin Munzir رضى الله عنه to check the number of people in the army. He returned and informed Rasulullah ﷺ of the number.

All night long, S'ad bin Mu'aaz رضى الله عنه, Usaid bin Hudhair رضى الله عنه and S'ad bin 'Ubaadah رضى الله عنه were on guard in Masjidun-Nabawi and other guards were placed all around the town as well.

This was on a Friday night. The next morning, Rasulullah ﷺ met with the Sahaabah رضى الله عنهم and asked them what they thought. The senior Muhaajireen and Ansaar felt that the Muslims should fight the enemy whilst from inside Madinah. However, the younger Sahaabah رضى الله عنهم, who did not take part in Badr and were hoping for martyrdom, suggested that they attack the enemy outside Madinah.

Since 'Abdullah bin Ubayy, the chief of the hypocrites, was an expert in war, he was also asked. He said: "It is our experience that whenever an enemy attacked Madinah and the people of Madinah fought the enemy from inside the city, the Madanis always won. However, whenever they fought the enemy on the outside, they were defeated. Do not step out of the boundaries of the city. By Allah! Whenever we stepped out of Madinah we suffered at the hands of the enemy and when the enemy attacked us whilst we were inside Madinah, the enemy suffered a great loss at our hands. Why don't you blockade and make the entire city safe and if, the enemy somehow manages to break through, the men will fight them with swords whilst the women and children will throw stones on them. If the enemy goes back without getting into the city, then we will be also successful."

Some of the senior Sahaabah رَضِيَ اللهُ عَنْهُم also agreed with the younger Sahaabah رَضِيَ اللهُ عَنْهُم and felt that the enemy be fought out of the city of Madinah. They said: "O Rasulullah! We were waiting for such a day and we begged Allah Ta'ala to show us this day soon. Now Allah Ta'ala has given us the chance and the journey is also a short one."

Hadhrat Hamzah رَضِيَ اللهُ عَنْهُ, S'ad bin 'Ubaadah رَضِيَ اللهُ عَنْهُ and Nu'maan bin Maalik رَضِيَ اللهُ عَنْهُ said: "O Rasulullah صَلَّى اللهُ عَلَيْهِ وَسَلَّم! If we defend ourselves whilst we are inside Madinah, our enemy will regard us as weak cowards in the path of Allah Ta'ala."

Hadhrat Hamzah رَضِيَ اللهُ عَنْهُ said: "I swear by the Being Who has sent the Qur'aan to you! I will not eat until I have fought the enemy with my sword out of Madinah."

Nu'maan bin Maalik Ansaari رَضِيَ اللهُ عَنْهُ said: "O Rasulullah! Please give us this opportunity to enter Jannah. I swear by the Being Who has sent you with the truth! I will surely enter Jannah." Rasulullah صَلَّى اللهُ عَلَيْهِ وَسَلَّم asked: "How is that?" Nu'maan رَضِيَ اللهُ عَنْهُ replied: "Because I believe that there is none worthy of worship but Allah and that you are His Nabi and also because I will not run away from the battlefield." According to another narration, he said: "Because I love Allah and His Rasool." To this Rasulullah صَلَّى اللهُ عَلَيْهِ وَسَلَّم replied: "You have spoken the truth."

When Rasulullah صَلَّى اللهُ عَلَيْهِ وَسَلَّم saw the excitement of the younger Sahaabah رَضِيَ اللهُ عَنْهُم to fight out of Madinah to earn Jannah and when he saw the desire for martyrdom from some of the senior Muhaajireen and Ansaar like Hadhrat Hamzah رَضِيَ اللهُ عَنْهُ and S'ad bin 'Ubaadah رَضِيَ اللهُ عَنْهُ, then Rasulullah صَلَّى اللهُ عَلَيْهِ وَسَلَّم also decided to do the same.

This happened on a Friday. After the Jumu'ah Salaah, Rasulullah ﷺ gave a talk in which he created the desire for Jihaad and commanded them to prepare for battle. The moment the sincere Muslims who were happy to meet Allah Ta'ala heard this, it was as though a new life was placed in their bodies and they felt that now the time had finally arrived for their freedom from the 'jail' of this world.

خرم آن روز کزیں منزل ویران بروم   راحت جان طلبم و زپے جانان بروم

Blessed be the day when I am to leave from this lonely place; When I will be at ease in front of my beloved.

Rasulullah ﷺ puts on the Armour

After 'Asr Salaah, Rasulullah ﷺ went into his room with Abu Bakr رضى الله عنه and 'Umar رضى الله عنه.

Rasulullah ﷺ had not come out from the room as yet when S'ad bin Mu'aaz رضى الله عنه and Usaid bin Hudhair رضى الله عنه spoke to the people and said: "You forced Rasulullah ﷺ to go out of the city and fight the enemy whereas wahi comes to him. It would be best to let him decide." In the meantime, Rasulullah ﷺ came out wearing two suits of armour. Astonished by this, the Sahaabah رضى الله عنهم said: "O Rasulullah ﷺ! We made a mistake by forcing you to choose our opinion. This was totally incorrect of us. Please do whatever you feel is right."

Rasulullah ﷺ replied: "It is not permissible for a Nabi to arm himself for war and thereafter remove his armour without fighting the enemy of Allah in war. Now I ask you to take the name of Allah and go ahead and do as I command you to do. Remember if you have taqwa and patience, you will certainly enjoy Allah's help and victory."

Rasulullah ﷺ leaves for battle

On Friday the 11th Shawwaal after 'Asr Salaah, Rasulullah ﷺ left Madinah Munawwarah with 1000 men. Rasulullah ﷺ was riding a horse with S'ad bin Mu'aaz رضي الله عنه and S'ad bin 'Ubaadah رضي الله عنه in full armour walking ahead of him whilst the rest of the Muslims were walking to his right and left. As he reached the outskirts of Madinah Munawwarah at a place called Shaykhayn, Rasulullah ﷺ inspected the army. The very young from them were sent back home.

Raaf'i bin Khadeej رضي الله عنه was also from these youngsters who were inspected by Rasulullah ﷺ. He was smart and stood on the tips of his feet to appear far taller than his age. Rasulullah ﷺ allowed him to join the army. It is also said that he was a very good archer.

Samurah bin Jundub رضي الله عنه was one of the children who was refused by Rasulullah ﷺ. Full of sadness, he cried before his stepfather, "O father! Raaf'i (who is my age) is allowed to join the army whilst I get left behind? I am far stronger than him and I am certain that I will beat him in wrestling." His father went up to Rasulullah ﷺ and said: "O Rasulullah! You allowed Raaf'i to take part and sent my son Samurah back whereas Samurah will surely be able to wrestle him to the ground." Rasulullah ﷺ then called both the youngsters for a wrestling match. When Samurah won, Rasulullah ﷺ permitted him as well.

Young and old, child or adult, every single one of them was ready for sacrifice. Even before they were actually martyred, they were martyred by the sword of love for Allah and his Rasulullah ﷺ.

Return of the Hypocrites

As Rasulullah ﷺ got closer to Uhud, the chief of the hypocrites, 'Abdullah bin Ubayy bin Salool, who came with a group of 300 decided to turn back saying: "You did not take my advice. Why should we now throw ourselves into danger for nothing? This is certainly not a war. If we believed this to be war, we would have definitely joined you."

Eventually only 700 Sahaabah ﷺ were left with Rasulullah ﷺ, of which only one hundred were dressed in body armour. The whole army had just two horses; one for Rasulullah ﷺ and the other belonged to another Sahaabi.

Drawing up the Battle Lines

Rasulullah ﷺ now turned his attention towards the army. Facing Madinah Munawwarah with Uhud behind him, Rasulullah ﷺ drew up the battle lines. This group of pious souls who, before this, were standing humbly before Allah Ta'ala, were now standing to sacrifice their lives in His path of Jihaad.

Baraa bin 'Aazib ﷺ says: "Rasulullah ﷺ placed a group of fifty archers at the back of Mount Uhud to stop any attack by the Quraysh from the back. He chose 'Abdullah bin Jubair ﷺ as their leader and warned them: "Do not move from this place even if you see us destroying the kuffaar and even if you see the kuffaar overpowering us, do not ever leave this place to come and help us." Rasulullah ﷺ warned them: "Even if you see us being picked apart by birds, then too do not move from here. Remain here and protect us from the back and even if you see us being killed, do not leave your positions to help us. If you see us gathering the war booty, then too stay where you are and do not dare join us."

Condition of the Qurayshi Army

The Quraysh army had already reached near Madinah Shareef on Wednesday and set up camp at the bottom of Mount Uhud. They had an army of 3000 men including 700 warriors with full armour. They had 200 horses and 3000 camels. Also with them were the wives of the noblemen of Makkah, who increased the courage of the warriors by singing poetry. The Quraysh chose Khaalid bin Waleed as the leader of the right side of the army, 'Ikramah bin Abi Jahal as the leader of the left side, Safwaan bin Umayyah or 'Amr bin 'Aas as the leader of the foot soldiers and 'Abdullah bin Abi Rabi'ah as the leader of the archers. All these five leaders later accepted Islam.

Rasulullah ﷺ Speaks to the Army

When the two armies lined up, Rasulullah ﷺ, held a sword in his hand, and asked the Sahaabah رضي الله عنهم:

"Who will take this sword with its due right?"

Many hands reached out to take the sword but Rasulullah ﷺ held it back. In the meantime, Abu Dujaanah رضي الله عنه stepped ahead and asked: "What is the right of this sword, O Rasulullah ﷺ?" Rasulullah ﷺ replied: "The right of this sword is that it be used to strike the enemies of Allah until they are defeated."

According to another narration, Rasulullah ﷺ said: "The right of this sword is that it is not to be used to kill a Muslim and that a person does not run away when fighting the kuffaar with this sword."

Abu Dujaanah رضي الله عنه said: "O Rasulullah ﷺ! I will take this sword with its due right." In other words, "I will try to fulfil its right." Rasulullah ﷺ handed over the sword to Abu Dujaanah رضي الله عنه.

Note: Hadhrat Abu Dujaanah رضي الله عنه was a brave, fearless warrior. During the heat of battle, he would walk very bravely and be ever ready to fight the enemy. Whilst fighting with the enemy, he would wear a red 'Amaamah (turban) and move swiftly and gracefully. Perhaps this is why Rasulullah ﷺ handed the sword over to him as he proved himself to be a fierce warrior.

The Battle Begins

From the side of the Quraysh, the first person to come onto the battlefield was Abu 'Aamir who was the leader of the Aws tribe (of Madinah) before Islam came to Madinah. Because he was a firm Christian, he was famously known as Raahib (the monk). When the light of Islam shorn in Madinah, he could not accept this and he left Madinah to settle down in Makkah. Instead of Raahib, Rasulullah ﷺ named him Faasiq (criminal).

This Faasiq came to Makkah and encouraged the Quraysh to go to war against Rasulullah ﷺ and he himself joined the Quraysh in this battle of Uhud. He told them that when the people of Aws see him, they would happily leave Rasulullah ﷺ and join up with him.

Thus Abu 'Aamir, stepped out as the first challenger and as he proudly walked onto the battlefield, he shouted: "O people of Aws! I am Abu 'Aamir."

May Allah Ta'ala cool the eyes of the Aws tribe, who immediately replied: "O Faasiq! May Allah never cool your eyes." On hearing this mocking reply, Abu 'Aamir quickly turned away, unsuccessfully and said: "After I left them, my people have become evil."

1. He was followed onto the battlefield by the flag-bearer (carrier) of the kuffaar, Talhah bin Abi Talhah and with pride, he challenged: "O Sahaabah of Muhammad! You believe that Allah Ta'ala would quickly send us into Jahannam with the help of your swords whilst He would enter you with the help of our swords into Jannat. So, is there anyone from amongst you who would like to be quickly put into Jannah with my sword or whose sword would quickly send me to hell?" On hearing this, Hadhrat Ali رضي الله عنه stepped foward and fought him in a swordfight. Hadhrat Ali رضي الله عنه gave a heavy blow to his leg and he fell face down to the ground in such a way that his satar (private part) could be seen. Full of shame Hadhrat Ali رضي الله عنه stepped back. Rasulullah ﷺ asked: "O Ali! What made you step back?" He

replied: "His satar (private parts) became open and I was very ashamed." Hadhrat Ali رضى الله عنه then struck him on his head so severely that his head split into two. This made Rasulullah صلى الله عليه وسلم very happy and he congratulated him by saying: "Allahu Akbar!" The Muslims also shouted out Allahu Akbar!

2. Thereafter, 'Usmaan bin Abi Talhah, holding the flag of the kuffaar, stepped forward onto the battlefield, saying the following poem: "It is the duty of the flag-bearer to see that his spear becomes red with the blood of the enemy or it breaks into pieces." Hadhrat Hamzah رضى الله عنه stepped forward and attacked him, cutting off both his arms at the shoulders. The flag fell and in an instant he was no more.

3. Thereafter, the flag was taken by Abu S'ad bin Abi Talhah. Hadhrat S'ad bin Abi Waqqaas رضى الله عنه shot an arrow towards him. It went through his neck with such force that his tongue was pushed out of his mouth. S'ad bin Abi Waqqaas رضى الله عنه then quickly finished him off.

4. Thereafter the flag was taken by Musaf'i bin Talhah bin Abi Talhah. With just one blow, Hadhrat 'Aasim bin Saabit رضى الله عنه put him to death.

5. The flag was then held by Haaris bin Talhah bin Abi Talhah. He too was finished off with just one blow by Hadhrat 'Aasim bin Saabit رضى الله عنه. Some historians say that he was killed by Hadhrat Zubair رضى الله عنه.

6. Kilaab bin Talhah bin Abi Talhah then stepped out with the flag. Hadhrat Zubair رضى الله عنه stepped forward and killed him.

7. Thereafter the flag was taken up by Julaas bin Talhah bin Abi Talhah. The moment he stepped out, Hadhrat Talha رضى الله عنه finished him off.

8. The flag was then taken by Artaat Shurahbil. Hadhrat Ali رضى الله عنه quickly finished him off.

9. Shuraih bin Qaariz then took the flag and stepped out. He too was immediately finished off. The killer of Shuraih is not known.

10. Thereafter, a slave by the name of Suwaab stepped out holding the flag. Either Hadhrat S'ad bin Abi Waqqaas رضي الله عنه or Hadhrat Hamzah رضي الله عنه or Hadhrat Ali رضي الله عنه killed him.

In this manner, twenty-two leaders of the Quraysh were killed.

The bravery of Abu Dujaanah رضي الله عنه

Abu Dujaanah رضي الله عنه, to whom Rasulullah ﷺ gave his blessed sword, was a fearless and brave warrior. Firstly, he took out a red 'Amaamah (turban) and tied it onto his head. He then walked onto the battlefield showing his bravery whilst reading the following poem:

أَنَا الَّذِىْ عَاهَدَنِىْ خَلِيْلِىْ ۞ وَنَحْنُ بِالسَّفْحِ لَدَى النَّخِيْلِ

"I am the one from whom my Khalil (my beloved i.e. Rasulullah ﷺ) had taken a promise whilst we were at the foot of the mountain close to the date orchard.

أَنْ لَّا أَقُوْمَ الدَّهْرَ فِى الْكُيُوْلِ ۞ أَضْرِبُ بِسَيْفِ اللهِ وَالرَّسُوْلِ

The promise was that I would never stand in the back rows and I would continue fighting the enemy with the sword of Allah and His Rasool."

When Rasulullah ﷺ saw Abu Dujaanah رضي الله عنه showing off his bravery in this manner he said: "Allah hates such a walk except on such occasions." In other words, when fighting the enemy, this (pride) is for the sake of Allah Ta'ala and His Rasool ﷺ and not for selfish reasons of pride.

Tearing through the lines of the enemy, whoever Abu Dujaanah رضي الله عنه came across would fall dead to the ground. He moved ahead until Hindah, the wife of Abu Sufyaan, challenged him. Abu Dujaanah رضي الله عنه lifted his sword to strike her but stopped himself thinking that it was not right for him to use Rasulullah's ﷺ sword against a woman.

According to another narration, when Abu Dujaanah رضي الله عنه came close to Hindah, she shouted for help but nobody came to help her. Abu Dujaanah رضي الله عنه says: "At that time I felt it incorrect to test the sword of Rasulullah ﷺ on a helpless woman."

Bravery and Martyrdom of Hadhrat Hamzah رضي الله عنه

The fearless attacks by Hadhrat Hamzah رضي الله عنه put the kuffaar into a severe panic. The moment he lifted his sword upon anyone, that persons body would fall to the ground.

Wahshi bin Harb was a slave of Jubair. During the battle of Badr, Jubair's uncle was killed by Hadhrat Hamzah رضي الله عنه. Jubair was heartbroken at the death of his uncle. Jubair promised Wahshi that if he killed Hamzah in revenge for his uncle, he would set him free. When the Quraysh left for the battle of Uhud, Wahshi also joined them.

When the two made their lines at Uhud and the battle started, Sib'a bin 'Abdul-'Uzza boastfully came onto the battlefield shouting: "Is there anyone who dares to challenge me?" Walking towards him, Hadhrat Hamzah رضي الله عنه replied: "O Sib'a! O son of the woman who does female circumcision! How dare you openly disobey Allah and His Rasool?" Saying this, Hadhrat Hamzah رضي الله عنه attacked him with his sword and in just a single blow, he quickly sent him to his death.

Meanwhile, Wahshi hid himself behind a boulder waiting for Hadhrat Hamzah رضي الله عنه. When Hadhrat Hamzah رضي الله عنه passed by, he struck him on his back with such force that his spear went through his stomach and came out from his navel. Hadhrat Hamzah رضي الله عنه managed taking a few steps but eventually fell as a martyr.

Wahshi says: "When I reached Makkah, I was set free (as promised). I went with the Quraysh only to kill Hadhrat Hamzah رضي الله عنه. I had absolutely no intention to take part in the actual battle. After I killed Hamzah, I separated myself from the army and sat down away from the fighting because I had no other intention (of fighting). I joined them only with the intention of becoming a free man by killing Hamzah رضي الله عنه."

The Archers Leave their Positions

When the group of archers who were chosen to guard the mountain pass saw the victory of the Muslims and saw them collecting the war booty, they also decided to leave their positions and come quickly to fetch the booty. Their Ameer, 'Abdullah bin Jubair رضي الله عنه, repeatedly asked them not to leave their positions and reminded them about Rasulullah's صلى الله عليه وسلم order about not leaving their positions at all. However, some of them did not agree and they left their positions and went to collect the booty. Thus only 'Abdullah bin Jubair رضي الله عنه and ten Sahaabah were left at this spot. Since the Muslims refused to listen to the command of Rasulullah صلى الله عليه وسلم, the victory quickly turned into defeat. When Khaalid bin Waleed, who was on the right hand side of the Mushrikeen, saw the empty gap, he attacked them from the back. This attack made 'Abdullah bin Jubair رضي الله عنه and ten of his companions as martyrs.

Martyrdom of Mus'ab bin 'Umair رضي الله عنه

This sudden and unexpected attack by the kuffaar left the Muslims in shock and the enemy managed to come very close to Rasulullah صلى الله عليه وسلم. The flag-bearer of the Muslims, Mus'ab bin 'Umair رضي الله عنه was standing close to Rasulullah صلى الله عليه وسلم. He bravely fought with the kuffaar to protect Rasulullah صلى الله عليه وسلم until he himself was martyred. Thereafter, Rasulullah صلى الله عليه وسلم gave the flag to Hadhrat Ali رضي الله عنه. Since Mus'ab bin 'Umair رضي الله عنه looked like Rasulullah صلى الله عليه وسلم, a certain shaytaan started shouting that Rasulullah صلى الله عليه وسلم was martyred. The moment they heard this terrible news, the Muslims began to panic. In this state of panic, they could not make out who was their friend and who was their enemy and they started attacking one another.

The Firmness of Rasulullah ﷺ

When Khalid bin Waleed attacked the Muslims, many of them lost their courage (bravery) but nothing could shake the firmness of Rasulullah ﷺ. How could anything shake his firmness because the Nabi of Allah can never be a coward. The mountains may move but the Ambiyaa of Allah Ta'ala will remain standing. The bravery of a single Nabi is much more than the bravery of the entire world of champions.

Hadhrat Miqdaad ﷺ says:

> "I swear by the Allah Who sent Rasulullah ﷺ with the truth, Rasulullah's ﷺ feet did not move an inch away from the kuffaar. A group of the Sahaabah ﷺ would sometimes come to help him and sometimes they would disappear and quite often I saw Rasulullah ﷺ firing arrows and throwing stones at the kuffaar until the enemy moved away."

Bodyguards of Rasulullah ﷺ

During this time of confusion, fourteen Sahaabah ﷺ stood firmly with Rasulullah ﷺ; seven from the Muhaajireen and seven from the Ansaar. They were:

Muhaajireen	Ansaar
1. Abu Bakr ﷺ	1. Abu Dujaanah ﷺ
2. 'Umar bin Khattaab ﷺ	2. Habbaab bin Munzir ﷺ
3. 'Abdur-Rahmaan bin 'Awf ﷺ	3. 'Aasim bin Saabit ﷺ

4. S'ad bin Abi Waqqaas رضى الله عنه	4. Haaris bin Sammah رضى الله عنه
5. Talhah رضى الله عنه	5. Suhail bin Hunaif رضى الله عنه
6. Zubair bin 'Awwam رضى الله عنه	6. S'ad bin Mu'aaz رضى الله عنه
7. Abu 'Ubaidah رضى الله عنه	7. Usaid bin Hudhair رضى الله عنه

Hadhrat Ali's رضى الله عنه name was not mentioned in the Muhaajireen because after the martyrdom of Mus'ab bin 'Umair رضى الله عنه, Rasulullah ﷺ gave him the flag of the Muslim army. He was busy fighting the enemy. These fourteen brave warriors were all the time with Rasulullah ﷺ.

Unexpected attack of the Quraysh

When the Quraysh suddenly attacked Rasulullah ﷺ, he called out: "Who will clear out these people and make himself my companion in Jannah?" Hadhrat Anas رضى الله عنه says: "There were seven Ansaar with Rasulullah ﷺ and every one of them fought bravely until, one by one, they were all made Shaheed."

According to another narration Rasulullah ﷺ called out: "Is there any man who is prepared to sell his life for us?" Immediately upon hearing this, Ziyaad bin Sakan رضى الله عنه and five other Ansaar answered this call. One after the other, each one of them sacrificed themselves and were made Shaheed. They gave their lives in exchange for Jannah. Ziyaad was blessed with something extra. When he fell wounded to the ground, Rasulullah ﷺ said: "Bring him closer to me." When the Sahaabah brought him to Rasulullah ﷺ, Ziyaad placed his cheek on the blessed foot of Rasulullah ﷺ and gave his life over to Allah Ta'ala.

إنا لله وإنا إليه راجعون

Attack of 'Utbah bin Abi Waqqaas

'Utbah bin Abi Waqqaas, the brother of S'ad bin Abi Waqqaas ﷺ found a chance and threw a stone upon Rasulullah ﷺ with such force that Rasulullah ﷺ lost a tooth and his bottom lip was injured. S'ad bin Abi Waqqaas ﷺ says: "I was not as eager to kill anyone else as much as I was eager to kill my brother 'Utbah bin Abi Waqqaas."

Attack of 'Abdullah bin Qumayyah

'Abdullah bin Qumayyah, a famous wrestler of the Quraysh, attacked Rasulullah ﷺ with such force that two pieces of his helmet pierced his cheek. Meanwhile, 'Abdullah bin Shihaab Zuhri threw a stone at Rasulullah ﷺ injuring his blessed forehead. When his blessed face started bleeding, Abu Sa'eed Khudri's ﷺ father Maalik bin Sinaan ﷺ sucked the blood and cleaned his blessed face. Rasulullah ﷺ promised: "The fire of Jahannam will never touch you." Abu Umaamah ﷺ says: "After causing this injury to Rasulullah ﷺ, Ibn Qumayyah teased:

'Here, take it! I am the son of Qumayyah.'"

Rasulullah ﷺ replied:

"May Allah disgrace and destroy you"

Just a few days later, Allah Ta'ala caused a mountain goat to attack him and tear him to pieces with its horns.

Support of Hadhrat Ali ﷺ and Hadhrat Talhah ﷺ to Rasulullah ﷺ

Since Rasulullah ﷺ was also wearing a pair of heavy steel armour, he fell into a hole dug by 'Abu 'Amir the Faasiq. Hadhrat Ali ﷺ held his hand and Hadhrat Talhah رضي الله عنه lifted his waist and only then did he manage to stand up.

Rasulullah صلى الله عليه وسلم: "If you wish to see a living martyr walking on the earth, take a look at Talhah."

When the two pieces of the helmet went into the cheeks of Rasulullah صلى الله عليه وسلم, Hadhrat Abu 'Ubaidah bin Jarrah رضي الله عنه gripped them with his teeth and pulled them out. He lost two of his teeth in the process.

When Rasulullah صلى الله عليه وسلم tried to climb onto the mountain, his tiredness and weakness increased because of his double armour. Hadhrat Talhah رضي الله عنه placed himself before Rasulullah صلى الله عليه وسلم. Placing his foot on Talhah رضي الله عنه, Rasulullah صلى الله عليه وسلم managed to climb up. Hadhrat Zubair رضي الله عنه says: "On this occasion, I heard Rasulullah صلى الله عليه وسلم saying: 'Talhah has made Jannah waajib for himself.'"

Qays bin Abi Haazim says: "I saw the hand of Hadhrat Talhah رضي الله عنه that he used as a shield in protecting Rasulullah صلى الله عليه وسلم on the day of Uhud. His hand was completely paralysed." On that day Hadhrat Talhah رضي الله عنه received thirty five or thirty nine wounds to his body. Whenever Abu Bakr رضي الله عنه spoke of the battle of Uhud, he would say: "That day belonged to Talhah."

Whilst blocking the attacks of the enemy, Hadhrat Talhah's رضي الله عنه fingers were cut off. Immediately he cried out: 'Hasan (good).' Upon this Rasulullah صلى الله عليه وسلم said:

> 'If you said Bismillah instead of Hasan, the angels would have raised you high up where the people would have been able to see you until they enter the sky with you.'"

Hadhrat Abu Bakr رضي الله عنه says: "On the day of Uhud, we counted more than seventy wounds on the body of Hadhrat Talhah رضي الله عنه."

Hadhrat Anas's ﷺ stepfather Hadhrat Abu Talhah ﷺ was protecting Rasulullah ﷺ with a shield. He was a master in archery. On that day, he broke two or three bows. Whoever happened to pass by with a quiver of arrows, Rasulullah ﷺ would say: "Go and empty out your quiver before Abu Talhah."

Whenever Rasulullah ﷺ planned to look over his head to check on the people, Abu Talhah ﷺ would beg him:

"May my parents be sacrificed for you, O Rasulullah ﷺ! Do not lift your head up. An arrow of the enemy may strike you. Rather it strikes my chest instead of yours."

S'ad bin Abi Waqqaas ﷺ too was an expert archer. On the day of Uhud, Rasulullah ﷺ pulled out all his arrows from his quiver and placed them before S'ad ﷺ and said:

"Go on S'ad, shoot the arrows. May my parents be sacrificed for you."

Hadhrat Ali ﷺ says: "I have not heard Rasulullah ﷺ saying 'may my parents be sacrificed for you' for anyone other than S'ad bin Abi Waqqaas ﷺ." On the day of Uhud, Hadhrat S'ad ﷺ fired 1000 arrows.

Abu Dujaanah ﷺ placed himself before Rasulullah ﷺ as a human shield with his back facing the enemy. Many arrows landed on his back but out of fear of an arrow wounding Rasulullah ﷺ, Abu Dujaanah ﷺ did not move an inch. Hadhrat Anas ﷺ says: "On the day of Uhud, Rasulullah ﷺ would continue wiping the blood off his blessed face and sadly say: 'How can a people who stained the face of their Nabi with blood ever be successful whilst the Nabi is inviting them towards their Rabb?'"

Abdullah bin Mas'ood رضى الله عنه says: "I can still clearly picture the scene where Rasulullah ﷺ was busy wiping the blood off his face and begging Allah:

$$\text{رَبِّ اغْفِرْ لِقَوْمِيْ فَاِنَّهُمْ لَا يَعْلَمُوْنَ}$$

"O my Rabb! Forgive my people because they do not know."

Martyrdom of Anas bin Nadr رضى الله عنه

Hadhrat Anas رضى الله عنه says: "My paternal uncle Anas bin Nadr رضى الله عنه was very sad because he did not take part in the battle of Badr. Once, he mentioned to Rasulullah ﷺ: 'O Rasulullah! How sad that I could not take part in the first battle of Islam against the kuffaar. If Allah Ta'ala gives me the ability to take part in another Jihaad, Allah Ta'ala will see my bravery and sacrifice.'"

During the battle of Uhud, when some people ran away from the battle, Anas bin Nadr رضى الله عنه made dua to Allah: "O Allah! I beg your forgiveness from what some of the Muslims have done – running away from the battlefield - and I have nothing to do with what the kuffaar have done."

Saying this, he moved towards the enemy with a sword in his hand. When he saw of S'ad bin Mu'aaz رضى الله عنه before him, he said:

$$\text{اَيْنَ يَا سَعْدُ اِنِّيْ اَجِدُ رِيْحَ الْجَنَّةِ دُوْنَ اُحُدٍ}$$

"Where are you going O S'ad?! I am finding the fragrance of Jannah at Uhud."

"Ah! I can smell the fragrance of Jannah coming out from the mountain of Uhud." Hadhrat Anas رضى الله عنه went forward and fought the enemy until he was martyred. More than eighty wounds of swords and arrows were found on his body.

The main reason for the suffering of the Muslims at Uhud was that they could not see Rasulullah ﷺ. People were spreading rumours (false news) that Rasulullah ﷺ had passed away.

The first person to recognise Rasulullah ﷺ during this confusion was K'ab bin Maalik ؓ. Rasulullah ﷺ was wearing a helmet that was covering his blessed face. K'ab ؓ says: "I recognised Rasulullah ﷺ from his shinning eyes. As soon as I saw him, I shouted: 'O Muslims! Good news for you. There is Rasulullah ﷺ over there.'" Lifting his hand to his face, Rasulullah ﷺ pointed to him to stay silent. After his announcement, few Muslims rushed off towards Rasulullah ﷺ. K'ab ؓ says: "Then Rasulullah ﷺ gave me his armour to wear whilst he wore my armour. Thinking that I am Rasulullah ﷺ, the enemy started firing arrows upon me. I received more than twenty wounds on this occasion."

As a few Muslims gathered around Rasulullah ﷺ, he went towards the mountain pass. With him were Abu Bakr, 'Umar, Ali, Talhah, Haaris bin Simmah ؓ and others. Rasulullah ﷺ tried to climb the mountain but because of weakness, exhaustion and the weight of the double armour, he could not climb up. This is why Hadhrat Talhah ؓ sat down before him. Placing his foot on Talhah ؓ, Rasulullah ﷺ climbed over.

Killing of Ubayy bin Khalaf

In the meantime, Ubayy bin Khalaf came galloping on his horse, a horse that he fed and fattened with the intention of sitting on it and killing Rasulullah ﷺ. When Rasulullah ﷺ heard of his intentions, he at once said: "Insha Allah, I will kill him." As he came closer to the Muslims, the Sahaabah ؓ asked Rasulullah's ﷺ permission to finish him off. Rasulullah ﷺ said: "Leave him. Allow him to get closer."

As he came up to them, Rasulullah ﷺ took a spear from Haaris bin Simmah رضي الله عنه and scratched him on his neck. He started screaming at the top of his voice and returned to his people shouting: "By Allah! Muhammad has killed me."

His people tried to comfort him saying: "It is nothing but a slight scratch. It is not such a serious wound that you have to scream like this." Ubayy replied: "Don't you know? Muhammad himself told me in Makkah: 'I will kill you'. Only my heart understands the severity of this 'scratch'. By Allah! If this scratch were to be distributed amongst the people of Hejaz, just this one poke would be sufficient for their destruction."

Ubayy continued shouting like this until he reached a place called Sarif where he died.

Hadhrat Ali رضي الله عنه and Hadhrat Faatimah رضي الله عنها clean the wounds of Rasulullah ﷺ

When Rasulullah ﷺ reached the valley, the battle had ended. He sat down whilst Hadhrat Ali رضي الله عنه brought some water and cleaned the blood off his blessed face. He also poured some water over his head. Rasulullah ﷺ then performed wudhu and led the Salaah whilst seated. The Sahaabah رضي الله عنهم also performed their Salaah whilst seated behind Rasulullah ﷺ.

Cutting the Bodies of the Muslims

During the battle, the kuffaar started cutting up the bodies of the Muslims. They cut their noses and ears. They ripped open their stomachs and cut off their private parts. Even the women joined the men in this terrible action.

Hindah, whose father was killed by Hadhrat Hamzah رضي الله عنه in the battle of Badr, cut the body of Hadhrat Hamzah رضي الله عنه. She cut his stomach open and sliced off a piece of his liver. She then tried to swallow it but since it refused to go down her throat, she spat it out.

Overjoyed with Hamzah's ﷺ death, she removed all her jewellery and gave it to Wahshi. She also made a necklace out of the ears and noses of the Muslims and hung it around her neck.

After the kuffaar left the battlefield, the Muslim women came out of Madinah to find out the conditions of the Muslims. Hadhrat Faatimah ﷺ saw blood running down the blessed face of Rasulullah ﷺ. Hadhrat Ali ﷺ fetched some water in his shield and Hadhrat Faatimah ﷺ cleaned his wound. However the more she cleaned the wound, the more it bled. They then burnt a piece of a grass-mat and filled its ash into the wound. This helped in stopping the blood.

Looking for the Body of Hadhrat Hamzah ﷺ

Rasulullah ﷺ went out to look for his uncle, Hadhrat Hamzah ﷺ. He found his body inside the valley. His nose and ears were cut off. His stomach and chest were ripped open. When he saw his body in this condition, Rasulullah ﷺ began to cry. He sadly said: "May Allah shower you with His mercy. As far as I know, you were very charitable and you kept up good family ties. If it was not for the pain of Safiyyah (1), I would have left you like this for the vultures and beasts. They would have eaten you up and on the day of Qiyaamah you would have been brought back to life from their bellies."

Hadhrat Jaabir ﷺ says that when Rasulullah ﷺ saw the body of Hadhrat Hamzah ﷺ, he burst out crying and in a crying voice he mentioned:

سَيِّدُ الشُّهَدَاءِ عِنْدَ اللهِ يَوْمَ الْقِيَامَةِ حَمْزَةُ

---

[1] Hadhrat Safiyyah ﷺ was the sister of Hadhrat Hamza ﷺ

"On the day of Qiyaamah, Hamzah would be the leader of all the martyrs in the sight of Allah."

This is why he was famously known as Sayyidus-Shuhadaa.

People of Madinah hurried to find out the condition of Rasulullah ﷺ

Since some terrible stories about the war had reached Madinah, the men, women, children and the old were eager to see Rasulullah ﷺ safe and sound, even more than their own relatives.

Hadhrat S'ad bin Abi Waqqaas ﷺ says: "After returning from this battle, Rasulullah ﷺ passed by an Ansaari woman who lost her husband, brother and father in this battle. When she was told of the death of her husband, brother and father, she said: 'No, tell me how is Rasulullah ﷺ?' The people replied: 'Alhamdulillah! He is well.' The lady replied: 'Show me his blessed face. I will be at ease only when I see him.' When the people pointed out Rasulullah ﷺ to her, she said: 'Every difficulty after (seeing) you is small and easy.'"

Kafn and Burial of the Martyrs

In this battle seventy Sahaabah ﷺ were martyred, most of them were from the Ansaar. They were so poor that they did not even have enough cloth to cover their dead. When Mus'ab bin 'Umair ﷺ was martyred, the sheet for his kafn was so short that when his head was covered, his feet would be open and when his feet were covered his face would be open. Rasulullah ﷺ told them to cover his head with the sheet and his feet with leaves.

Hadhrat Hamzah's ﷺ feet also had to be covered with leaves. Some of the martyrs did not even have a single sheet of cloth. Sometimes one cloth was used to cover two martyrs. When it was time to bury them two or three

Sahaabah were buried in one grave. At the time of burial, Rasulullah ﷺ would ask: "Who knows more of the Qur-aan Shareef from them?" He would then place whoever was pointed out to him towards the front of the grave facing the Qiblah. The others would then be placed behind him. Rasulullah ﷺ would then say:

$$\text{اَنَا شَهِيْدٌ عَلٰى هٰؤُلَاءِ يَوْمَ الْقِيَامَةِ}$$

"I will be a witness for them on the day of Qiyaamah."

Rasulullah ﷺ also instructed them to bury these martyrs without ghusl in their same blood-soaked clothing.

Some of the Sahaabah رضي الله عنهم wanted to take the bodies of their loved ones back to Madinah for burial but Rasulullah ﷺ refused and asked them to bury their dead where they were martyred.

CHAPTER 15
INCIDENT OF RAJ'EE

During the month of Safar, some people of the 'Adal and Qaarah tribes came to Rasulullah ﷺ and said: "O Rasulullah! We have accepted Islam. Please send us someone who would teach us the knowledge of the Qur-aan and the rules of Islam." Rasulullah ﷺ sent ten Sahaabah رضى الله عنهم with them.

Rasulullah ﷺ chose 'Aasim bin Saabit رضى الله عنه as their Ameer. When these Sahaabah رضى الله عنهم reached Raj'ee, these tribes broke their promise (which they had made to Rasulullah ﷺ) and sent a message to the Banu Lihyaan tribe who sent two hundred warriors, including one hundred archers. As they came closer, Hadhrat 'Aasim رضى الله عنه and his friends climbed up a hillock.

The Banu Lihyaan called out to the Muslims: "Come down, we promise you safety and protection." Hadhrat 'Aasim رضى الله عنه replied: "I will never accept the protection of a kaafir." He then made the following dua:

"O Allah! Inform Rasulullah ﷺ of our situation."

Allah Ta'ala accepted the dua of Hadhrat 'Aasim رضى الله عنه and through wahy, he immediately informed Rasulullah ﷺ about their condition. Rasulullah ﷺ then informed the Sahaabah رضى الله عنهم.

One of the duas Hadhrat 'Aasim رضى الله عنه made was:

Chapter Fifteen – Incident of Rajee

"O Allah! Today I am protecting Your Deen. I beg you to save my flesh (my body from the kuffaar)."

Thereafter, Hadhrat 'Aasim رضي الله عنه, together with seven of his friends, were martyred whilst fighting the enemy.

The kuffaar promised safety to the remaining three Sahaabah '(Abdullah bin Taariq رضي الله عنه, Zaid bin Dasinah رضي الله عنه and Khubaib bin 'Adi رضي الله عنه). Therefore they came down from the hill. However, the moment they came down, the kuffaar tied them up. Abdullah bin Taariq رضي الله عنه said: "This is the first broken promise. You are acting dishonestly right from the beginning; I wonder what promises you are going to break in the future?"

Saying this, he refused to go with them. The kuffaar dragged him on the ground and killed him. His other two friends, Hadhrat Khubaib رضي الله عنه and Hadhrat Zaid رضي الله عنه were taken to Makkah where they were sold as slaves.

Safwaan bin Umayyah (whose father Ummayyah bin Khalaf was killed at Badr) bought Hadhrat Zaid رضي الله عنه with the intention of killing him in revenge for the death of his father. Haaris bin 'Aamir was killed in Badr by Hadhrat Khubaib رضي الله عنه. Thus the sons of Haaris bought Khubaib.

Safwaan wanted to kill Hadhrat Zaid رضي الله عنه immediately. Thus he sent Hadhrat Zaid رضي الله عنه with his slave Nastaas out of the Haram area to a place called Tan'eem to kill him. A group of the Quraysh also gathered to watch this. When Hadhrat Zaid رضي الله عنه was brought for killing, Abu Sufyaan mockingly asked: "O Zaid! I ask you to take an oath in the name of Allah, would you be happier to be set free and Muhammad killed in your place whilst you are relaxing comfortably in your home?" Hadhrat Zaid رضي الله عنه replied: "By Allah! I will not tolerate even a thorn poking Muhammad ﷺ on his foot whilst I am relaxing at home." Abu Sufyaan said: "I have not seen anyone loving another person more than the love that the Sahaabah have for Muhammad." Thereafter, Nastaas killed Hadhrat Zaid رضي الله عنه. Later on in life, Nastaas accepted Islam.

Hadhrat Khubaib ؓ, on the other hand, was kept alive until the end of the month of Muharram. As he was close to his date of killing, he asked Zainab bint Haaris (who later accepted Islam) for a blade to clean himself. She gave him a blade and got busy with her housework. Zainab says: "A little while later I was shocked to see my son calmly sitting on Khubaib's lap with a blade in his (Khubaib's) hand. I was totally shocked at this sight."

Hadhrat Khubaib ؓ said: "Are you afraid that I will kill this child? Never! Insha Allah, I will never do something like this. We are not such mean people."

Hadhrat Zainab ؓ would often remember this moment and say:

> *"I have not seen a prisoner better than Khubaib. I noticed him eating from a bunch of grapes whereas there was no fresh fruit available in Makkah at that time. Furthermore, he was tied in chains. He could not have brought those grapes from anywhere. This was nothing but the help of Allah to him."*

As he was brought to Tan'eem for killing, he asked them to allow him to read two Rakaats of Salaah. They allowed him and when he completed his two Rakaats, he spoke to the kuffaar saying: "I did not read a long Salaah because you may think that I am afraid of dying." He then lifted his hands and made the following dua:

اَللّٰهُمَّ اَحْصِهِمْ عَدَدًا ، وَاقْتُلْهُمْ بَدَدًا ، وَلَا تُبْقِ مِنْهُمْ اَحَدًا

"O Allah, one by one kill them all and do not leave anyone behind."

He then read the following poem:

لَسْتُ اُبَالِيْ حِيْنَ اُقْتَلُ مُسْلِمًا   عَلٰى اَيِّ شِقٍّ كَانَ لِلّٰهِ مَصْرَعِيْ

"I am not worried in the least if I am killed as a Muslim, on which side I fall on as long as it is for Allah alone.

$$\text{وَذٰلِكَ فِيْ ذَاتِ الْاِلٰهِ وَاِنْ يَّشَأْ يُبَارِكْ عَلٰى اَوْصَالِ شِلْوٍ مُمَزَّعِ}$$

And this is only for the pleasure of Allah. If He wishes, He can bless every joint of my broken body."

Hadhrat Khubaib رضى الله عنه was then martyred. He is the one who started the good practice of reading two Rakaat Salaah for every person sentenced to death.

Allah protects the body of Aasim رضى الله عنه

In the battle of Uhud, Hadhrat 'Aasim رضى الله عنه killed two sons of Salaafah bint Sa'eed. Wanting to take revenge, she vowed to drink wine in the skull of 'Aasim رضى الله عنه. Some people went to fetch 'Aasim's head hoping to sell his head to Salaafah for a good amount of money. Salaafah announced that the person who brings 'Aasim's head will be rewarded with a prize of a hundred camels.

Hadhrat 'Aasim رضى الله عنه had already made dua for the safety and protection of his body. Allah Ta'ala sent a swarm of wasps around his body. No kaafir could go nearby. When they saw the wasps around his body they said: "We will return at night when the wasps disappear and then we will cut off his head." However, in the evening, a sudden flood washed his body away leaving them all very disappointed. Hadhrat 'Aasim رضى الله عنه had promised Allah Ta'ala that neither should he touch a mushrik (kaafir) nor should a mushrik touch him.

Whenever Hadhrat 'Aasim رضى الله عنه was mentioned in the presence of Hadhrat 'Umar رضى الله عنه, he would say: "Allah Ta'ala protects some of His special servants even after their death as He protected them during their lifetime."

Hadhrat Khubaib's رضى الله عنه body was left on the cross by the kuffaar of Makkah. Rasulullah ﷺ sent Hadhrat Zubair رضى الله عنه and Hadhrat

Miqdaad رضي الله عنه from Madinah Munawwarah to Makkah Mukarramah to bring his body down. When they came to Tan'eem, they saw forty guards lying asleep around the cross. They went very quickly, brought his body down from the cross and loaded it on their horse. Although he was hanging for forty days on the cross, his body was still fresh without any change.

When the guards opened their eyes and found the body missing, they rushed about looking for it. They eventually caught Hadhrat Zubair رضي الله عنه and Hadhrat Miqdaad رضي الله عنه. Hadhrat Zubair رضي الله عنه gently lowered the body to the ground and almost immediately the ground opened up and swallowed his body. This is why Hadhrat Khubaib رضي الله عنه was known as Bali'ul-Ard (one swallowed by the earth).

According to another narration, when Hadhrat Khubaib رضي الله عنه was martyred, his face was facing the Qiblah. Whenever the kuffaar tried to turn his face away from the Qiblah, his face turned back towards the Qiblah. They tried this many times but they eventually left him alone.

CHAPTER 16
THE STORY OF BI'R MA'UNAH

In the month of Safar, a person by the name of Abu Baraa came to Rasulullah ﷺ and offered him a gift, but Rasulullah ﷺ did not accept it. Rasulullah ﷺ then invited him to Islam but Abu Baraa neither accepted nor denied Islam but said: "If you send some of your sahaabah towards Najd (the Arabian highlands) with the intention of inviting others to Islam, I have great hope that they will all accept Islam." Rasulullah ﷺ replied: "I am worried about the difficulty my sahaabah may face from the people of Najd." Abu Baraa replied: "I give you my word. I guarantee their safety."

Rasulullah ﷺ sent seventy Sahaabah رضى الله عنهم with him. This noble group was known as the Qurra (the Qaaris). Rasulullah ﷺ chose Munzir bin Amr Saa'idi رضى الله عنه as the Ameer over them.

This was a very sincere and loyal group of Muslims. During the day they would collect firewood, which they would sell in the evening and buy food for the Ashaabus Suffah. Part of the night they would spend in learning and teaching the Qur-aan Shareef and part of it in Tahajjud Salaah.

This group of pious people reached a place called Bi'r Ma'unah. Rasulullah ﷺ wrote a letter to 'Aamir bin Tufail (leader of the Banu 'Aamir tribe and the nephew of Abu Baraa) and gave this letter over to Haraam bin Milhaan رضى الله عنه, the uncle (mother's brother) of Hadhrat Anas رضى الله عنه.

When they reached Bi'r Ma'unah, Haraam bin Milhaan came to 'Aamir bin Tufail with this blessed letter, however, even before 'Aamir bin Tufail could read the letter, he pointed to another person to kill him. This person poked a spear from the back that went right through him. At this moment, the following words were on his tongue:

$$\text{اَللّٰهُ اَكْبَرُ! فُزْتُ وَ رَبِّ الْكَعْبَةِ}$$

"Allahu Akbar! Allah is the Greatest. I swear by the Rabb of the K'abah, I am victorious."

'Aamir bin Tufail then encouraged his people to kill the rest of the Sahaabah رضى الله عنهم as well; but due to the promise made by 'Aamir's uncle, Abu Baraa, the Banu 'Aamir tribe refused to support him.

When 'Aamir bin Tufail noticed that his people were not going to help him, he came to the Banu Sulaim tribe for help. The tribes of 'Usayyah, R'al and Zakwaan agreed to support him. All together, they cruelly killed all the Sahaabah. Only K'ab bin Zaid Ansaari رضى الله عنه was saved. He was unconscious and they thought that he was dead. He later recoverd and lived for some time thereafter. He was martyred in the battle of Khandaq (trench). Besides him, another two Sahaabah also survived; Munzir bin Muhammad رضى الله عنه and 'Amr bin Umayyah رضى الله عنه. These two Sahaabah were grazing the animals in the fields when suddenly they saw a huge flock of birds in the sky. They realised that something was not right. As they came close to their camp, they found all their companions martyred and 'soaked in blood'. They discussed with one another about what to do. 'Amr bin Umayyah suggested that they return to Madinah and inform Rasulullah صلى الله عليه وسلم about this. Munzir replied: "He صلى الله عليه وسلم will somehow get the news. Why should we lose out on martyrdom?"

Nonetheless, they went forward to face the enemy in battle. Hadhrat Munzir رضى الله عنه was martyred whilst fighting and 'Amr bin Umayyah رضى الله عنه was captured.

They handed over 'Amr bin Umayyah رضى الله عنه to 'Aamir bin Tufail, who shaved off his hair and freed him saying: "My mother promised to free a slave. Therefore, I set you free."

In this journey, Abu Bakr's رضى الله عنه freed slave, 'Aamir bin Fuhayrah رضى الله عنه was also martyred and his body was lifted to the heavens.

When Rasulullah ﷺ was informed of the killing of his Sahaabah رضى الله عنهم in this journey, he was very sad and upset. For an entire month he continued cursing these people in the Qunoot of Fajr Salaah. He then said to the Sahaabah رضى الله عنهم: "Your friends were martyred. They asked Allah Ta'ala to inform me that they have met their Rabb and that they are pleased with Him and He is pleased with them."

Battle of Banu Nazeer - Rabi'ul-Awwal 4 A.H.

As Amr bin Umayyah Damari رضى الله عنه (one of the survivors from the Bi'r Ma'unah) was returning to Madinah, two kuffaar from the Banu 'Aamir tribe joined him on his journey. When they reached a place called Qanaat, they rested in one of the orchards. When these two kuffaar fell off to sleep, 'Amr bin Umayyah Damiri thought to himself that the leader of their tribe, 'Aamir bin Tufail, killed seventy Muslims. It was not possible to take revenge for the deaths of all of them. Why don't I at least kill some of them, he thought. Therefore, he killed both of them whereas Rasulullah ﷺ had a peace agreement with this tribe. However 'Amr bin Umayyah Damiri did not know about this agreement.

When he reached Madinah Shareef and told Rasulullah ﷺ about what he had done, Rasulullah ﷺ said: "We had a peace agreement with them. We will have to pay the blood money for both of them." Rasulullah ﷺ then paid the blood money to their tribe.

Since the Banu Nazeer tribe were also friends of the Banu 'Aamir, they had to pay part of the blood money, as this was in accordance to the peace treaty. In order to get some help in paying this blood money, Rasulullah

ﷺ decided to speak to the Banu Nazeer. He left with Abu Bakr, 'Umar, 'Usmaan, Zubair, Talhah, 'Abdur-Rahmaan bin 'Awf, S'ad bin Mu'aaz, Usaid bin Hudhair and S'ad bin 'Ubaadah رضى الله عنهم.

Rasulullah ﷺ sat in the shade of a wall. The Banu Nazeer received Rasulullah ﷺ very warmly and promised to help in paying the blood money but secretly planned to send someone on top of the roof and roll a heavy boulder onto his head and kill him.

However, Sallaam bin Mishkam warned his people: "No! Don't ever do that! By Allah, his Rabb will surely inform him of your evil intentions. Furthermore, this will break of our peace treaty with him."

Jibraa'eel عليه السلام came with wahi, informing Rasulullah ﷺ about their terrible intentions. Rasulullah ﷺ immediately got up and started moving towards Madinah. Rasulullah ﷺ made it seem as though he was getting up for a short while. This is why the Sahaabah رضى الله عنهم continued sitting in the same place. When the Jews heard about Rasulullah's ﷺ leaving, they lost hope. Kinaanah bin Huwayraa said: "Don't you know why Muhammad got up from there? By Allah, he was informed about your evil plan. By Allah, he is a Nabi of Allah."

When Rasulullah ﷺ did not return, the Sahaabah رضى الله عنهم also got up and went out to look for him towards Madinah. Rasulullah ﷺ told them about the plan of the Jews and commanded them to attack the Banu Nazeer.

After choosing 'Abdullah ibn Ummi Maktum رضى الله عنه as the Ameer over Madinah, Rasulullah ﷺ left for the Banu Nazeer and surrounded them. The Banu Nazeer quickly rushed into their fortresses and shut the doors. On the one hand they felt safe in their strong fortresses and on the other hand 'Abdullah bin Ubayy and the other hypocrites promised them that they will give them their full support. However, none of them dared to come out and fight the Muslims.

The Banu Nazeer then sent a message to Rasulullah ﷺ asking him to come with three people for a discussion with three of their rabbis (Jewish priests). They promised Rasulullah ﷺ that if these rabbis accept Islam, all of them will also accept Islam. However, secretly they asked the three rabbis to hide daggers in their clothing and at the first chance, they should kill Rasulullah ﷺ.

Even before they could come for this discussion, Rasulullah ﷺ was informed of their plan (by Allah Ta'ala).

In short, all these evil plans of the Banu Nazeer forced Rasulullah ﷺ to attack them. The siege lasted for fifteen days. Rasulullah ﷺ also ordered their trees and orchards to be set on fire. Eventually, full of worry about losing their trees and orchards, they begged for mercy.

Rasulullah ﷺ replied: "You have ten days to empty out your homes. You may take your wives, families and children wherever you wish. You may also carry away as much goods as your camels and animals can carry, but you cannot take your weapons."

Out of greed, they even removed the doors and door-frames of their houses and where possible, took them away on their camels. In this way, they were chased from Madinah. Most of them moved to Khaybar whilst some of them settled down in Syria. Their leaders, Huyayy bin Akhtab, Kinaanah bin Rab'i and Sallaam bin Abil-Haqeeq were from amongst those who decided to settle down in Khaybar.

Rasulullah ﷺ then divided their remaining goods amongst the Muhaajireen in order to make it easy for the Ansaar (because the Ansaar were looking after the Muhajireen in their homes). Rasulullah ﷺ then called the Ansaar and spoke to them. He said: "O people of the Ansaar! If you wish I am prepared to divide the wealth of the Banu Nazeer equally between you and the Muhaajireen and they will continue sharing your wealth as before or if you wish, I will divide it only amongst the Muhaajireen and they will then leave your homes."

S'ad bin 'Ubaadah رضى الله عنه and S'ad bin Mu'aaz رضى الله عنه, the leaders of the Ansaar agreed to this by saying: "O Rasulullah صلى الله عليه وسلم! From the bottom of our hearts, we would be more than happy if you divide this wealth amongst the Muhaajireen only and even after this, they are free to live in our homes and eat our meals, as before."

According to another narration, the Ansaar agreed by saying: "O Rasulullah صلى الله عليه وسلم! You may divide this wealth only amongst the Muhaajireen. Also, we would be very happy if you take whatever you wish from our wealth and divide it amongst them."

Such beautiful words pleased Rasulullah صلى الله عليه وسلم and he made the following dua for them:

اللّٰهُمَّ ارْحَمِ الْأَنْصَارَ وَأَبْنَاءَ الْأَنْصَارِ

"O Allah! Shower Your special mercy on the Ansaar and the children of the Ansaar."

A man tries to kill Rasulullah صلى الله عليه وسلم

After returning from Zaatur Riqaa, Rasulullah صلى الله عليه وسلم took rest under a shady tree on which he had hung his sword. A kaafir came silently to him, took Rasulullah's صلى الله عليه وسلم sword and shouted: "Tell me, who will save you from me?" Rasulullah صلى الله عليه وسلم calmly replied: "Allah." Jibraa'eel عليه السلام suddenly gave a punch to the man's chest. The sword fell out of his hands. Rasulullah صلى الله عليه وسلم picked it up and asked: "Who will save you from me?" The man replied: "Nobody." Rasulullah صلى الله عليه وسلم said: "Go! I have forgiven you." This man later accepted Islam, returned to his people and invited them towards Islam. Many of his people accepted Islam. This man's name was Ghawrith bin Haaris.

A Sahaabi is wounded in Salaah

When he left this area, Rasulullah ﷺ then stopped at a mountain pass. He asked 'Ammaar bin Yaasir رضي الله عنه and 'Abbaad bin Bishr رضي الله عنه to guard the pass. The two of them agreed that 'Abbaad would stand guard for the first half of the night and 'Ammaar the second half. Therefore, 'Ammaar bin Yaasir رضي الله عنه took a rest whilst 'Abbaad bin Bishr رضي الله عنه stood up and started his salaah. A kaafir saw him and understood that this man is the night guard. He fired an arrow that struck Abbaad رضي الله عنه. He did not break his salaah but continued reading his Salaah in the same calm manner. He calmly pulled out the arrow and threw it aside. The enemy fired a second arrow and he removed that arrow as well and threw it aside. The enemy then fired a third arrow. Abbaad رضي الله عنه then became worried about the safety of Rasulullah ﷺ and the sahaabah. Therefore, he completed his Salaah and woke his friend up saying: "Get up, I am wounded." When the enemy saw him getting his friend up, he ran away. When 'Ammaar bin Yaasir رضي الله عنه got up and saw the blood flowing down his body, he said: "Subhaanallah! Why did you not get me up when the first arrow struck you?" He replied: "I was busy reading a certain Surah of the Qur-aan and I felt it incorrect to cut it short. When the arrows started coming one after the other, I completed my Salaah and got you up. I swear by Allah, if it was not for the commands of Rasulullah ﷺ, I would have rather died than cutting short my Salaah."

CHAPTER 17
BATTLE OF KHANDAQ (TRENCH)

اَللّٰهُمَّ لَا عَيْشَ اِلَّا عَيْشُ الْاٰخِرَةِ

The battle of Khandaq took place in the year 5 A.H. Whilst returning from the battle of Uhud, Abu Sufyaan made a promise to the Muslims warning them that he would fight them the following year. Saying this he returned to Makkah. In the following year, as the time to carry out his promise came closer, he gave some excuses and did not prepare an army. A year later, he tried to attack Madinah Munawwarah with an army of ten thousand men. This battle is known as the battle of Khandaq or the battle of Ahzaab.

The reason for this battle was that after the Banu Nazeer were chased out of Madinah, Huyayy bin Akhtab and Kinnanah bin Rab'i went to Makkah and encouraged the Quraysh to fight against Rasulullah ﷺ. Then they came to meet the people of Ghitfaan and also got them ready to go to war against Rasulullah ﷺ. This is how Abu Sufyaan, with an army of ten thousand, set out towards Madinah to finish off the Muslims once and for all.

When Rasulullah ﷺ heard of them leaving from Makkah, he made mashwara (consulted) with the Sahaabah رضي الله عنهم. Hadhrat Salmaan Faarsi رضي الله عنه suggested the digging of trenches around the city. He felt that it would be difficult to fight them on an open field. Fighting them from the safety of the trenches would be better. Everybody liked this idea.

Rasulullah ﷺ himself marked the area of the trench, drew lines and fixed ten people for every nine meters for the digging of the trenches. The trenches were dug so deep that the water of the soil could be seen. The trenches were completed in six days. Rasulullah ﷺ also joined the Sahaabah رضي الله عنهم in digging the trenches. He struck the very first pick to the ground with his blessed hands and the following words were on his blessed tongue:

$$\text{بِسْمِ اللهِ وَبِهِ بَدِيْنَا وَلَوْ عَبَدْنَا غَيْرَهُ شَقِيْنَا حَبَّذَا رَبًّا وَحَبَّذَا دِيْنًا}$$

"Bismillah, we start in the name of Allah. If we believe in anyone besides Him, we would surely be unfortunate. O! What a wonderful Rabb He is and what a beautiful Deen we have!"

It was during the middle of winter. Icy cold winds were blowing and they were starving for a few days but the loyal Muhaajireen and Ansaar were happily digging the trenches. Whilst busy moving the heaps of sand, they would say the following words:

$$\text{نَحْنُ الَّذِيْنَ بَايَعُوْا مُحَمَّدًا عَلَى الْجِهَادِ مَا بَقِيْنَا أَبَدًا}$$

"We are those who took bay'at at the hands of Muhammad (and we have sold our lives to Allah for Rasulullah ﷺ) that we would continue fighting in Jihaad as long as we have life within us."

In reply to these words, Rasulullah ﷺ would say:

$$\text{اَللّٰهُمَّ لَا عَيْشَ اِلَّا عَيْشُ الْاٰخِرَةِ فَاغْفِرْ لِلْاَنْصَارِ وَالْمُهَاجِرَةِ}$$

"O Allah! There is really no true life but the life of the aakhirat. So forgive the Ansaar and the Muhaajireen."

Baraa bin 'Aazib رضي الله عنه says: "On the day of the trench, Rasulullah ﷺ himself was busy carrying the sand of the trenches so much so that his blessed stomach turned dusty. Whilst carrying the sand, he would say the following words:

$$\text{وَاللهِ، لَوْ لَا اللهُ مَا اهْتَدَيْنَا وَلَا تَصَدَّقْنَا، وَلَا صَلَّيْنَا}$$

By Allah! If it was not for the divine guidance of Allah, we would not have been guided, and we would not have performed our Salaah or given charity.

$$\text{فَاَنْزِلَنْ سَكِيْنَةً عَلَيْنَا وَثَبِّتِ الْاَقْدَامَ اِنْ لَاقَيْنَا}$$

O Allah! Shower us with peace and keep us firm when we face the enemy.

$$\text{اِنَّ الْاُلٰى قَدْ بَغَوْا عَلَيْنَا   اِذَا اَرَادُوْا فِتْنَةً اَبَيْنَا}$$

They have been cruel to us. If they wish to trap us into any temptation, we will flatly refuse." (At the end, the words Abaynaa, Abaynaa are repeated (we will refuse, we will refuse).

Hadhrat Jaabir ﷺ says: "Whilst digging the trenches, we came to a huge boulder. When we mentioned this problem to Rasulullah ﷺ, he replied: 'Wait, I will go down into the trench myself.' Due to severe hunger, Rasulullah ﷺ had tied a stone to his mubaarak stomach. We also had not tasted anything for three days. Rasulullah ﷺ took the pickaxe with his blessed hands and struck the boulder, turning it into a heap of sand."

The Muslims had just completed the digging of the trenches when the ten-thousand men of the army of the Quraysh arrived just outside Madinah. They set up camp near Mount Uhud. With an army of 3000 Sahaabah ﷺ, Rasulullah ﷺ came out to face them and set up camp near Mount Sil'a. The trenches were separating both the armies. Rasulullah ﷺ moved all the women and children into a safe fort.

Up until that moment, the Banu Qurayzah (Jews living in Madinah) were still neutral (did not join anyside). However, the leader of the Banu Nazeer,

Huyayy bin Akhtab tried every possible way to make them join the kuffaar army. He went to Kʻab bin Asad, the leader of the Banu Qurayzah tribe who had already signed a peace agreement with Rasulullah ﷺ. When Kʻab saw Huyayy coming, he quickly closed the door of the fort. Huyayy shouted: "Open the door. (I wish to speak to you)." Kʻab responded:

"Shame on you, O Huyayy! You are certainly an evil man. I have an agreement with Muhammad ﷺ and I will definitely not break this agreement because I have not seen anything from him but truthfulness, honesty and fulfilling his promises."

Huyayy begged him: "Allow me to offer you something that would guarantee you great honour. I have brought the armies of the Quraysh and Ghitfaan right up to your doorstep. All of us have promised never to move an inch until Muhammad and his companions are totally destroyed."

Kʻab replied: "By Allah! You always bring disgrace and shame to yourself. I will never ever break the agreement with Muhammad. I haven't seen anything from him but truthfulness, honesty and fulfilling his promises." However, Huyayy did not give up. He continued convincing Kʻab until Kʻab finally agreed to break his agreement with Rasulullah ﷺ.

When Rasulullah ﷺ was informed of their breaking the agreement, he sent Sʻad bin Muʼaaz ؓ, Sʻad bin ʻUbaadah ؓ and ʻAbdullah bin Rawaahah ؓ to check and make sure. He also advised them: "If this news is correct, return and inform me in unclear words so that an ordinary person would not be able to understand its meaning and if this news is incorrect, there is no problem in saying it clearly."

When this group went to Kʻab bin Asad and reminded him about their agreement, he said: "What agreement? Who is Muhammad? I do not ever remember making an agreement with him."

When this group returned to Rasulullah ﷺ, they only said: "ʻAdal and Qaarah." In other words, just as the tribes of ʻAdal and Qaarah were dishonest with Hadhrat Khubaib رَضِىَ اللّٰهُ عَنْهُ and his companions, similarly, these Jews are also being dishonest.

Rasulullah صَلَّى اللّٰهُ عَلَيْهِ وَسَلَّم was very worried and disapointed. Now the Muslims were surrounded by the kuffaar from all sides. Outside Madinah, more than 10 000 kuffaar were camped and waiting whilst inside Madinah, the Banu Qurayzah had also joined them. In short, the Muslims were facing lots of difficulties and to make things worse, the nights were very cold and they were starving for a number of days.

Two weeks passed like this without any actual fighting. During these two weeks, both sides shot arrows at one another. Eventually, a few warriors of the Quraysh; 'Amr bin 'Abduwudd, 'Ikramah bin Abi Jahal, Hubairah bin Abi Wahab, Diraar bin Khattaab and Nawfal bin 'Abdullah, stepped out to fight the Muslims. When they reached the trenches, they said: "By Allah! We've never seen such plans (the digging of trenches) from the Arabs before this."

One part of the trench was a bit narrow. They managed to jump over and challenged the Muslims to step out for battle. Amr bin 'Abduwudd, who had been wounded in the battle of Badr, was in a full-body armour covering him from head to toe. In a loud voice, he screamed: "Is there anyone who dares to fight me?" The lion of Allah, Hadhrat Ali رَضِىَ اللّٰهُ عَنْهُ stepped forward and said: "O 'Amr! I call you to Allah and His Rasool. I invite you towards Islam." 'Amr mockingly replied: "I have no need for such things." Hadhrat Ali رَضِىَ اللّٰهُ عَنْهُ said: "Okay, I now invite you to fight me." 'Amr replied: "You are still a youngster. Send me someone older than you. I hate killing someone as young as you." Hadhrat Ali رَضِىَ اللّٰهُ عَنْهُ replied: "But I would love to kill you." This made him very angry. He jumped off his horse and marched up to Hadhrat Ali رَضِىَ اللّٰهُ عَنْهُ. At once, he attacked Hadhrat Ali رَضِىَ اللّٰهُ عَنْهُ with his sword. Hadhrat Ali رَضِىَ اللّٰهُ عَنْهُ managed to block the strike with his shield but was slightly wounded on his forehead. Hadhrat Ali رَضِىَ اللّٰهُ عَنْهُ then suddenly attacked him and finished him off for good. He shouted out the Takbeer of Allahu Akbar! This was a sign for the Muslims of his victory over his enemy.

Chapter Seventeen – Battle of Khandaq (Trench)

Nawfal bin 'Abdullah who was sitting on a horse, also came forward with the sole intention of killing Rasulullah ﷺ. He tried to jump across the trench but he fell into it and broke his neck. The kuffaar offered ten thousand Dirhams to Rasulullah ﷺ in exchange of Nawfal's body but Rasulullah ﷺ replied: "He was filthy and the diyat (blood money) offered is also filthy. Allah's curse is on him and his blood money. We have absolutely no need for his ten thousand nor for his body." Rasulullah ﷺ then handed over his body free of charge.

In this battle Hadhrat S'ad bin Mu'aaz رضي الله عنه was struck on his neck by an arrow. He then made the following dua:

O Allah! If this battle with the Quraysh is going to last (for some time) then allow me to live a bit longer because I have no wish greater than fighting the people who troubled your Nabi, didn't believe in him and threw him out from the safe Haram. O Allah! If this is the end of the war, make this injury a source of my martyrdom but do not take my life away until I am able to see the disgrace of the Banu Qurayzah."

This was one of the fiercest days of the battle. Most of the day passed in shooting arrows and throwing rocks. In this commotion, Rasulullah ﷺ missed four Salaahs.

Rasulullah ﷺ had placed the women and children safely in one of the forts. The fort was near the area of one of the Jewish tribes. Hadhrat Safiyyah رضي الله عنها, Rasulullah's ﷺ father's sister was also in this fort. Hadhrat Hassaan رضي الله عنه was chosen to guard the fort. Hadhrat Safiyyah رضي الله عنها saw a Jew walking near the fort. She thought that he may be a spy or he may have evil intentions. She said to Hadhrat Hassaan رضي الله عنه: "Go out and kill him. He should not give any information about us to the enemy." He replied: "Don't you know? I am not chosen for killing anyone and I am not able to do such a thing." Hadhrat Safiyyah رضي الله عنها then decided to sort the problem out herself. She took a tent peg and struck the jew with such force that his head cracked open. She told Hassaan رضي الله عنه: "He is a man and

I am a woman. I cannot touch him. Go and take off his weapons." Hadhrat Hassaan رضى الله عنه replied: "I have no need for his weapons and goods."

During the course of the battle, one of the chiefs of the Ghitfaan tribe, Nu'aim bin Mas'ood came to Rasulullah صلى الله عليه وسلم and said: "O Rasulullah! I have accepted Islam and I believe in you. My people do not know I have accepted Islam. If you agree, I wish to use a plan that would end this blockade." Rasulullah صلى الله عليه وسلم replied: "Sure. You are a man of great experience. If such a plan is possible, go for it because after all 'war is deception'."

Thereafter, Nu'aim رضى الله عنه came up with such a plan that caused a split between the Banu Qurayzah and the Quraysh. This forced the Banu Qurayzah to totally stop supporting the Quraysh.

After the deaths of 'Amr bin Abduwudd and Nawfal, the remaining Qurayshi warriors turned around in defeat.

Abu Sa'eed Khudri رضى الله عنه says: "After looking at the harshness and difficulty of this blockade, we asked Rasulullah صلى الله عليه وسلم to make dua for us. Rasulullah صلى الله عليه وسلم replied: "Make the following dua:

$$\text{اَللّٰهُمَّ اسْتُرْ عَوْرَاتِنَا وَآمِنْ رَوْعَاتِنَا}$$

"O Allah! Hide our mistakes and remove our fear."

Allah Ta'ala accepted this dua of Rasulullah صلى الله عليه وسلم and sent upon the Quraysh and Ghitfaan such a strong wind which caused the tent-ropes to break and the tents to become loose. The pots and other containers overturned. Sand began blowing into the eyes, which caused confusion in the entire army of the kuffaar. Allah Ta'ala had sent 'an army, which they could not see' i.e. the angels who put fear and worry into the hearts of the kuffaar whilst strengthening the hearts of the Muslims. In this way, a ten-thousand-strong army of the kuffaar became very confused and ran away.

Chapter Seventeen – Battle of Khandaq (Trench)

Huzaifah bin Yamaan ﺭﺿﻰﺍﻟﻠﻪﻋﻨﻪ says: "Rasulullah ﷺ instructed me to gather some information about the Quraysh. I said: "I fear being caught by the enemy." Rasulullah ﷺ replied: "Never! You will never be caught." Rasulullah ﷺ then made the following dua for me:

$$\text{اَللّٰهُمَّ احْفَظْهُ مِنْ بَيْنِ يَدَيْهِ وَ مِنْ خَلْفِهِ وَ عَنْ يَمِيْنِهِ وَ عَنْ شِمَالِهِ وَ مِنْ فَوْقِهِ وَ مِنْ تَحْتِهِ}$$

Because of this dua of Rasulullah ﷺ, all my worries went away and with a feeling of happiness I left. As I was leaving, Rasulullah ﷺ warned me: "Huzaifah! Don't do anything that I didn't ask you to do."

When I sneaked into their camp, the wind was blowing so strongly that everything was flying about and the night was so dark that nothing could be seen. As I came closer to them, I heard Abu Sufyaan talking: "O people of the Quraysh! This is not a place to be staying. Our animals have died, the Banu Qurayzah have left us and this wind has caused so much of confusion. Moving about and even sitting here is almost impossible. It is best for us to return immediately." Saying this, Abu Sufyaan sat on his camel. Huzaifah ﺭﺿﻰﺍﻟﻠﻪﻋﻨﻪ says: "At that moment I thought of shooting an arrow at him but the words of Rasulullah ﷺ came to mind that, 'Huzaifah! Don't do anything that I didn't ask you to do'. I then returned to our camp."

As the Quraysh started leaving, Rasulullah ﷺ said: "From now on we will attack them and they will not attack us."

Early the next morning Rasulullah ﷺ began preparing to return to Madinah and the following words were on his blessed tongue:

> "There is none worthy of worship but Allah. He has no partner. To Him belongs all power and praise and He has complete control over everything. We have returned, we are making towbah, we make sajda before our Rabb and we praise Him Alone. Allah has fulfilled His promise, helped His servant and overpowered the enemies all Alone."

The siege lasted for fifteen days. In this battle, three kuffaar were killed and six Muslims were martyred.

CHAPTER 18
HUDAYBIYYAH

Hudaybiyyah is the name of a well. A village next to this well became well known with this name. This village is about nine miles from Makkah Mukarramah. Rasulullah ﷺ saw a dream in which he saw himself and a few of his sahaabah entering Makkah Mukarramah very safely. They performed Umrah and some of the sahaabah shaved their heads whilst the others had cut their hair. When the sahaabah heard of this dream, the love for Baitullah (the ka'bah) which was deep down in their hearts made them desire to visit the Ka'bah.

On Monday 1st Zul-Qa'dah 6 A.H. Rasulullah ﷺ left Madinah Munawwarah towards Makkah Mu'azzamah with the intention of Umrah. About 1500 Muhaajireen and Ansaar joined Rasulullah ﷺ on this journey. Since Rasulullah ﷺ had no intention of battle, they did not carry too many weapons. They only carried a few weapons normally carried by travellers which were safely kept in their sheaths.

When Rasulullah ﷺ reached Ghadir Ashtaat, his spy told him that the Quraysh had started gathering their army as soon as they heard of Rasulullah's ﷺ leaving Madinah. He also said that this time, the Quraysh were determined to fight and they agreed amongst themselves to refuse Rasulullah ﷺ entry into Makkah.

Rasulullah ﷺ also learnt that Khaalid bin Waleed, together with 200 mounted (riding) soldiers, had already reached a place called Ghameem, as the first part of the army. When Rasulullah ﷺ heard this information, he turned away from this route and took another road towards Makkah, until he reached Hudaybiyyah. From this point on, as Rasulullah ﷺ tried to move his camel towards Makkah, the camel sat down. The people shouted out: "Hal! Hal!" trying every possible trick to get it to stand, but it remained stubbornly seated. Some people said: "Qaswa has become stubborn!" Rasulullah ﷺ replied: "This is not its habit but actually Allah Ta'ala has stopped it from moving ahead."

Then Rasulullah ﷺ said: "I swear by the Being in whose control is my life, whatever the Quraysh ask me which is according to the Sha'aair (main qualities) of Islam, I am fully prepared to accept."

Saying this, Rasulullah ﷺ tapped the camel with his whip. At once she got up. From here Rasulullah ﷺ moved towards the edge of Hudaybiyyah and set up camp there. It was a very hot summer's day. The Sahaabah رضي الله عنهم were suffering from severe thirst and there was a shortage of water. Whatever water was available in the nearby well had long since been drawn out. When the Sahaabah رضي الله عنهم told Rasulullah ﷺ the water problem, he took out an arrow from his quiver and instructed them to place it inside the well. When the arrow was placed into the well, so much of water started gushing out that the whole army had more than enough.

Once he set up camp in Hudaybiyyah, Rasulullah ﷺ sent Khiraash رضي الله عنه on a camel to the people of Makkah, informing them that the Muslims came to Makkah only to visit the Baitullah and not to fight in any way.

When Khiraash رضي الله عنه reached Makkah Shareef and gave the message of Rasulullah ﷺ, they slaughtered his camel and if it was not for the last minute help of some of the people, they would have killed him too. Hadhrat Khiraash رضي الله عنه escaped, returned to Rasulullah ﷺ and told him what had happened.

Rasulullah ﷺ then decided to send Hadhrat 'Umar رضى الله عنه with this message to the people of Makkah. However, Hadhrat 'Umar رضى الله عنه excused himself saying: "O Rasulullah ﷺ! You know how angry the people of Makkah are with me. They really hate me. No one from my family lives in Makkah and nobody will be able to speak for me. If you send Usmaan رضى الله عنه, who has family in Makkah, it would be much better." Rasulullah ﷺ accepted this suggestion. He called Hadhrat Usmaan رضى الله عنه and instructed him: "Give our message (of our intentions) to Abu Sufyaan and the leaders of Makkah and also give good news to those Muslims who are hiding their Islam that they should not panic, soon Allah Ta'ala will give the Muslims victory and make His Deen overpower."

Hadhrat Usmaan رضى الله عنه entered Makkah where he gave the message of Rasulullah ﷺ and gave good news to the weak Muslims.

When Hadhrat 'Usmaan رضى الله عنه gave Rasulullah's ﷺ message to the leaders of Makkah, they said: "This year he (Rasulullah ﷺ) would not be allowed to enter Makkah. Yes, if you ('Usmaan) wish to perform Tawaaf on your own, you may do so." Hadhrat 'Usmaan رضى الله عنه said: "I will definitely not perform Tawaaf without Rasulullah ﷺ." On hearing this, the Quraysh remained silent but held Hadhrat 'Usmaan رضى الله عنه back.

Whilst Hadhrat 'Usmaan رضى الله عنه was being delayed in Makkah, a rumour (false news) started in Hudaybiyyah that the Quraysh had killed 'Usmaan رضى الله عنه. When Rasulullah ﷺ heard about this, he was very sad and said: "I will not leave from here until I take revenge for his death."

Bay'atur-Ridwaan

Rasulullah ﷺ started taking bay'at (promise of following) right there under the acacia tree in whose shade he was sitting. This bay'at was that they would fight the kuffaar as long as they had life in their bodies. They promised to die rather then running away.

The first person to take this promise was Abu Sinaan Asadi رَضِيَ ٱللَّهُ عَنْهُ. He said: "O Rasulullah صَلَّى ٱللَّهُ عَلَيْهِ وَسَلَّمَ! Give me your hand so that I may make a promise." Rasulullah صَلَّى ٱللَّهُ عَلَيْهِ وَسَلَّمَ asked: "On what would you like to make this promise?" He replied: "On whatever is in my heart." Rasulullah صَلَّى ٱللَّهُ عَلَيْهِ وَسَلَّمَ asked: "And what is within your heart?" He replied: "O Rasulullah صَلَّى ٱللَّهُ عَلَيْهِ وَسَلَّمَ! In my heart is that I will continue striking my sword (against the enemy) until Allah Ta'ala gives you victory or until I am killed in His path." Rasulullah صَلَّى ٱللَّهُ عَلَيْهِ وَسَلَّمَ then accepted his bay'at and everyone else also took bay'at. Hadhrat Salamah bin Akw'a رَضِيَ ٱللَّهُ عَنْهُ took this promise thrice; once at the beginning, once in the middle and once at the end.

When Rasulullah صَلَّى ٱللَّهُ عَلَيْهِ وَسَلَّمَ finished off with the bay'at, he placed his left hand over his right hand and said: "This promise is for 'Usmaan."

The right hand was for himself whilst his left hand was for 'Usmaan رَضِيَ ٱللَّهُ عَنْهُ. Whenever Hadhrat 'Usmaan رَضِيَ ٱللَّهُ عَنْهُ would mention this incident, he would say: "Rasulullah's صَلَّى ٱللَّهُ عَلَيْهِ وَسَلَّمَ left hand was far more greater than my right hand."

Later on they heard that the news of Hadhrat 'Usmaan's رَضِيَ ٱللَّهُ عَنْهُ murder was false. When the Quraysh heard about this bay'at, they became terrified.

Budail bin Waraqa, together with a few of his people came to Rasulullah صَلَّى ٱللَّهُ عَلَيْهِ وَسَلَّمَ and said: "The Quraysh have gathered a huge army just outside Hudaybiyyah near the big water-springs to make sure that you do not enter Makkah. They also have many milking camels with them." (In other words, they plan to camp there for a long time. They will eat, drink and prepare to fight.)

Rasulullah صَلَّى ٱللَّهُ عَلَيْهِ وَسَلَّمَ said: "We have not come here to fight. We have come with the only purpose of performing Umrah. War has weakened the strength of the Quraysh. If they wish, I am prepared to write out a treaty for some time. Within that time, we will not interfere with one another. They should leave the Arabs and me alone. If, by the grace of Allah, I am victorious, you (the Quraysh) are invited to enter this Deen and for now you will be given a few days of grace. But if the Arabs (non-Muslims) are victorious then your job is done. However, let me inform you that, Allah Ta'ala will definitely make sure that His Deen is victorious. The promise that He has made about helping this Deen, that promise will surely be fulfilled. If the Quraysh refuse to accept this, I swear by the Being in whose control lies my life, I will certainly wage Jihaad against them until my neck is separated from my body."

Budail then went to the Quraysh telling them: "I have just heard a suggestion from that man. If you wish I will explain it to you?" The foolish from amongst them said: "We have no need for him. We do not want to listen to what he has to say." However, the intelligent ones from them said: "Sure, why not? Tell us what he has to say."

Budail said: "You people are rushing. Muhammad has not come here to fight but to perform Umrah. He wants peace with you." The Quraysh replied: "Definitely he has not come to fight but whatever his intention may be, he will not be allowed to enter Makkah."

Urwah bin Mas'ood stood up and spoke to them saying: "O people! Am I not like a father to you and are you not like my children?" "Surely", they replied, "why not?" 'Urwah then asked: "Do you have any bad thoughts about me?" They replied: "Absolutely not!" 'Urwah then said: "This man (Muhammad Rasulullah ﷺ) has made a suggestion for our own good. I feel that we should accept his suggestion. Why don't you allow me to meet with him (Rasulullah ﷺ) and speak with him directly?" The people accepted.

When 'Urwah came to Rasulullah ﷺ, he made the same suggestion that he had made to Budail. 'Urwah said: "O Muhammad! Have you ever heard of anyone destroying his own people? Also if the situation was the other way (i.e. if the Quraysh were to be victorious) I think that the people who are with you, will leave you and run away."

Hadhrat Abu Bakr ﷺ who was sitting behind Rasulullah ﷺ, said: "What? Can we ever leave Rasulullah ﷺ and run away?"

'Urwah asked: "Who is this man?" When the people replied that it was Abu Bakr, 'Urwah asked: "I swear by Allah, had it not been for your favour towards me – which I haven't as yet paid back – I would have definitely replied to you."

Saying this, he continued talking to Rasulullah ﷺ. Whenever he said something, he would hold the beard of Rasulullah ﷺ."

Mughirah bin Shu'bah ﷺ ('Urwah's brother's son) who was standing holding a sword behind Rasulullah ﷺ, couldn't bear this behaviour of his uncle in front of Rasulullah ﷺ. He said: "Remove your hand from the beard of Rasulullah ﷺ. A Mushrik (kaafir) should not touch the blessed beard of Rasulullah ﷺ."

During this meeting with Rasulullah ﷺ, 'Urwah saw such love of the Sahaabah ﷺ for Rasulullah ﷺ which he had never seen anywhere else before. He saw that whenever Rasulullah ﷺ asked for something, each one of his sahaabah would compete with one another to be the first to do it. Whenever he needed to spit, the sahaabah would not allow it to fall to the ground. They would quickly catch it with their hands and rub it on to their faces. When he made wudhu, they would not let his used-water fall to the ground. They would push one another to grab it as though a fight was about to start. If a hair fell from his blessed body, they would rush forward to take it. When he spoke, there would be complete silence. Nobody looked at him in the eye. How can those who have such love ever leave Rasulullah ﷺ and run away?

When 'Urwah returned from Rasulullah ﷺ back to the Quraysh, he said to them: "O people! By Allah! I have been to Caesar, Chosroes, Negus and other great rulers but I swear by Allah that I have never seen such an amazing amount of love and honour."

Suhail bin 'Amr came to Rasulullah ﷺ from the Quraysh to discuss a peace treaty. When Rasulullah ﷺ saw Suhail coming, he said to the Sahaabah ﷢: "Qad Sahula Lakum min Amrikum (Your problem has been made easy)."

Rasulullah ﷺ then said: "The Quraysh now want a peace treaty. They sent this person to discuss peace with us."

Rasulullah ﷺ and Suhail had a long discussion about a peace treaty and the conditions of a peace treaty. After discussing the conditions of the peace treaty, Rasulullah ﷺ instructed Hadhrat Ali ﷢ to write it down. He instructed him to write Bismillahir-Rahmaanir-Raheem at the beginning of the document.

Usually, the Arabs used to write 'Bismikallahumma' at the beginning of their letters. This is why Suhail said: "I do not know what this Bismillahir-Rahmaanir-Raheem is all about. Just write Bismika-Allaahumma as we usually do." Rasulullah ﷺ said: "Fine, write that down then."

Rasulullah ﷺ then instructed Hadhrat Ali ﷢ to write the following:

هٰذَا مَا قَضٰى عَلَيْهِ مُحَمَّدٌ رَسُوْلُ اللّٰهِ

"These are the conditions on which Muhammad, the Rasool of Allah, has decided a peace treaty."

Suhail said: "If we knew that you were the Rasool of Allah, we would not have stopped you from the Baitullah nor would we have fought with you. Instead of 'Muhammad, the Messenger of Allah', write: Muhammad, the son of 'Abdullah."

Rasulullah ﷺ said: "By Allah! I am the Rasool of Allah even though you do not believe in me."

He then instructed Hadhrat Ali ﷺ to erase this and write his name as Suhail wanted. Hadhrat Ali ﷺ said: "O Rasulullah ﷺ! I will never erase your name." Rasulullah ﷺ said: "Okay, then show me where the words 'the Rasool of Allah' are written. I will erase them myself." Once Hadhrat Ali ﷺ pointed it out to him, Rasulullah ﷺ erased the words with his own hand and commanded Hadhrat Ali ﷺ to write 'Muhammad, the son of 'Abdullah'.

The conditions of the peace treaty were as follows:

Terms of the Treaty of Hudaybiyyah

- All fighting will stop for the next ten years.
- Anyone of the Quraysh who runs away to Madinah without the permission of his master or guardian will be returned even though he is a Muslim.
- Any Muslim who goes to Makkah from Madinah will not be returned to the Muslims.
- During these ten years, none of them will be dishonest with the other.
- This year Muhammad ﷺ will return to Madinah without performing Umrah. He will not be allowed to enter Makkah this year. He will be allowed to enter Makkah next year for three days only. He should go back home after performing Umrah. The Muslims will not be allowed to enter Makkah with any weapons except with sheathed swords.
- The other tribes from the Arab Peninsula have the choice of joining themselves to whichever party they wish.

The Banu Khuzaa'ah tribe joined themselves with Rasulullah ﷺ whilst the Banu Bakr joined the Quraysh. Whilst this treaty was being written out, Suhail's son, Abu Jandal, escaped from Makkah and came to Rasulullah ﷺ with his legs still in chains. He had already accepted

Islam before this and the kuffaar of Makkah were really troubling him. When Suhail saw him, he happily said: "Well, well, well. This is the first person to be returned to us."

Rasulullah ﷺ said: "The treaty has not been signed as yet." In other words, the treaty is only valid when it is written out completely and signed. Rasulullah ﷺ begged Suhail many times to hand over Abu Jandal رضي الله عنه to the Muslims, but Suhail was stubborn. Finally, Rasulullah ﷺ returned him over to Suhail.

The kuffaar of Makkah were putting him to great suffering. This is why Abu Jandal, in a sad voice, said to the Muslims: "What a pity, O Muslims! I am being handed over to the kuffaar?"

Rasulullah ﷺ comforted Abu Jandal by saying: "O Abu Jandal! Be patient and put your hopes in Allah, as we do not want to break the treaty. However, remember that Allah Ta'ala will surely find a way out for you from your difficulty."

His return to the kuffaar was not liked by the Muslims. Hadhrat 'Umar رضي الله عنه was unable to control himself and said: "O Rasulullah ﷺ! Are you not the true Messenger of Allah?" "Surely!" replied Rasulullah ﷺ. Hadhrat 'Umar رضي الله عنه asked: "Are we not on the true path whilst they are on falsehood?" Rasulullah ﷺ replied: "No doubt about it." Hadhrat 'Umar رضي الله عنه in amazement asked: "Then why do we have to tolerate this disgrace?" Rasulullah ﷺ replied: "I am the Rasool and true Messenger of Allah Ta'ala. I am not going to break His command. He is my helper and supporter."

Hadhrat 'Umar رضي الله عنه then asked: "Okay, but did you not promise us that we would perform Tawaaf of the Baitullah?" Rasulullah ﷺ replied: "When did I promise that we will perform Tawaaf this year?" Hadhrat 'Umar رضي الله عنه then went to Hadhrat Abu Bakr رضي الله عنه and had the same talk with him as well. Hadhrat Abu Bakr رضى الله عنه gave him exactly the same reply, word for word as Rasulullah ﷺ.

Hadhrat 'Umar رضى الله عنه says: "After this, I was very ashamed of myself. To cover up for this behaviour, I performed many Salaahs, kept a lot of fasts, gave a lot of charity and freed many slaves."

Hadhrat Anas رضى الله عنه says that the Sahaabah رضى الله عنهم asked: "O Rasulullah ﷺ! How can this condition of the treaty be acceptable? How can we accept that a person who runs away from us Muslims and joins the kuffaar will not be returned to us?"

Rasulullah ﷺ replied: "Yes, if anyone of us joins them, we do not need him. Allah Ta'ala has put such a person far away from His mercy. As for the person who runs away from them and comes to us, although, according to the treaty, he will be returned to them, there is nothing to be frightened of. Shortly, Allah Ta'ala will make a way out for him from his difficulty." (Also, Alhamdulillah so far no one escaped from Madinah to Makkah.)

After signing this treaty, Rasulullah ﷺ instructed the Sahaabah رضى الله عنهم to slaughter their animals and shave off the hair of their heads. However, the Sahaabah رضى الله عنهم were so disappointed and saddened by the treaty that although Rasulullah ﷺ repeated his instructions thrice, not one of them listened.

When Rasulullah ﷺ saw this, he came to Umme Salamah رضى الله عنها and sadly told her what was happening. She said: "O Rasulullah ﷺ! This treaty is extremely difficult for the Muslims. This is why they are so dissapointed that they cannot carry out your instructions. Do not say anything to anyone. You yourself go outside, slaughter your Qurbaani animal and shave off your hair. Automatically the people will follow you."

This is exactly what happened. When Rasulullah ﷺ began to slaughter his Qurbaani animals, all the Sahaabah ﷺ slaughtered their animals.

May Allah Ta'ala reward Umme Salamah ﷺ greatly. Her brilliant idea solved the problem that Rasulullah ﷺ found himself in.

After staying in Hudaybiyyah for two weeks, Rasulullah ﷺ left for his return journey to Madinah. Whilst he was between Makkah and Madinah, Surah Fatah (victory) was revealed.

Rasulullah ﷺ gathered all the Sahaabah ﷺ and read the Surah to them. The Sahaabah ﷺ felt that this treaty was a type of defeat for them but Allah Ta'ala called it as a clear victory. Surprised by this, they asked: "O Rasulullah ﷺ! Is this really a victory?" Rasulullah ﷺ replied: "I swear by the Being in Whose complete control is my life, this is definitely a clear victory."

A little while after Rasulullah ﷺ reached Madinah, Abu Baseer ﷺ escaped from the kuffaar of Makkah and came to Madinah. The Quraysh quickly sent two men to Rasulullah ﷺ to bring him back. According to the treaty, Rasulullah ﷺ handed Abu Baseer ﷺ to them and said to Abu Baseer ﷺ saying: "I cannot break the peace treaty. It is best if you return." Shocked, Abu Baseer ﷺ asked: "Are you returning me to the kuffaar who want to change my religion and who put me through all kinds of suffering?"

Rasulullah ﷺ comforted him by saying: "Be patient and have hope in Allah Ta'ala. Soon Allah Ta'ala will find a way out for you from your difficulty."

Finally, these two people took Abu Baseer ﷺ and left. They stopped over at Zul-Hulayfah to take a small rest and eat some dates that they carried with them. Abu Baseer ﷺ said to one of them: "Your sword seems very nice." Taking the sword out of its sheath, the man boasted: "I swear by Allah that this is a very nice sword. I have used it many times." Abu Baseer ﺭﺿﻰ ﺍﻟﻠﻪ ﻋﻨﻪ asked: "May I have a look at it?" As soon as the man gave it to Abu Baseer ﺭﺿﻰ ﺍﻟﻠﻪ ﻋﻨﻪ, he snatched it from him and killed him with one shot. On seeing what happened to his friend, the other man quickly ran away and went back to Madinah where he came to Rasulullah ﷺ and said: "O Rasulullah ﷺ! My friend has been killed and now it's my turn."

A little later, when Abu Baseer ﺭﺿﻰ ﺍﻟﻠﻪ ﻋﻨﻪ came to Rasulullah ﷺ, he said: "O Rasulullah ﷺ! Allah Ta'ala has fulfilled your part of the treaty. You had handed me over to them and now Allah Ta'ala has freed me from them. O Rasulullah ﷺ! You know that if I had to return to Makkah, these people would force me to leave Islam. I had done whatever I had done only for this reason. There is no treaty between me and them." Rasulullah ﷺ replied: "This man is going to cause a war if he has any friends with him."

Abu Baseer ﺭﺿﻰ ﺍﻟﻠﻪ ﻋﻨﻪ understood from this that if he had to stay here any longer he would be handed back to the non-Muslims. This is why he quickly left Madinah Munawwarah and settled in a place along the coast through which the Qurayshi caravans would pass during their travels to Syria.

When the oppressed and helpless Muslims of Makkah Mukarramah heard of this, they quietly started going and joining Abu Baseer's hideout. Abu Jandal ﺭﺿﻰ ﺍﻟﻠﻪ ﻋﻨﻪ also came there. In this way, a group of seventy men settled there. Whenever a Qurayshi caravan passed by, they would stop them and they would take their goods.

The Quraysh, were forced to send some people to Rasulullah ﷺ and begged him in the name of Allah and their blood relationship to call Abu Baseer and his group back to Madinah. They also promised not to interfere if anyone of the people of Makkah accepted Islam and ran away to Madinah.

Rasulullah ﷺ then wrote a letter to Abu Baseer رضي الله عنه. However, the letter reached Abu Baseer رضي الله عنه as he was about to pass away. As he began reading this letter, his happiness and joy continued increasing until he finally passed away whilst the blessed letter was on his chest. According to another narration, he passed away whilst holding the letter in his hand.

Abu Jandal رضي الله عنه did the ghusl, kafan, janaazah salaah and buried him there. He built a Masjid nearby as well. Thereafter, Abu Jandal رضي الله عنه, together with his friends left for Madinah.

After this treaty with the Makkans, any Muslim male who escaped from Makkah to Madinah was sent back to Makkah by Rasulullah ﷺ because of the treaty. Sometime later, a few women also escaped from Makkah to Madinah. The Makkans insisted that they also be returned according to the treaty. However, through wahi, Allah Ta'ala stopped Rasulullah ﷺ from sending the women back, explaining that this condition was for the males only and that the women were not included in this treaty. According to some narrations, the actual words of the treaty were: "No Rajul (man) will run away to you from us but he will be returned." Obviously the word Rajul clearly referred to men only. How could women be included in this?

The kuffaar remained silent and did not ask again for the return of the women.

CHAPTER 19
INVITATION LETTERS TO THE KINGS OF THE WORLD

After returning from Hudaybiyyah in Zul-Hijjah 6 A.H., Rasulullah ﷺ decided to send letters of invitation to the kings of the world. He gathered the Sahaabah رضي الله عنهم and spoke to them saying:

"O People! I have been sent as a mercy to the whole universe. Give this message to the world and Allah will shower His mercy on you. Do not fight with one another like the followers of Isa عليه السلام. When they were instructed to travel to a close by area, they would happily go, but when told to travel to a far place, they would sit down on the ground as though they could not move." The Sahaabah رضي الله عنهم were obedient, loyal and ready to sacrifice even in the most difficult of situations. That's what gave them the highest positions in the eyes of Rasulullah ﷺ.

The Sahaabah رضي الله عنهم gave a very good suggestion to Rasulullah ﷺ saying: "O Rasulullah ﷺ! The kings and rulers of this world do not accept a letter without an official seal stuck to it. In fact, they would not even bother to look at it."

Therefore Rasulullah ﷺ had a seal engraved on a ring. The ring, as well as the seal on it, were made of silver, in the Abyssinian style. The words "Muhammad, Rasool Allah" were written on the seal as follows:

Muhammad was right at the bottom with the word Allah right on the top and Rasool in between.

Rasulullah ﷺ then sent letters to the different rulers of the world inviting them to the truth and informing them that they would be responsible if their people were misguided. This happened after the treaty of Hudaybiyyah but before the conquest of Makkah. And Allah Ta'ala knows best.

(1) Letter to Hiraql (Heraclius) the king of Rome

This letter was taken to Hiraql by Hadhrat Dihya Kalbi (radiyallahu anhu). When Hadhrat Dihyaa رضي الله عنه, gave the king the letter of Rasulullah ﷺ he placed it on his head and his eyes and respectfully kissed it. He then opened it and after reading it he said: "I will think about it and give an answer by tomorrow."

He then asked his servants to bring to him anyone whom they could find who was from the same family as Rasulullah ﷺ, as he wanted to find out more from them. It so happened that Abu Sufyaan, was on business in Shaam. He was camped at Ghazzah. Abu Sufyaan had not yet accepted Islam. The king's messenger fetched him from Ghazzah and brought him to the king. All the Roman noblemen, priests, monks and other important people were present. He asked him many questions about Rasulullah ﷺ until eventually the king was sure that this is really the messenger of Allah ﷺ. The king then called all his people and read the letter out to them. When he did this, there was a lot of commotion. People began screaming from all around and were very unhappy. The king quietened them down by saying that he just wanted to test them to see their love for their religion.

The king then called Hadhrat Dihyaa Kalbi رضي الله عنه in private and explained to him: "I swear by Allah and believe that your friend is definitely the Nabi of Allah. However, I am afraid of my people killing me. If it were not for this worry, I would certainly follow him. Go to Daghaatir, the archbishop (high priest) of Rome. He is a very learned man. His knowledge is much more than mine. Furthermore, he is more respected by the Romans than me. Go to him and tell him about this Nabi."

Hadhrat Dihyaa Kalbi ﷺ went to Daghaatir and described to him Rasulullah ﷺ. Daghaatir replied by saying: "By Allah! He is a Nabi. We have read about his characteristics, conditions and qualities in our holy books." Saying this, he went into his room, removed the black clothing he was wearing and changed into white clothing. Holding a stick in his hand, he went to the church where he spoke to the people: "O Romans! A letter has come to us from Ahmad (ﷺ) in which he invites us towards Allah, the Almighty. I believe that there is none worthy of worship besides Allah and Ahmad (ﷺ) is His slave and messenger." When the people heard this announcement they attacked him and beat him to death. Hadhrat Dihyaa ﷺ returned to the king and explained whatever he had seen. The king replied: "I also have the same fear. I am afraid of them treating me in the same way."

He then told Hadhrat Dihyaa ﷺ: "I believe and do recognise him to be the true Prophet, just as Daghaatir had done, but if I had to announce this, I would lose my kingdom and my people will kill me."

With great respect, the king hid this blessed letter of Rasulullah ﷺ in a box made out of gold. However he did not accept Islam and died as a kaafir.

(2) Letter to Chosroe Parvez, the king of Persia

Rasulullah ﷺ sent this letter with Abdullah bin Huzaafah Sahmi ﷺ. When Chosroe saw this letter, he became very angry. He tore the letter to pieces and shouted: "This man has the guts to write a letter like this? He is inviting me to accept Islam whereas he is my slave." Abdullah bin Huzaafah Sahmi ﷺ returned and explained to Rasulullah ﷺ

what happened. Rasulullah ﷺ said: "Chosroe's country has fallen to bits and pieces."

Chosroe then wrote to Baazaan, the governor of Yemen to send two powerful men to arrest this man who had written this letter to him. He instructed Baazaan to arrest him and bring him to his palace. Baazaan immediately sent two men with a letter to Rasulullah ﷺ. When these two men came with Baazaan's letter to Rasulullah ﷺ, they were so affected by the awe (fear) of Rasulullah ﷺ that they started shivering. Shivering with fear, they gave the letter to Rasulullah ﷺ. After hearing the letter read out to him, Rasulullah ﷺ smiled and invited both of them to accept Islam and asked them to return to him the following day. When they returned to Rasulullah ﷺ the following day, he said: "Last night at a certain time, Allah Ta'ala made Sherwayh conquer his father, Chosroe. Sherwayh killed his father Chosroe." This happened on Tuesday the 10th of Jumaadal-Ula 7 A.H. Rasulullah ﷺ instructed both of them to return to Baazaan and explain to him what had happened. He also said: "Also inform Baazaan that my religion and my rule will reach as far as the kingdom of Chosroe had reached."

On hearing this, Baazaan said: "These definitely seem like the words of a prophet. If this information is true then I swear by Allah that this man is a Nabi." Eventually, the words of Rasulullah ﷺ turned out to be true. Baazaan, together with his family, friends and near and dear ones, all accepted Islam. He also informed Rasulullah ﷺ of him accepting Islam.

(3) Letter to Negus, the King of Abyssinia

This letter was sent by Rasulullah ﷺ with Hadhrat 'Amr bin Umayyah Damiri رضي الله عنه who handed this letter over to the king. When Negus read the letter he immediately stood up and said, "I believe that he is the same unlettered Prophet who has been awaited by the people of the book. Just as Musa عليه السلام gave the good news of 'Isa عليه السلام by speaking about him as the rider of the donkey, similarly, he had given the good news of Muhammad ﷺ by speaking about him as the rider of the camel. I have such firm belief in his Prophethood that even after seing him myself, it would not increase my Imaan in him one bit." Negus then accepted the letter of Rasulullah ﷺ, placed it over his eyes in respect, came down from his throne and sat down on the ground. He then accepted Islam and believed in the truth. Thereafter, he wrote a letter in reply to Rasulullah's ﷺ letter confirming his Imaan and promising to obey Rasulullah ﷺ and informing him that he will send his son to him.

Negus sent his son with sixty other Abyssinians to Rasulullah ﷺ. However, the ship they were travelling on sank (drowning all passengers on board). This is the same Negus towards whom the Muslims made hijrat in the 5th year of prophethood. His name was As-hamah (اصحم). He accepted Islam at the hands of Hadhrat Ja'far رضي الله عنه and he passed away in Rajab 9 A.H. Rasulullah ﷺ informed the Sahaabah رضي الله عنهم of his death on the very day that he passed away. Rasulullah ﷺ, together with the Sahaabah رضي الله عنهم performed his 'absent' Janaazah Salaah in the Eid-Gaah.

(4) Letter to Muqawqis, Governor of Egypt and Alexandria

Rasulullah ﷺ sent Haatib bin Abi Balta'ah رضي الله عنه with this letter to the governor of Egypt. The governor was in Alexandria (a city in Egypt). When Haatib رضي الله عنه reached Alexandria, he saw the governor sitting on a balcony facing the sea. From the bottom, Haatib رضي الله عنه pointed towards the letter. The governor asked him to join him at the top. Haatib رضي الله عنه went up and gave the letter to him. He received the letter very warmly and respectfully read through it.

Hadhrat Haatib رضي الله عنه says: "Thereafter the governor of Alexandria kept me as a special guest in one of the royal homes. One day, he called all the priests and leaders and sent for me. After asking a few questions, Muqawqis, said: "I have been thinking about this Prophet for a long time and I found that he commands good and stops the people from evil. He does not encourage evil things and does not stop good. He is not a magician and he is not misguided. He is not a fortune-teller or a liar. I find clear signs of Prophethood in him such as his news of the unseen. Nonetheless, allow me to think about this some more." He then placed this blessed letter in an ivory box and instructed his treasurer to keep it safely. Thereafter he called for his scribe (writer) and instructed him to write a reply to Rasulullah's ﷺ letter in Arabic.

Bismillahir-Rahmaanir-Raheem

To Muhammad bin 'Abdullah, from Muqawqis the head of the Copts.

Salaam upon you. I have read your letter and understood what you mentioned in it about accepting Islam.

I was certain that a final Nabi is yet to come but I thought that he would come from Shaam.

Nonetheless, I have received your Messenger with great respect. As a gift to you, I am sending with him two slave girls, a few sets of clothing and a mule for you to ride.

Wassalaam."

The name of one of these slave girls was Maariyah Qibtiyyah (the Copt). She became part of the family of Rasulullah ﷺ. Rasulullah's ﷺ son, Ibraaheem رضي الله عنه, was born from her. The name of the other slave girl was Shireen and she was given to Hassaan bin Saabit رضي الله عنه. The name of the mule was Duldul. Muqawqis received the messenger of Rasulullah ﷺ with great honour and showed great respect towards his blessed letter and although he agreed that Rasulullah ﷺ was the final Nabi, he did not accept Islam. He remained a Christian. When Haatib bin Abi Balta'ah رضي الله عنه returned to Rasulullah ﷺ and explained the whole incident, Rasulullah ﷺ said: "Kingdom stopped him from accepting Islam but his kingdom will not last forever." Later on, the Muslims conquered Egypt when Hadhrat 'Umar ﷺ was the Khalifa.

(5) Letter to Munzir bin Sawa, the Governor of Bahrain

Rasulullah ﷺ sent a letter of invitation towards Islam to Munzir bin Sawa and sent it with 'Alaa bin Hadrami ﷺ.

'Alaa bin Hadrami ﷺ says: "When I reached Munzir with the blessed letter of Rasulullah ﷺ, I spoke to him saying: 'O Munzir! In worldly things you are very intelligent. Do not become foolish in matters of the aakhirat. This religion of fire-worship is the most shameless religion. It does not have the nobility of the Arabs nor the knowledge of the people of the book. The followers of this religion marry their own sisters, which is so shameful to even speak about it. They eat such things that are disgusting to normal people. They worship the fire of this world whereas in the aakhirat, the same fire will burn them. O Munzir! You are not foolish. Think properly. Why do you delay in believing in Allah Ta'ala?

Munzir replied: "The religion that I follow is only concerned about this world and not about the aakhirat. When I think about your religion, I find it to be excellent for both this world as well as the aakhirat. So what stops me from accepting this religion? It promises to give you the comforts of this life and the comforts of death. Until now I was disgusted by those who accept this religion of Islam but now I am angry with those who do not accept this true religion."

Munzir bin Sawa accepted Islam and replied to Rasulullah's ﷺ letter:

> "O Rasulullah! I read out your letter to the people of Bahrain. Some of them love Islam. They found it very attractive and have accepted Islam. However, some of them do not want to accept Islam.

Chapter Nineteen – Invitation Letters to the Kings

(6) Letter to the Ruler of Oman

Rasulullah ﷺ sent 'Amr ibnul 'Aas ؓ with a letter inviting the two sons of Julandi; 'Abd and Jayfar to Islam. Hadhrat 'Amr bin 'Aas ؓ says: "I reached Oman with this letter where I first met with 'Abd. He was a very patient and good-natured person. I explained to him that I am the messenger of Rasulullah ﷺ and that Rasulullah ﷺ instructed me to give this letter to him and his brother. 'Abd said: "My elder brother Jayfar is the ruler. I will arrange a meeting for you with him. You should give this letter to him."

Thereafter, 'Abd took me to his brother Jayfar. I gave him the sealed letter of Rasulullah ﷺ. He took the letter from me, broke the seal and read through it. After asking me to take a seat, he asked about the conditions of the Quraysh etc. After a few days of thinking, both brothers accepted Islam and many other people also accepted Islam with them. Jizyah (tax) was fixed on those who did not accept Islam.

'Amr bin 'Aas ؓ then spoke to Julandi (their father) and also invited him to accept Islam. Julandi replied: "I have thought about this unlettered Prophet and found that whatever he invites towards, he is the first to practice it and he does not stop anything evil but he is the first to stay away from it. When he defeats his enemies, he does not become proud and when he is defeated he does not become restless. He fulfils his promises and honours his word. I now believe that he is, certainly, the messenger of Allah."

(7) Letter to the Chief of Yamaamah, Huzah bin Ali

Rasulullah ﷺ gave this letter to Salit bin 'Amr ؓ and sent him off to Huzah bin Ali the leader of Yamaamah. Huzah read this blessed letter and recieved Salit ؓ with royal honour and much respect. Salit ؓ spoke to Huzah saying:

"O Huzah! Rotting bones (those who passed away long time ago) have chosen you as a leader. In reality, a leader is the one with Imaan and has Taqwa (fear of Allah). I wish to command you to do something that is excellent and I wish to stop you from something that is most terrible. I command you to worship Allah alone and I stop you from worshipping shaytaan. If you accept this, all your wishes will be fulfilled and you will be safe from all worries. However, if you refuse, then in Qiyaamah it will be decided between you and us."

Huzah replied: "Give me some time and allow me to think about this."

He then replied to the blessed letter of Rasulullah ﷺ as follows:

> "What you are inviting to is so brilliant. The Arabs respect my position. So allow me some rule and then I will follow you."

As he was leaving with this reply, Huzah offered Hadhrat Salit ؓ some gifts that included some fine cloth made in Hajar. When he reached Madinah Munawwarah and explained the incident to Rasulullah ﷺ, he said: "By Allah! Even if he has to ask for a single (hand) span of land I will refuse. He and his country both are destroyed."

After his return from the conquest of Makkah, Jibraa'eel ؑ informed Rasulullah ﷺ about the death of Huzah. He then gave this information to the Sahaabah ؓ and said: "Soon a liar, who will claim to be a Nabi will come out from Yamaamah and he will be killed after my death." This is exactly what happened.

(8) Letter to the Ruler of Damascus, Haaris Ghassaani

Shuj'a bin Wahhaab ؓ took the letter of Rasulullah ﷺ and reached Damascus. At that moment, the governor Haaris Ghassaani, was busy preparing to recieve Caesar, the Roman Emperor. To show thanks for his victory over the Persian Empire, Caesar had just arrived at Baitul-

Muqaddas (Jerusalem) walking barefoot all the way from Hims. Many days passed by without Hadhrat Shuj'a ﷺ meeting with Haaris, the governor.

Hadhrat Shuj'a ﷺ says: "I told the doorkeeper of Haaris's court: 'I am a messenger of Rasulullah ﷺ and I wish to meet the governor.' The doorkeeper replied: 'The governor will come to us in a few days time. You will be able to meet him then. The doorkeeper was from Rome and his name was Murri. He started asking me questions about Rasulullah ﷺ. As I continued describing to him who Rasulullah ﷺ was, he continued weeping. On being informed about the conditions of Rasulullah ﷺ, he said: 'I have read the Injeel (bible) and I have seen his (Rasulullah's ﷺ) name and qualities in it. I bring Imaan in him and believe that he is the true messenger of Allah. I fear that Haaris the governor will kill me (for accepting Islam).' Nonetheless, the doorkeeper treated me with great respect and went out of his way in looking after me as his guest."

Finally Haaris came to the royal court. Wearing the royal crown on his head, he sat down in front. Hadhrat Shuj'a ﷺ was allowed to enter the royal court. Hadhrat Shuj'a ﷺ gave the letter to him. After reading the letter, Haaris turned red in anger and throwing the letter aside he shouted in anger: "Who is this man who wants to take away my country from me? I will march against him." He then commanded that his horses be prepared for battle. He also sent a letter to the Roman king. The king replied: "Hold your horses and cancel your plans."

After receiving the reply of the Emperor, Haaris called Shuj'a ﷺ and asked him when he would be returning home. He replied that he planned to leave the next day. Haaris gave him 100 Misqaals of gold as a gift.

Hadhrat Shuj'a ﷺ says: "The doorkeeper also gave something as a gift and asked me to give his Salaams to Rasulullah ﷺ. I returned to Madinah Munawwarah and mentioned the whole incident before Rasulullah ﷺ who said: "His country is destroyed." I then gave the Salaam of

Murri the doorkeeper and also informed Rasulullah ﷺ about what he said. Rasulullah ﷺ replied: "He has spoken the truth."

اَنَا الَّذِیْ سَمَّتْ نِیْ اُمِّیْ حَیْدَرَۃْ

CHAPTER 20
BATTLE OF KHAYBAR

Rasulullah ﷺ returned from Hudaybiyyah to Madinah Shareef where he remained for Zul-Hijjah and the beginning of Muharram. During this time, Rasulullah ﷺ ordered an attack against the Jews who lived in Khaybar. These Jews had deceived the Muslims and helped the kuffaar of Makkah against the Muslims in the battle of Khandaq (trench). Allah Ta'ala also informed Rasulullah ﷺ that when the hypocrites hear about the conquest of Khaybar, they too would beg to join him in this battle. Allah Ta'ala commanded Rasulullah ﷺ: "Never! These people should never join you on this journey."

Rasulullah ﷺ left for Khaybar with 1400 foot soldiers and 200 riders towards the end of Muharram 7 A.H. Hadhrat Umme Salamah رضي الله عنها joined him on this journey.

Salamah bin Akw'a رضي الله عنه says: "On the night that we left for Khaybar with Rasulullah ﷺ, the famous poet 'Aamir bin Akw'a رضي الله عنه was infront of us reading poetry.

Rasulullah ﷺ asked: "Who is this reading this poetry." When the people informed him that it was 'Aamir bin Akw'a, he said: "May Allah forgive him." Whenever Rasulullah ﷺ made a special dua of forgiveness for someone, that person would soon die as a martyr. This is why Hadhrat 'Umar رضي الله عنه said: "Jannah is waajib for him. If only you allowed us to take advantage of 'Aamir's bravery for a few more days."

Hadhrat Abu Musa Ash'ari ﷺ says: "I was close to the camel of Rasulullah ﷺ when he heard me answer لَاحَوْلَ وَلَاقُوَّةَ اِلَّابِاللّٰهِ. He called: 'O 'Abdullah bin Qays!' I quickly answered: 'I am at your service O Rasulullah!' Rasulullah ﷺ asked: 'Should I not tell you about the treasures of Jannah?' I replied: 'May my parents be sacrificed for you, surely, why not O Rasulullah!' Rasulullah ﷺ said: 'Laa Hawla wa laa Quwwata Illaa Billah.' In other words, these words are the treasures of Jannah."

Rasulullah ﷺ first made dua and then instructed the Sahaabah ﷺ: "Go foward in the name of Allah!"

Hadhrat Anas ﷺ says: "Rasulullah ﷺ reached Khaybar at night. It was his noble habit not to attack at night. He would wait until the morning. If he heard the Azaan, he would not attack otherwise he would attack. Therefore at Khaybar, Rasulullah ﷺ waited for the Azaan of Fajr. When he did not hear the Azaan of Fajr, he made preparations to attack. When it was morning, the Jews, holding their picks and spades, came out to work (on their fields). When they saw the attacking army, they shouted in fear: "Muhammad and the Khamis. (Muhammad and his whole army is here)."

When he saw these people, Rasulullah ﷺ lifted his hands in dua:

اَللّٰهُ اَكْبَرُ! خَرِبَتْ خَيْبَرُ اِنَّا اِذَا نَزَلْنَا بِسَاحَةِ قَوْمٍ فَسَاءَ صَبَاحُ الْمُنْذَرِيْنَ

"Allah is great. Khaybar is destroyed. Verily when we come into the courtyard (in the midst) of a nation then terrible is the morning of those who had been warned."

When the Jews saw Rasulullah ﷺ, they went into their fortresses with their wives and children. Rasulullah ﷺ began attacking these fortresses and conquering them one after the other.

These fortresses were as follows:

(1) Naeem Fort

The first fort that the Muslims conquered in this battle was Naeem Fort. Mahmud bin Maslamah ﷺ was standing at the bottom of the fort when the Jews dropped a millstone onto him, thus making him a martyr.

(2) Qamus Fort

After conquering the Na'im fort, the Qamus fort was then conquered. This was one of the strongest forts of Khaybar. When the Muslims surrounded this fort, Rasulullah ﷺ could not go himself to the battlefield as he was suffering from a severe headache. Thus he gave the battle-flag to Hadhrat Abu Bakr Siddeeq ﷺ. After trying very hard, he was unable to conquer the fort and he returned. The following day, Rasulullah ﷺ handed over the flag to Hadhrat 'Umar ﷺ and sent him off to battle. He too fought with great efforts but he too returned without conquering the fort.

On that day Rasulullah ﷺ said: "Tomorrow I will hand over this flag to a person who loves Allah and His Rasool and Allah and His Rasool also love him and at his hands this fort will be conquered."

Every person was eagerly waiting to see who this blessed person was. They passed the whole night full of hope. The next morning Rasulullah ﷺ called Hadhrat Ali ﷺ. At that time he was suffering from an infection of the eye. Rasulullah ﷺ applied his blessed saliva to his eyes and read a dua. He was cured immediately as though nothing had troubled his eyes. Rasulullah ﷺ handed over the flag to him saying: "Before fighting them in battle, invite them towards Islam. Inform them about the commands of Allah. I swear by Allah, if Allah guides just one person through you, it is far better for you than red camels." Holding the flag up high, Hadhrat Ali ﷺ set out and eventually the fort was conquered at his hands.

One of the most famous heroes of the Jews, Murahhib, walked out onto the battlefield and proudly read the following poem:

$$\text{قَدْ عَلِمَتْ خَيْبَرُ اَنِّىْ مَرْحَبُ ۞ شَاكِىْ السِّلَاحِ بَطَلٌ مُجَرَّبُ}$$

"The people of Khaybar know very well that I am Marhabu, well armed, brave and an experienced fighter (of war)."

In reply, Hadhrat 'Aamir bin Akw'a ﷺ stepped out to challenge him whilst reading the following rhyme:

$$\text{قَدْ عَلِمَتْ خَيْبَرُ اَنِّىْ عَامِرُ ۞ شَاكِىْ السِّلَاحِ بَطَلٌ مُغَامِرُ}$$

"The people of Khaybar know very well that I am 'Aamir, well armed, a hero and brave."

Hadhrat 'Aamir ﷺ was about to strike him on his leg when the sword twisted back onto his own knee causing a serious wound. He eventually passed away at Khaybar.

Hadhrat Salamah bin Akw'a ﷺ (his brother) says: "Whilst returning from this battle, Rasulullah ﷺ noticed that I was very sad and when he asked for the reason, I replied: 'O Rasulullah! People are saying that all 'Aamir's good deeds are cancelled because he died with his own sword.' Rasulullah ﷺ said: 'Whoever said this is mistaken. He was an execellent warrior.' Thereafter, pointing with his two fingers, Rasulullah ﷺ said: 'He will get a double reward; one for being a martyr and secondly because Nabi ﷺ performed his Janaazah Salaah.

After this very sad incident with 'Aamir ﷺ, Hadhrat Ali ﷺ stepped out onto the battlefield whilst reading the following poem:

$$\text{اَنَا الَّذِىْ سَمَّتْنِىْ اُمِّىْ حَيْدَرَةْ ۞ كَلَيْثِ غَابَاتٍ كَرِيْهِ الْمَنْظَرَةْ}$$

> "I am the man who was named Haydar (lion) by his mother. I am as terrifying as the lions of the jungles."

As Hadhrat Ali ؓ was busy reciting these verses, he struck Murahhib with his sword using such force that split his head into two. Thereafter, the fort was captured.

Then, Murahhib's brother Yaasir decided to step foward onto the battlefield. Hadhrat Zubair ؓ stepped out and quickly finished him off.

This fort was conquered at the hands of Hadhrat Ali ؓ after a siege of twenty days. Besides the war booty, many people were taken as prisoners. From the prisoners was Hadhrat Safiyyah bint Huyayy bin Akhtab ؓ, the daughter of the leader of the Banu Nazeer and the wife of Kinaanah bin Rab'i.

(3) S'ab bin Mu'aaz Fort

After conquering the Qamus fort, the S'ab bin Mu'aaz fort was then conquered. Lots of grain, fat and other food were stored in this fort. All this came into the hands of the Muslims.

The Muslims were short of provisions and they asked Rasulullah ﷺ to make dua for them. The day after he made dua for them, S'ab bin Mu'aaz fort was conquered. They received a lot of provisions which helped them throughout this battle.

(4) Qullah Fort

The Jews then took protection in the Qullah fort which was also very strong and well-protected. It was built right on the peak of a mountain, hence the name Qullah fort. The word Qullah means 'mountain-top. This fort was later on known as Zubair Fort because it was part of the share of Hadhrat Zubair ؓ when the spoils of war were distributed amongst the Muslims.

For three days Rasulullah ﷺ surrounded this fort. A Jew came suddenly before Rasulullah ﷺ and said: "O Abul-Qaasim! Even if you had to surround these people for a whole month it would not affect them in the least. They have water springs flowing beneath them. They come out at night, fill up their containers and quickly go back into the fort. If you cut off their water supply, you will be able to succeed." Rasulullah ﷺ managed to cut off their water supply. They were then forced to come out from the fort. After a severe battle with the Jews, ten Jews were killed and a few Muslims were also martyred but the fort was eventually conquered.

(5) Watih and Salalim

After conquering the Qullah fort, Rasulullah ﷺ moved ahead to the other forts of the area. Only when all the other forts were occupied, Rasulullah ﷺ finally went to Watih and Salalim. The Muslims now controlled all the other forts. These two forts were left. The Jews put a lot of effort to protect these last two forts. The Jews, running away from the surrounding areas, all took protection in these forts. After surrounding them for fourteen days, the Jews were forced to ask for a peace treaty. Rasulullah ﷺ accepted their offer. The Jews chose Ibn Abul-Haqiq to discuss the peace treaty. Finally, Rasulullah ﷺ left them on condition that they immediately leave the area, leaving behind their gold, silver, weapons and other equipments of war. He also warned them not to hide anything and carry it away. He also warned them that if they break any of these conditions, Allah and His Rasool were free of any responsibility. (i.e. The peace treaty will be broken)

However, although they promised not to break this agreement, the Jews continued with their mischief. They somehow managed to hide away a leather bag belonging to Huyayy bin Akhtab. This bag had all their jewellery. Rasulullah ﷺ called Kinaanah bin Rab'i and asked him about the bag. He replied that it was used up in the battles. Rasulullah ﷺ warned them: "If this bag is found, none of you will be safe."

Saying this, Rasulullah ﷺ instructed an Ansaari to go to a certain tree in a certain area and dig out this bag from its roots. The Sahaabi went and brought this bag. The value of its jwellery was about 10 000 Dinaars (gold coins). These people were killed for this crime. One of the main culprits was the husband of Hadhrat Safiyyah رضى الله عنها, Kinaanah bin Rab'i.

An Attempt to Poison Rasulullah ﷺ

After the conquest of Khaybar, Rasulullah ﷺ stayed for a few days more at Khaybar. During this period, Zaynab bint Haaris, the wife of Salaam bin Mushkim, gifted to Rasulullah ﷺ a grilled goat mixed with poison. As soon as he tasted it, Rasulullah ﷺ pulled his hand back. However, Bishr رضى الله عنه, who was sitting with Rasulullah ﷺ, ate part of it. Rasulullah ﷺ warned him: "Hold it! This goat is poisoned."

Rasulullah ﷺ called Zaynab and asked her the reason for this terrible action. She explained: "Yes, the meat was poisoned because if you are truly a Nabi, Allah Ta'ala would surely inform you about it and if you are a false Prophet then the people would be saved from you." Since Rasulullah ﷺ never took revenge for himself, he left her. However, when Bishr رضى الله عنه passed away with this poison, Rasulullah ﷺ handed her over to Bishr's family. They killed her in exchange for the murder of Bishr.

Return Journey

Thereafter Rasulullah ﷺ returned to Madinah Munawwarah. On the way, Rasulullah ﷺ stopped to rest in one of the valleys during the last part of the night. It so happened that none of them woke up for Fajar Salaah until the sun had already turned bright in the sky. Rasulullah ﷺ was the first to get up. With great concern he woke the Sahaabah

رَضِىَ اللهُ عَنْهُم up and ordered them to move from this valley immediately, because of the strong effect of shaytaan there.

They moved out of the valley and stopped at a spot further on. Rasulullah ﷺ instructed Hadhrat Bilal رَضِىَ اللهُ عَنْهُ to call out the Azaan. After performing wudhu, Rasulullah ﷺ and the Sahaabah رَضِىَ اللهُ عَنْهُم read two Rakaats of Fajr Sunnats. Thereafter, Hadhrat Bilal رَضِىَ اللهُ عَنْهُ called out the Iqaamah and the Qadhaa Salaah of Fajr was performed with Jamaat.

Umratul-Qadaa – Zul Q'adah 7 A.H.

According to the Treaty of Hudaybiyyah, the Muslims would return home that year without performing Umrah. The Quraysh had promised to allow them to perform Umrah the next year on condition that they return home within three days. When the moon of Zul Q'adah was seen, Rasulullah ﷺ instructed the Sahaabah رَضِىَ اللهُ عَنْهُم to set out to perform Qadaa of this Umrah. He also said that all those who participated at Hudaybiyyah should go for Umrah. Thus, besides those who had been martyred or passed away, none of those who took part in Hudaybiyyah remained behind.

Thus, together with 2000 people, Rasulullah ﷺ left for Makkah Mukarramah. Seventy camels were also taken with Rasulullah ﷺ on this journey. When they reached Zul-Hulayfah, Rasulullah ﷺ and the Sahaabah رَضِىَ اللهُ عَنْهُم entered the Musjid in the state of Ihraam. Thereafter, reading the Labbayk, they began moving towards Makkah. They had their weapons with them but since one of the conditions of the treaty of Hudaybiyyah was that they would come unarmed, they left their weapons in the valley of Ya'jaj, which is about eight miles from Makkah Mukarramah. Rasulullah ﷺ also left behind a group of two hundred men to guard these weapons. Saying the Talbiyah, Rasulullah ﷺ, together with his beloved Sahabah رَضِىَ اللهُ عَنْهُم, moved towards the Haram Shareef.

During this time, Hadhrat 'Abdullah bin Rawaahah رضى الله عنه, holding the rope of Rasulullah's ﷺ camel, Qaswaa, was walking infront whilst reading poetry. Hadhrat 'Umar رضى الله عنه scolded: "O Ibn Rawaahah! You have the guts to read poetry infront of Rasulullah ﷺ and in the area of the Haram of Allah?" Rasulullah ﷺ said: "O 'Umar! Let it go. This poetry is more painful to the kuffaar than firing a volley of arrows upon them." He then instructed 'Abdullah bin Rawaahah رضى الله عنه to read the following words:

لَا اِلٰهَ اِلَّا اللهُ وَحْدَهُ نَصَرَ عَبْدَهُ وَاَعَزَّ جُنْدَهُ وَهَزَمَ الْاَحْزَابَ وَحْدَهُ

> "There is none worthy of worship besides Allah Who is alone. He assisted His servant, He honoured His army and He defeated the enemies all alone."

The Sahaabah رضى الله عنهم also joined 'Abdullah bin Rawaahah رضى الله عنه in saying this sentence. In this way, they entered Makkah, performed Tawaaf, made Sa'ee between Safa and Marwah, slaughtered their animals, shaved their heads and came out of Ihraam. Thereafter, Rasulullah ﷺ asked some of them to return to the valley of Ya'jaj (where the weapons were kept) and to tell those who were guarding their weapons to come and perform Tawaaf and Sa'ee. Then Rasulullah ﷺ entered the K'abah Shareef and remained inside until Zuhr. According to Rasulullah's ﷺ instructions, Hadhrat Bilal رضى الله عنه called out the Zuhr Azaan on the roof of the K'abah. Although the Quraysh, had allowed Rasulullah ﷺ to perform Tawaaf but due to their anger and jealousy they were unable to see this taking place. This is why the leaders of Quraysh left Makkah Mukarramah and went to the mountains.

CHAPTER 21
BATTLE OF MUTA

Muta is the name of a place in Shaam. When Rasulullah ﷺ sent letters to the kings and rulers of the world, he also wrote to Shurahbeel bin 'Amr Ghassaani. When Hadhrat Haaris bin 'Umair رضي الله عنه, the messenger of Rasulullah ﷺ reached Muta with the letter of Rasulullah ﷺ, Shurahbeel had him killed. For this reason, Rasulullah ﷺ sent an army of three-thousand towards Muta in the month of Jumaadul-Ula 8 A.H.

Rasulullah ﷺ chose Zaid bin Haarisah رضي الله عنه as the Ameer (leader) of the army and said: "If Zaid رضي الله عنه is killed, Ja'far bin Abi Taalib رضي الله عنه will be the leader of the army and if Ja'far رضي الله عنه is killed, 'Abdullah bin Rawaahah رضي الله عنه will be the leader and if 'Abdullah رضي الله عنه is killed too, the Muslims may choose an Ameer themselves."

Rasulullah ﷺ gave a white flag to Zaid bin Haarisah رضي الله عنه and instructed: "Go to the area where Haaris bin 'Umair was killed and invite the local people towards Islam. If they accept this invitation well and good otherwise make dua to Allah and fight them in Jihaad."

Rasulullah ﷺ joined this army right up to Saniyatul-Wadaa to see them off. At Saniyatul-Wadaa, Rasulullah ﷺ stopped a little while and gave the army the following advice: "At all times, have taqwa (Allah-consciousness) and piety. Always wish well for your friends. Go for Jihaad in the path of Allah with the name of Allah against those who disbelieve in Allah. Do not be deceived and do not deceive others. Do not ever kill a child, woman or an elderly person."

Chapter Twenty One – The Battle of Muta

As the people were bidding farewell to the leaders of this army, Hadhrat 'Abdullah bin Rawaahah رضي الله عنه burst out crying. When asked what made him weep, he replied: "Listen! I swear by Allah, it is not my love for this world nor my love for you that makes me weep but it is because I heard Rasulullah ﷺ reading the following Qur-aanic aayat: 'Everyone of you will have to pass over Jahannam and this has been certainly decided by your Rabb.' So I do not know whether I will be able to pass over Jahannam."

When the army was about to leave, the Muslims made this dua: "May Allah Ta'ala bring you back safe and victorious." To this, Hadhrat 'Abdullah bin Rawaahah رضي الله عنه replied in the following poem:

> "I do not wish to return but I beg the forgiveness of Allah and I hope for a deep sword-wound that froths. I wish for a wound by a razor-sharp spear or that an arrow goes right through my intestines and liver. (I wish to be wounded) such that when people pass my grave, they may congratulate me and say: 'Ah! Congratulations! What a brilliant warrior, what a success he made of his life.'"

When Shurahbeel heard about this army, he gathered more than 100 000 soldiers to fight the Muslims. To help Shurahbeel, the Roman emperor, Heraclius, himself came to Balqa with another 100 000 soldiers. When the Muslims reached Ma'an, they heard that a huge army of 200 000 soldiers were waiting for the 3000 Muslims at Balqa. The Mulsim army camped over for two nights at Ma'an whilst thinking about what to do. One group suggested that Rasulullah ﷺ be informed about this and that the Muslims should wait for his instructions and help. Hadhrat 'Abdullah bin Rawaahah رضي الله عنه said:

> "O people! I swear by Allah that the thing which you are afraid of is the same martyrdom that you came for. We neither fight the kuffaar on the basis of power nor on the strength of numbers. Our fighting is only on the basis of this Deen that Allah has honoured us with. So get up and move because you will get either one of two good things; either you will get victory over the kuffaar or you will get martyrdom."

To this, the people replied: "By Allah! Ibn Rawaahah has spoken the truth."

Saying this, this loyal group of 3000 men moved towards Muta to fight an army of 200 000 enemies of Allah Ta'ala.

When they reached the battlefield of Muta and both armies faced one another, Hadhrat Zaid bin Haarisah رضي الله عنه, holding the flag of Islam, stepped out to fight the enemy. He continued fighting bravely until he was martyred. Thereafter, Hadhrat Ja'far رضي الله عنه, climbed on to a horse and stepped out with the flag in his hand. When he was completely surrounded by the enemy and his horse was wounded, he jumped off and cut off his horse's legs and continued fighting them.

Note: He cut off the legs of the horse so that the enemies do not take it for themselves.

As he was fighting the enemy, he would go on reading the following couplets:

> "How beautiful and pure is Jannah! And how cool is its water! As for the Romans, their punishment is very close. They are kuffaar and their lineage (family history) is far from ours. (In other words, they do not enjoy any family relationship with us.) When they challenge me, I am happy to strike them."

As he was fighting, his right hand was chopped off. He then held the flag with his left hand. When the enemy chopped off his left hand too, he held the flag to his chest until he too was martyred. In return, Allah Ta'ala gave him a pair of wings with which he flies with the angels in Jannah.

'Abdullah bin 'Umar رضي الله عنه says that when Hadhrat Ja'far's رضي الله عنه body was found, he had more than ninety arrow and sword wounds on his body and every one of them was at the front of his body. He had not a single wound on the back of his body.

After the martyrdom of Hadhrat Ja'far رضي الله عنه, Hadhrat 'Abdullah bin Rawaahah رضي الله عنه took the flag and moved towards the enemy. He was sitting on a horse. For a few moments, he hesitated. He then spoke to himself and read the following couplets:

> *"O Nafs! I swear that you will jump off from the horse and fight the enemies of Allah whether you like it or not. If the people are screaming and crying, (let them do so). Why do I see you disliking Jannah? (In other words, why are you not moving quickly forward? The fact that you are hesitating in going forward shows that you do not like Jannah. (He said this only to scold himself.) You (O Nafs!) were always comfortable. What happened to you now? You were nothing but a small drop of fluid in your mothers stomach. (You are hesitating in the path of Allah just for this small drop?) O Nafs! Even if you are not killed today, you are definitely going to die one day. This is the reality of death. What you had wanted is now available to you (and that is the opportunity of martyrdom in the path of Allah). If you can get what Zaid and Ja'far ﴿رضي الله عنهما﴾ recieved, then you will be well-guided."*

Saying this, he jumped off his horse. His cousin offered him a bone with meat saying: "Why don't you eat this. Get some energy to fight. You are starving for a number of days now." Ibn Rawaaha ﴿رضي الله عنه﴾ took the bone, sucked on it just once and threw it aside saying: "O Nafs! People are fighting in Jihaad and you are busy eating." He then took his sword and went onto the battlefield. He continued fighting bravely until he was martyred and the flag of Islam fell from his hand. At once, Saabit bin Akhram ﴿رضي الله عنه﴾ took the flag and spoke to the Muslims: "O Muslims! Choose an Ameer over you." The people replied: "You are our Ameer. We are pleased with you as our Ameer." Saabit ﴿رضي الله عنه﴾ said: "I am not worthy of this." Saying this, he threw the flag into the hands of Khaalid bin Waleed ﴿رضي الله عنه﴾ and said: "You are an expert in war."

Khaalid bin Waleed ﴿رضي الله عنه﴾ did not want to accept the post of Ameer but all the Muslims insisted on him being the Ameer. Holding the flag of Islam, Hadhrat Khaalid bin Waleed ﴿رضي الله عنه﴾ fought against the enemy with great courage and bravery.

Hadhrat Khaalid bin Waleed ﷺ himself says: "In the battle of Muta whilst fighting the enemy, nine swords were broken at my hands. Only a single Yemeni sword remained."

On the second day of the battle, Hadhrat Khaalid ﷺ changed the arrangement of the army. He switched the front of the army with back and the right side of the army with the left. On seeing this change in the army, the enemy became terrified. They thought that more soldiers had arrived to strengthen the Muslims.

Ibn S'ad Abu 'Aamir ﷺ says: "When Khaalid bin Waleed ﷺ attacked the Roman forces, he crushed them so severely that never before have I seen such an amazing defeat. The Muslims were able to swing their swords wherever they wished to."

As these warriors of Islam were being martyred on the battlefield of Muta, Allah Ta'ala, in His absolute power, made it possible for Rasulullah ﷺ to witness the entire battle whilst he was sitting in Madinah Munawwarah. Rasulullah ﷺ gathered the Sahaabah ﷺ by announcing: "As-Salaatu Jaami'ah". When the Sahaabah ﷺ were gathered, Rasulullah ﷺ climbed on to the mimbar and said: "Zaid has taken the flag of Islam in his hand and he fought the kuffaar until he was martyred and entered Jannah. Then, Ja'far took the flag and he also fought the enemies of Allah bravely until he was martyred and he too entered Jannah. He is now flying with the angels in Jannah with the help of his two wings." "Thereafter 'Abdullah bin Rawaahah picked up the flag." Saying this, Rasulullah ﷺ remained silent for some time. He ﷺ then said: "'Abdullah bin Rawaahah ﷺ has also fought the kuffaar. He also fought bravely until he was martyred. All three of them were raised into Jannah and all three are relaxing on golden thrones".

Whilst Rasulullah ﷺ was describing this scene of the battlefield, his eyes were flowing with tears. He then said: "After them, a 'sword from the swords of Allah' (Khaalid bin Waleed) has taken hold of the flag of Islam. He fought until Allah Ta'ala granted the Muslims victory."

They also earned some spoils of war (booty). After defeating the Romans, Hadhrat Khaalid bin Waleed رَضِيَ اللهُ عَنْهُ did not feel it wise to chase them any further, and together with his small group of men, he returned to Madinah Munawwarah. In this battle, twelve Muslims were martyred.

After describing the battle, Rasulullah صَلَّى اللهُ عَلَيْهِ وَسَلَّمَ went to the house of Hadhrat Ja'far رَضِيَ اللهُ عَنْهُ. He called his children and as Rasulullah صَلَّى اللهُ عَلَيْهِ وَسَلَّمَ was patting them with his blessed hands over their heads, his eyes were flowing with tears. Hadhrat Ja'far's رَضِيَ اللهُ عَنْهُ wife, Hadhrat Asma bint 'Umais رَضِيَ اللهُ عَنْهَا realised that something was wrong. She asked: "O Rasulullah صَلَّى اللهُ عَلَيْهِ وَسَلَّمَ! May my parents be sacrificed for you. Why are you crying? Have you heard something about Ja'far رَضِيَ اللهُ عَنْهُ and his friends?" Rasulullah صَلَّى اللهُ عَلَيْهِ وَسَلَّمَ replied: "Yes, today he was martyred." Hadhrat Asma bint 'Umais رَضِيَ اللهُ عَنْهَا says: "The moment I heard this heartbreaking news, I began to scream loudly. Many women gathered around me (to comfort and console me)."

Rasulullah صَلَّى اللهُ عَلَيْهِ وَسَلَّمَ then returned to his house and asked his family to prepare meals for the family of Ja'far رَضِيَ اللهُ عَنْهُ as they were very much in grief. This incident had a great effect on Rasulullah صَلَّى اللهُ عَلَيْهِ وَسَلَّمَ as well. Saddened by this heartbreaking incident, Rasulullah صَلَّى اللهُ عَلَيْهِ وَسَلَّمَ stayed for three days in the Masjid. On their return from Muta, as Hadhrat Khaalid bin Waleed رَضِيَ اللهُ عَنْهُ and his companions neared Madinah, Rasulullah صَلَّى اللهُ عَلَيْهِ وَسَلَّمَ and the Muslims came out to give them a warm welcome.

CHAPTER 22
CONQUEST OF MAKKAH

When the peace treaty was signed at Hudaybiyah between Rasulullah ﷺ and the Quraysh, then the different tribes were given the choice of joining either of the two parties (of the peace treaty). The Banu Bakr joined the Quraysh while the Banu Khuzaa'ah joined Rasulullah ﷺ. Both these tribes were enemies of one another for many years. They kept on killing people from each other's tribes. Because of the peace treaty that was signed in Hudaybiyyah, the two groups now felt safe from each other. The Banu Bakr who were the friends of the Quraysh unfortunately broke their agreement. They got together with their friends and attacked the Khuzaa'ah tribe. It was at night when some people of the Khuzaa'ah tribe had stopped over at a spring where they had been sleeping. The Quraysh secretly helped the Banu Bakr in this attack. The Khuzaa'ah escaped to the safety of the Haram Shareef but they were not left alone over here as well. The Quraysh helped the Banu Bakr in every way possible. They supplied them with weapons and men as well.

The Quraysh thought that Rasulullah ﷺ would not come to know of their involvement. The next morning, the Quraysh regretted their actions and realised that they went against the peace treaty, and that through this mistake, they broke their promises which they made with Rasulullah ﷺ at Hudaybiyah.

Amr ibn Saalim Khuzaa'i went to Madinah Munawwarah with a group of 40 people and came to Rasulullah ﷺ who was in the Masjid at that time. He explained the entire incident of how they were attacked at night and how the Quraysh helped and assisted them in this evil deed. They begged Rasulullah ﷺ for help and assistance against these wrong doers.

After hearing all these incidents, Rasulullah ﷺ promised to help and assist them. This group then returned. Rasulullah ﷺ sent a Sahabi رضي الله عنه to the Quraysh in Makkah and asked him to give the message: "Either they pay the blood money for those who were killed from the Banu Khuzaa'ah or they announce that the peace treaty of Hudaybiyah is now cancelled."

When the Sahabi رضي الله عنه gave this message, the Quraysh said: "We will not pay the blood money to the Banu Khuzaa'ah, but we are prepared to cancel the treaty of Hudaybiyah." However, when the Sahabi رضي الله عنه returned, the Quraysh regretted this. They immediately sent Abu Sufyaan to Madinah in order to renew the treaty and to increase the period of the treaty.

Abu Sufyaan goes to Madinah

As Abu Sufyaan left Makkah and headed towards Madinah in order to renew the peace treaty, Rasulullah ﷺ informed the Sahaabah رضي الله عنهم that Abu Sufyaan was coming from Makkah in order to increase the period of the treaty. On reaching Madinah, Abu Sufyaan went straight to the house of his daughter, Ummul-Mu'mineen Umm-e-Habibah رضي الله عنها. He said to her: "O my daughter! You have folded up the sitting mat. Do you think that the mat is not worthy of me or am I not worthy of it?" She replied: "This is the bedding of Rasulullah ﷺ. A kaafir who is impure and filthy with the filth of shirk cannot sit on it." Abu Sufyaan shouted out saying: "O my daughter! By Allah, you have learnt some bad ways after leaving me." She replied: "Rather, I have come out of the darkness of kufr and went into the light and guidance of Islam. I am surprised at you that although you are one of the leaders of the Quraysh, you worship stones that cannot hear or see."

Abu Sufyaan got up and went to the Masjid. He came to Rasulullah ﷺ and said: "I have come on behalf of the Quraysh in order to renew the peace treaty and to increase the period of the treaty." Rasulullah ﷺ did not give any reply. When he got no answer from Rasulullah ﷺ, he went to Hadhrat Abu Bakr رضى الله عنه and asked him to speak on his behalf. He replied: "I cannot help you in any way." He then went to 'Hadhrat Umar ibn al-Khattaab رضى الله عنه and asked him to speak on his behalf. 'Hadhrat Umar رضى الله عنه replied: "Allah is the greatest! If I do not find a single person in the entire world to join me, I am prepared to go out and fight in Jihaad all by myself." On hearing this, he went to Hadhrat Ali رضى الله عنه who was sitting with his wife, Hadhrat Faatimah رضى الله عنها and his son, Hadhrat Hasan رضى الله عنه. He spoke to Hadhrat Ali رضى الله عنه saying: "O father of Hasan! You are the closest family to me. I have come with an urgent need. I cannot go back unsuccessful. You should therefore speak on my behalf to Rasulullah ﷺ." Hadhrat Ali رضى الله عنه replied: "I swear by Allah that Rasulullah ﷺ has already made his decision. It is now impossible for anyone to say anything." On hearing this, he spoke to Faatimah رضى الله عنها saying: "O daughter of Muhammad! If you order this child (Hasan رضى الله عنه) to announce that he has given safety to the Quraysh, he will forever be recognised as a leader of the Arabs." She replied: "First of all, he is very young (giving safety is the responsibility of adults). Secondly, who can give safety against the pleasure of Rasulullah ﷺ?" Abu Sufyaan spoke to Ali رضى الله عنه saying: "The problem has become very serious. Please show me a way out." He replied: "I cannot think of anything except that you should go into the Masjid and announce: 'I have come to renew the peace treaty of Hudaybiyah, to further strengthen it, and to increase the period of the treaty.' After saying this, go back to your city." Abu Sufyaan left, went to the Masjid and made this announcement in a loud voice: "I am renewing the peace treaty and increasing the period of the treaty." After saying this, he returned to Makkah.

After reaching Makkah and telling the entire story to the Quraysh, they asked him: "Did Muhammad accept this announcement of yours?" He

Chapter Twenty Two – The Conquest of Makkah

replied: "No." The Quraysh said: "How can you feel pleased and satisfied without the agreement of Muhammad? You have come back with something useless. By Allah, Ali mocked you (when he told you what to do). You have not come with any news about the peace treaty so that we can feel safe, nor have you come with any news of war so that we could prepare."

When Abu Sufyaan left (Madinah), Rasulullah ﷺ ordered the Sahaabah رضي الله عنهم to secretly prepare for the journey to Makkah and to get their weapons ready for war. He instructed that this should be kept a secret, it should not be announced. He also sent a message to the surrounding tribes to prepare for war.

The story of Haatib ibn Abi Balta'ah رضي الله عنه

During this time, Haatib ibn Abi Balta'ah رضي الله عنه wrote a letter to the people of Makkah informing them that Rasulullah ﷺ was preparing to attack Makkah. He secretly sent this letter with a woman going to Makkah. Allah Ta'ala informed Rasulullah ﷺ of this through wahy. He sent Hadhrat Ali رضي الله عنه, Hadhrat Zubayr رضي الله عنه and Hadhrat Miqdaad رضي الله عنه instructing them to continue travelling till they reach a place called Raudah-e-Khaakh where they will find a woman riding a camel. She will have a letter written by Haatib ibn Abi Balta'ah رضي الله عنه addressed to the people of Makkah. They should bring the letter back to Madinah. They said: "We reached this place, found a woman there, made her camel sit down and we searched her. However, we did not find the letter. We said to ourselves: 'By Allah! Rasulullah ﷺ can never be wrong.' We said to the woman: 'It would be better if you hand over the letter to us. If not, we will strip you naked and take the letter from you.' The woman then removed the letter from her hair and handed it over to us. We returned with it to Rasulullah ﷺ. He called Haatib ibn Abi Balta'ah رضي الله عنه and asked him for an explanation. He replied: 'O Rasulullah ﷺ! Do not be quick in punishing me. I am not related to the Quraysh. I only have an understanding with them. My family is living in Makkah. They have no one to protect or help them there. On the other hand, the Muhaajireen whose families are there have other relatives living there as well. Their families are protected. I thought that since I have no family with the Quraysh, I should do them a favour and they would protect my family. I take an oath in the name of Allah that I did not turn away from Islam nor have I chosen kufr after having accepted Islam. My only reason was what I just mentioned.'"

On hearing his explanation, Rasulullah ﷺ said:

$$\text{أَمَا إِنَّهُ قَدْ صَدَقَكُمْ}$$

"Listen! He has surely spoken the truth to you."

'Umar ؓ said: "O Rasulullah ﷺ! Permit me to chop off the neck of this hypocrite." Rasulullah ﷺ replied: "He took part in the battle of Badr and Allah Ta'ala addressed those who took part in Badr, saying: 'Do whatever you wish, for I have forgiven you.'"

On hearing this, 'Umar's ؓ eyes were filled with tears and he said: "Allah Ta'ala and His Rasool ﷺ know best."

Leaving from Madinah

On the 10th of Ramadhaan, Rasulullah ﷺ together with a group of 10 000 Sahaabah left Madinah Munawwarah after the Asr Salaah with the intention of conquering Makkah. From his noble wives, Hadhrat Umme Salmah ؓ and Hadhrat Maymunah ؓ joined him.

When he reached Zul Hulayfah or Juhfah, he met Hadhrat Abbaas ؓ and his family, who left Makkah with the intention of shifting to Madinah.

Abu Sufyaan ibnul Haaris and 'Abdullah ibn Abi Umayyah were at a place called Abwa'. They left Makkah Mukarramah for Madinah with the intention of accepting Islam. Abu Sufyaan ibnul Haaris ibn 'Abd al-Muttalib was the cousin of Rasulullah ﷺ, as well as his foster brother. He was also breast-fed by Halimah Sa'diyyah ﷺ. He was a friend of Rasulullah ﷺ before Islam and was always with him. However, when Rasulullah ﷺ became a Nabi, he became his bitter enemy. He sang poetry disgracing Rasulullah ﷺ. These lines of poetry were replied to by Hassaan ibn Saabit ﷺ. Abu Sufyaan's son, Ja'far, was also with him.

Abdullah ibn Abi Umayyah was also the cousin of Rasulullah ﷺ. He was the son of Rasulullah's ﷺ aunt, 'Aatikah bint 'Abdul-Muttalib. He was also a bitter enemy of Rasulullah ﷺ. They both wanted to meet Rasulullah ﷺ but because they both had caused a lot of suffering on him, he turned away from them and did not allow them to meet him. Umme Salamah ﷺ spoke on their behalf and said: "O Rasulullah ﷺ! One is your uncle's son and the other is your aunt's son." He replied: "I have no need to meet them. My uncle's son disgraced me. As for my aunt's son, he is the one who had said to me while I was in Makkah: 'By Allah! I will never believe in you till you get a ladder going up to the heavens and I see you climbing up with my very own eyes. Then you must come down with a written command from above, with four angels who will confirm that Allah Ta'ala has chosen you as His Messenger. Even then, I do not think that I will believe in you.'"

Umme Salamah ﷺ replied: "O Rasulullah! It is hoped of your noble character that both your cousins will enjoy your favour. When your mercy and pardon is so wide-spread, why should these two be left out?"

On the other side, Abu Sufyaan ibnul Haaris said: "If you do not meet with me, I will take my son, Ja'far, to a desert and die there out of hunger and thirst." On hearing Umme Salamah ﷺ and the remorse of these two, Rasulullah ﷺ allowed them to meet him. The moment they entered, they accepted Islam and joined the Muslims towards Makkah Mukarrmah.

Hadhrat Ali ﷺ advised Abu Sufyaan ibnul Haaris to stand before Rasulullah ﷺ and to say the words that the brothers of Yusuf عَلَيْهِ السَّلَام had said to Yusuf عَلَيْهِ السَّلَام:

$$\text{تَاللّٰهِ لَقَدْ اٰثَرَكَ اللّٰهُ عَلَيْنَا وَاِنْ كُنَّا لَخٰطِئِيْنَ}$$

"We take an oath by Allah that Allah has certainly chosen you over us. And surely we are in error." [Surah Yusuf, verse 91]

Rasulullah ﷺ replied:

$$\text{لَا تَثْرِيْبَ عَلَيْكُمُ الْيَوْمَ ۖ يَغْفِرُ اللّٰهُ لَكُمْ ۖ وَهُوَ اَرْحَمُ الرَّاحِمِيْنَ}$$

"There is no blame on you today. May Allah forgive you, and He is the most merciful of those who show mercy." [Surah Yusuf, verse 92]

Abu Sufyaan's ﷺ tawbah was accepted, and according to the Hadith "Islam wipes out all that was done before accepting Islam", his heart became so pure that no filth whatsoever remained in it. The qualities of Imaan, goodness, sincerity and yaqeen (conviction) were filled into his heart in such a way that no dust or atom of kufr could reach into his heart.

It is said that whenever he was with Rasulullah ﷺ, Abu Sufyaan ﷺ did not look at him directly in the face out of modesty. Rasulullah ﷺ used to give him the good news of Jannah. May Allah be pleased with him.

Rasulullah ﷺ then left and reached Marruz-Zahraan at about Isha time. On reaching there, he got off and ordered that each person should light a fire outside his tent. This was an old Arab custom. Due to their breaking the treaty, the Quraysh were on their guard as to when Rasulullah ﷺ would attack them. Abu Sufyaan ibnul Harb, Budayl ibn Warqaa' and Hakeem ibn Hizam came out of Makkah in order to get whatever information they could. When they came close to Marruz-Zahraan, they saw the army there and became very worried.

The moment the night watchmen of Rasulullah ﷺ saw these three people, they arrested them. These three people (who were arrested) asked them as to who they were, and they replied that Rasulullah ﷺ and his companions were among them. While they were still talking, 'Abbaas رضي الله عنه was on the donkey of Rasulullah ﷺ moving about. He recognised the voice of Abu Sufyaan and said: "How terrible, O Abu Sufyaan! This is the army of Rasulullah ﷺ. By Allah, if he is victorious over you, he will chop off your head. It would be better for the Quraysh if you ask for peace and agree to obey him." Abu Sufyaan says: "On hearing this voice, I turned in that direction until I found 'Abbaas رضي الله عنه. I said to him: 'O Abu al-Fadl! May my parents be sacrificed for you. How can I save myself and what is the way out?'" 'Abbaas رضي الله عنه replied: "Climb onto this donkey with me. I will take you to Rasulullah ﷺ in order to seek safety for you." 'Abbaas رضي الله عنه took him and left while showing him around the Muslim army.

Rasulullah ﷺ ordered 'Abbaas رضي الله عنه to take Abu Sufyaan to his tent and to bring him back the next morning. Abu Sufyaan remained in the tent the entire night while Hakeem ibn Hizaam and Budayl ibn Warqaa' came to Rasulullah ﷺ and accepted Islam. Rasulullah ﷺ remained with them for some time asking them about the present conditions in Makkah. After accepting Islam, they both returned to Makkah in order to inform the people of Makkah of Rasulullah's ﷺ arrival.

Abu Sufyaan ibnul Harb accepts Islam

The next morning, 'Abbaas رضي الله عنه took Abu Sufyaan to Rasulullah ﷺ. He addressed Abu Sufyaan saying: "O Abu Sufyaan! Has the time not come for you to believe that there is none worthy of worship except Allah?" He replied: "May my parents be sacrificed for you. You are extremely tolerant, kind and one who keeps good family relations. I take an oath by Allah that had there been any god besides Him, he would have helped us today and I would have asked for his help against you."

Rasulullah ﷺ said: "O Abu Sufyaan! Has the time not come that you recognise me as the Prophet of Allah?" He replied: "May my parents be sacrificed for you. You are extremely tolerant, kind and one who keeps good family relations. You are still showing your kindness. Although I am your enemy, you are still showing your kindness to me. I have a slight doubt about you being a Prophet or not."

Abbaas رضي الله عنه cleared out his doubts and Abu Sufyaan رضي الله عنه accepted Islam. After this, 'Abbaas رضي الله عنه said: "O Prophet of Allah! Abu Sufyaan is from the leaders of Makkah. He likes position. Therefore give him something that would be a source of honour, nobility and position for him." Rasulullah ﷺ replied: "Certainly, make this announcement that whoever enters the house of Abu Sufyaan رضي الله عنه will be safe." Abu Sufyaan رضي الله عنه said: "O Prophet of Allah! How will all the people fit in my house?" Rasulullah ﷺ replied: "Whoever enters the Haram Shareef will also be safe." Abu Sufyaan رضي الله عنه said: "O Messenger of Allah! Even the Haram Shareef will not be enough." Rasulullah ﷺ replied: "Okay, whoever enters his house and keeps his door shut will also be safe." Abu Sufyaan رضي الله عنه replied: "Yes, there is much leniency in this."

When Rasulullah ﷺ began preparations to leave from Marruz-Zahraan, he ordered 'Abbaas رضي الله عنه to take Abu Sufyaan رضي الله عنه to the mountain pass, so that he would be able to see the Muslim army in full view. As a result, when the different tribes began passing him, group after group, he was amazed and said to 'Abbaas رضي الله عنه: "The kingdom of your nephew has really grown." 'Abbaas رضي الله عنه replied: "This is not kingship. Rather, it is prophethood."

As each tribe used to pass by, Abu Sufyaan رضي الله عنه would ask as to who that particular tribe was. Khaalid ibn Waleed رضي الله عنه was the first to pass by with an army of 900 to 1000. After him, other tribes passed by. Eventually, the group of Rasulullah ﷺ passed by with a fully armed group of the Muhaajireen and Ansaar. The flag of the Muhaajireen was carried by

Zubayr ﷺ while that of the Ansaar was carried by Sa'd ibn 'Ubaadah ﷺ. When he passed by and saw Abu Sufyaan ﷺ, he became very excited and shouted out:

$$\text{اَلْيَوْمَ يَوْمُ الْمَلْحَمَةِ الْيَوْمَ تُسْتَحَلُّ الْكَعْبَةُ}$$

"Today is the day of war. Today the laws of the holiness of the Ka'bah will not apply."

On hearing this, Abu Sufyaan ﷺ became worried and asked about these people. Hadhrat 'Abbaas ﷺ replied that they were the Muhaajireen and Ansaar together with Rasulullah ﷺ.

When Rasulullah ﷺ passed by, Abu Sufyaan ﷺ asked: "O Rasulullah ﷺ! Have you ordered Sa'd ibn 'Ubaadah ﷺ to kill your people?" He then mentioned what Sa'd ﷺ had said and asked: "O Rasulullah ﷺ! I ask you in the name of Allah and our family ties, for you are the one who takes care of family relations the most." Rasulullah ﷺ replied:

$$\text{يَا اَبَا سُفْيَانَ اَلْيَوْمَ يَوْمُ الْمَرْحَمَةِ يُعِزُّ اللّٰهُ فِيهِ قُرَيْشًا}$$

"O Abu Sufyaan! Today is the day of mercy, in which Allah will honour the Quraysh."

Rasulullah ﷺ said:

$$\text{كَذَبَ سَعْدٌ وَلٰكِنْ هٰذَا يَوْمٌ يُعَظِّمُ اللّٰهُ فِيهِ الْكَعْبَةَ وَيَوْمٌ تُكْسٰى فِيهِ الْكَعْبَةُ}$$

"Sa'd is wrong. Today is the day in which Allah Ta'ala will honour the Ka'bah and the Ka'bah will be given a covering."

Rasulullah ﷺ then ordered that the flag be taken from Sa'd ibn 'Ubaadah ﷺ and be given to his son, Qays.

Abu Sufyaan رضى الله عنه then left Rasulullah صلى الله عليه وسلم and rushed towards Makkah. On reaching there, he made the following announcement: "Muhammad is coming with an army. According to me, there is no one who can fight against him. Accept Islam and you will be safe. The person who enters the Haram Shareef will be safe. The person who enters my house will be safe. The person who shuts himself in his house, or hands over his weapons will be safe." His wife Hindah caught him by his moustache and announced: "O Banu Kinaanah! This old man has become mad and stupid. He does not even know what he is saying." She said many other bad words to him. Many people gathered around them. Abu Sufyaan رضى الله عنه said to them: "Such talk will not help in any way. O people! Don't be bluffed by this woman."

"There is no one who can fight Muhammad صلى الله عليه وسلم. The person who enters the Haram Shareef is safe. The person who enters my house is also safe." The people replied: "O foolish one! How many people can fit into your house?" Abu Sufyaan replied: "The person who shuts himself in his house is also safe."

Abu Sufyaan رضى الله عنه told his wife: "It is best that you also accept Islam or else you will be killed. Go into your house and shut your door. I am speaking the truth." On hearing this, some people began rushing to the Haram Shareef while others ran towards their homes.

Entry into Makkah

Rasulullah صلى الله عليه وسلم then entered Makkah. On entering Makkah, he fully showed his respect and honour to the Ka'bah Shareef. He entered with humility, with his head bowing down. He did not enter proudly like kings. 'Abdullah ibn Mughaffal رضى الله عنه says: "I saw Rasulullah صلى الله عليه وسلم on the day of the conquest of Makkah. He was sitting on his camel and reciting Surah al-Fatah in a most beautiful voice."

At that time, although Rasulullah صلى الله عليه وسلم was very happy and in high spirits, humility, modesty and peace were also seen on his mubarak face. He was sitting on his camel with his head lowered out of humility to such an extent that his blessed beard was touching the saddle. His attendant (helper), Usaamah ibn Zaid رَضِيَ اللَّهُ عَنْهُ was sitting with him.

Hadhrat Anas رَضِيَ اللَّهُ عَنْهُ says that when Rasulullah صَلَّى اللَّهُ عَلَيْهِ وَسَلَّمَ entered Makkah Mukarramah as a conqueror, all the people were looking at him but he had his face lowered out of humility.

Hadhrat Abu Sa'eed Al-Khudri رَضِيَ اللَّهُ عَنْهُ says that on the day of the conquest of Makkah, Rasulullah صَلَّى اللَّهُ عَلَيْهِ وَسَلَّمَ said: "This is the day which Allah Ta'ala had promised me." He then read Surah Nasr.

Rasulullah صَلَّى اللَّهُ عَلَيْهِ وَسَلَّمَ was thinking about the time when he had to leave this city weak and poor. Now the time has come that through the help of Allah Ta'ala, he is entering the same city as a conqueror with much power and rule. This is the gift of Allah Ta'ala which He gives to whom so ever He wills.

It is for this reason that Rasulullah's صَلَّى اللَّهُ عَلَيْهِ وَسَلَّمَ head was lowered and placed on the saddle – bowing before Allah Ta'ala out of thanks. Out of his extreme happiness, he was reciting Surah Fatah and Surah Nasr in a very beautiful voice. In so doing, he was saying that this clear victory, help, power and rule are all only the blessings of Allah Ta'ala. Truth has overpowered and falsehood has been destroyed. The light of Islam and Imaan shone while the darkness of kufr was removed. The holy land (of Makkah) was cleaned from the filth of kufr and shirk.

Rasulullah صَلَّى اللَّهُ عَلَيْهِ وَسَلَّمَ passed through the place of Kada' and entered from the upper section of Makkah. He ordered Khaalid ibn Waleed رَضِيَ اللَّهُ عَنْهُ to enter from Kuda' – the lower section of Makkah, and Zubayr رَضِيَ اللَّهُ عَنْهُ to enter from Kada' – the upper section of Makkah. He commanded both of them not to start any fighting. They should only fight the person who attacks them first. He then entered Makkah Mukarramah very respectfully.

When he entered Makkah, he first went to the house of Umme Hani bint Abi Taalib رَضِىَ اللهُ عَنْهَا. He took a bath and read eight Rakaats of Salaah – this was the time of chasht – mid-morning.

Umme Hani رَضِىَ اللهُ عَنْهَا said to Rasulullah ﷺ: "O Nabi of Allah! Two relatives of my husband have ran away and took safety in my house. I have given them safety. However, my brother Ali رَضِىَ اللهُ عَنْهُ wants to kill them." Rasulullah ﷺ replied: "I give safety to those whom Umme Hani رَضِىَ اللهُ عَنْهَا has given safety to. Ali should not kill those two people."

After finishing his Salaah, Rasulullah ﷺ went to his tent at Shi'b Abi Taalib. The Sahaabah رَضِىَ اللهُ عَنْهُمْ had asked Rasulullah ﷺ the day before he could enter Makkah Mukarramah as to where he would like to stay. He replied: "At the place where the Quraysh had boycotted the Banu Haashim and the Banul-Muttalib and made an agreement and promise that they would stop all business dealings, marriage, etc. with the Banu Haashim and the Banu Muttalib as long as they do not hand over Muhammad (ﷺ) to them." This place is known as Shi'b Abi Taalib.

Entering the Haram Shareef

After the victory, Rasulullah ﷺ entered the Haram Shareef and made Tawaaf of the Ka'bah Shareef. 'Abdullah ibn 'Umar رَضِىَ اللهُ عَنْهُ says that when Rasulullah ﷺ entered the Masjid, 360 idols were placed around the Ka'bah. Rasulullah ﷺ pointed to each one with a stick and read the words:

$$\text{جَآءَ الْحَقُّ وَ زَهَقَ الْبَاطِلُ}$$

"The truth has come, and falsehood is defeated."

As he said this, each idol began falling one after the other.

When Rasulullah ﷺ entered the Masjid, he was on his camel. He made Tawaaf of the Ka'bah Shareef whilst sitting on the camel. After completing the Tawaaf, he called 'Usmaan ibn Talhah, took the key of the Ka'bah Shareef from him and opened it. He saw that there were idols inside. He ordered all these to be removed. When they were all removed and the inside of the Ka'bah Shareef was washed with zam zam water, he went in and read Salaah inside.

He went to all the corners of the Ka'bah Shareef and recited 'Allahu Akbar'. Hadhrat Bilal رضي الله عنه and Hadhrat Usaamah رضي الله عنه were both with him at that time. Then he opened the door and stepped outside. He saw that the Haram Shareef was filled with people and that they were waiting for him to speak to them about the criminals and enemies. This was the 20th of Ramadhaan. He was standing at the door of the Ka'bah with its key in his hand. He then gave a speech from the door of the Ka'ba Shareef. After giving the speech he spoke to the Quraysh:

Rasulullah ﷺ gives a speech from the door of the Ka'bah

ثُمَّ قَالَ يَا مَعْشَرَ قُرَيْشٍ مَا تَرَوْنَ أَنِّيْ فَاعِلٌ بِكُمْ قَالُوْا خَيْرًا أَخٌ كَرِيْمٌ وَابْنُ أَخٍ كَرِيْمٍ. قَالَ فَإِنِّيْ أَقُوْلُ لَكُمْ كَمَا قَالَ يُوْسُفُ لِإِخْوَتِهِ لَا تَثْرِيْبَ عَلَيْكُمُ الْيَوْمَ اِذْهَبُوْا فَأَنْتُمُ الطُّلَقَاءُ

He then said: 'O group of Quraysh! What do you think I am going to do to you?' They replied: 'We think that you will be good to us. You are a noble brother who is the son of a noble brother.' He said: 'I am speaking to you in the same way which Yusuf عليه السلام spoke to his brothers: 'There is no blame on you today. Go, for you are all free.'"

The Arabs were very proud of their noble families. In this speech, Rasulullah ﷺ cancelled this pride. It was explained that in Islam, everyone is equal. True honour and nobility is only through taqwa (piety). Rasulullah ﷺ was sent as a mercy to the world for the guidance of the entire universe. His only purpose was guidance. Taking revenge from enemies is the way of kings (and not true Prophets of Allah Ta'ala).

After his speech, Rasulullah ﷺ sat down in the Masjid. The key to the Ka'bah was in his hand. Hadhrat Ali رضي الله عنه stood up and asked: "O Nabi of Allah! Give the key to us so that together with providing zam zam to the Hajis, we will also have the honour of guarding the Ka'bah." This aayat was then revealed:

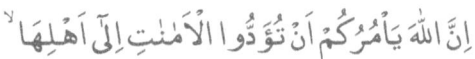

"Surely Allah Ta'ala commands you to discharge (give back) the trusts to their owners." *[Surah an-Nisaa', verse 58]*

Rasulullah ﷺ called for 'Usmaan ibn Talhah and returned the key to him. He then said to him: "Take this key forever." In other words, it will remain in your family forever. "I am not giving it to you from my own side. Rather, it is Allah who has given it to you. No one but a cruel ruler will take it away from you."

The Azaan is given at the door of the Ka'bah

When it was the time for Zuhr Salaah, Rasulullah ﷺ ordered Hadhrat Bilal رضي الله عنه to climb the door of the Ka'bah and call out the Azaan. The Quraysh of Makkah were looking at this clear victory of Islam from the mountain tops of Makkah.

The leaders of the Quraysh who could not see the disgrace of kufr and shirk and the honour of Islam, hid their faces in shame. Abu Sufyaan, A'ttaab and Khalid (the two sons of Usaid), Haaris bin Hishaam (who later on became Muslims) and other Qurayshi leaders were sitting in the courtyard of the Ka'bah. A'ttaab and Khalid said: "Allah honoured our forefathers by taking them away from this world before they could hear this call (of the Azaan)." Haaris said: "I take an oath by Allah that if I were sure that you are on the truth, I would certainly follow you." Abu Sufyaan said: "I am remaining silent. If I were to say anything, these pebbles would inform him about it." Rasulullah ﷺ was informed of all these conversations through wahi from Allah Ta'ala. When he passed by these people he said to them: "I have been informed of all that you have been speaking through wahi." He then told them all that they had been speaking. Haaris and 'Itaab said: "We bear witness that you are certainly the Prophet of Allah, for none of us informed you of what we were speaking. (We are now sure that it was Allah alone who told His Nabi of all that we were speaking.)"

After 'Itaab ibn Usayd accepted Islam, Rasulullah ﷺ chose him as the governor of Makkah. He was 21 years old at that time. Rasulullah ﷺ ordered that he should be paid one Dirham per day.

After the Tawaaf, Rasulullah ﷺ went to Mt. Safa, faced the Ka'bah Shareef and remained in dua and praising Allah Ta'ala for a long time. A group of Ansaar was also present. Some of them said: "Allah Ta'ala allowed Rasulullah ﷺ to conquer his city and homeland. It may well be that he will decide to remain behind and settle down in this city and not come back to Madinah." They continued speaking like this when they saw the effects of wahy on Rasulullah's ﷺ face. It was the habit of the Sahaabah رضى الله عنهم that when wahy was coming to Rasulullah ﷺ, they would not look at him. When the wahi was completed, he said: "O Ansaar! Is this what you said?" They replied: "Yes, O Nabi of Allah." He replied: "Understand well that this can never happen. I am the servant and Nabi of Allah Ta'ala. I made hijrat through the command of Allah Ta'ala. My life is your life and my death is your death." After hearing this, the Ansaar began crying and said: "O Nabi of Allah! We feared that the light which lit us will be taken away from us. We are servants who are prepared to sacrifice our lives (for Allah Ta'ala and His Rasool ﷺ) and we are prepared to choose others over our own selves, but we are extremely miserly when it comes to Allah Ta'ala and His Messenger ﷺ. (We are not prepared to share them with anyone else)."

باسایه ترا نمی پسندم   عشق است وہزار بدگمانی

*I am in love with your actual being not with your shadow,
when I am deeply in love with you I end up having thousands of
doubts*

Rasulullah ﷺ replied: "Allah Ta'ala and His Rasool know that you are true in this regard and excuse you in this regard."

Forgiveness for one and all

After the conquest of Makkah, Rasulullah ﷺ made the announcement of general forgiveness. Rasulullah ﷺ completely forgave those who had thrown thorns in his path, those who had thrown stones at him, those who were violent towards him, and those who had caused his legs and feet to be covered in blood. However, there were a few who had been extremely disrespectful towards Rasulullah ﷺ and caused him much pain. Allah Ta'ala ordered that these people must be killed:

مَلْعُوْنِيْنَ ۛ اَيْنَمَا ثُقِفُوْۤا اُخِذُوْا وَقُتِّلُوْا تَقْتِيْلًا ۝ سُنَّةَ اللهِ فِى الَّذِيْنَ خَلَوْا مِنْ قَبْلُ ۚ وَلَنْ تَجِدَ لِسُنَّةِ اللهِ تَبْدِيْلًا ۝

*"(They are) cursed. Wherever they are found, they should be arrested
and put to death. Such has been the way of Allah with those who
passed from before. And you will not find Allah's way changing."*
[Surah Ahzaab, verses 61-62]

To respect and honour Rasulullah ﷺ and to help and defend him is a fardh duty on the entire ummah. Showing disrespect to him means disrespect to the religion of Allah Ta'ala.

Abu Quhaafah accepts Islam

Rasulullah ﷺ was in the Holy Masjid when Abu Bakr رضى الله عنه brought his old father before Rasulullah ﷺ and made him sit in front of him. Rasulullah ﷺ said:

هَلَّا تَرَكْتَ الشَّيْخَ فِىْ بَيْتِهٖ حَتّٰى اَكُوْنَ اَنَا آتِيْهِ فِيْهِ

"Why did you not leave this old person at home so that I would have gone personally to meet him?"

Hadhrat Abu Bakr رضى الله عنه replied:

يَا رَسُوْلَ اللهِ هُوَ اَحَقُّ اَنْ يَّمْشِىَ اِلَيْكَ مِنْ اَنْ تَمْشِىَ اِلَيْهِ اَنْتَ

"O Messenger of Allah! It is more proper that he comes to you than your going to him."

Rasulullah ﷺ then passed his blessed hand on the chest of Abu Quhaafah and made him read the kalimah. Due to his old age, all his hair was white. When Abu Quhaafah accepted Islam, Rasulullah ﷺ congratulated Hadhrat Abu Bakr رضى الله عنه. Hadhrat Abu Bakr رضى الله عنه replied: "O Nabi of Allah! I take an oath in the name of that Being who sent you with the truth, that had Abu Taalib accepted Islam, I would have been more pleased."

Small armies are sent to destroy idols

After the conquest of Makkah, Rasulullah ﷺ remained in the city for about 15 days. The idols that were in the Ka'bah Shareef were destroyed and this announcement was made: "Whoever believes in Allah and the last day should not have any idol in his house." When Makkah Mukarramah was cleaned of all idols and they were all destroyed, small groups were sent to the surrounding areas to destroy all the other idols. On the 25 Ramadhaan

8 A.H. Khaalid ibnul Waleed رضي الله عنه was sent with a group of 30 riders to Nakhlah to destroy the idol by the name of Uzza. This place was one nights' journey from Makkah. 'Amr ibn 'Aas رضي الله عنه was sent to destroy the idol named Suwa' which was about three miles from Makkah. When 'Amr رضي الله عنه reached that place, the guardian of this idol asked him the reason for which he had come. He replied: "I am following the orders of Rasulullah ﷺ to destroy this idol." On hearing this, the guardian said: "You will never be able to do this. The god of Suwa' will personally stop you from doing this." 'Amr رضي الله عنه replied: "How sad that you are still holding on to such useless beliefs. Can this idol hear and see that it will be able to stop me?" After saying this, he struck it with one blow and broke it to pieces. He then spoke to the guardian saying: "Did you see what happened?" After seeing this, the guardian immediately accepted Islam.

CHAPTER 23
BATTLE OF HUNAYN

Hunayn is the name of a place between Makkah and Taa'if where the Hawaazin and Saqeef tribes lived. These tribes loved war and were very good archers. After the conquest of Makkah, they thought that Rasulullah ﷺ might attack them. They therefore decided to attack the Muslims before they could attack them. Their leader, Maalik ibn Auf left with an army of 20 000 in order to attack the Muslims.

Maalik ibn 'Auf commanded all the soldiers that each one should bring his wife and children with, so that he would fight with passion and no one would leave his wife and children behind and run from the battlefield. When they reached the valley of Autaas, Darid who was an old wise man asked, "What place is this? The people replied that it was the valley of Autaas. Darid replied that this place was very good for battle. The ground is neither too hard, nor too soft whereby the feet would sink in. He then asked:

مَالِيْ أَسْمَعُ رُغَاءَ الْبَعِيْرِ وَنُهَاقَ الْحَمِيْرِ وَبُكَاءَ الصَّغِيْرِ وَثَغَارَ الشَّاءِ

"What is this that I hear the sounds of the camels, the braying of donkies, the crying of children and the bleating of sheep?"

The people replied that Maalik ibn 'Auf had instructed them to bring their wives, children, animals, etc. so that the people would not run away from the battlefield. On hearing this, Darid said: "This is a serious mistake. Do those who are defeated ever take back anything? Nothing but spears and swords are of use in battle. If you are defeated, it would be a cause of disgrace for all your families. It would be better to keep all the families behind the actual army. If we are victorious, we would all meet again. If we are defeated, our families will be safe from the attacks of the enemy."

However, due to his youth, Maalik ibn 'Auf did not accept this advice. Instead, he said: "I swear by Allah that I will not change my decision. This person has lost his mind due to old age. If the Hawaazin and Saqeef follow my decision, well and good. If not, I will commit suicide (kill myself) right now." All the people replied that they were with him.

When Rasulullah ﷺ heard of this army, he sent 'Abdullah ibn Abi Hadr to find out about them. 'Abdullah learnt all the conditions from a distance and returned to inform Rasulullah ﷺ of all their preparations. After hearing all the facts, Rasulullah ﷺ also made preparations for war. He borrowed 100 coats of armour from Safwaan ibn Umayyah.

Rasulullah ﷺ left Makkah on the 8th of Shawwaal 8 A.H. with 12 000 men and headed towards Hunayn. 10 000 were those loyal followers who joined him from Madinah. Some non Muslims also joined him.

When this fully equipped army of 12 000 moved towards Hunayn, a person exclaimed:

$$\text{لَنْ نُغْلَبَ الْيَوْمَ مِنْ قِلَّةٍ}$$

"Today we will not be defeated because of small numbers."

This sentence, which was filled with pride, was disliked by Allah Ta'ala. In this world usually a big army defeats a small army. Therefore, on seeing their large number, some Sahaabah ﵁ made this statement that they will not be defeated because of small numbers. In other words, if they are defeated on this occasion, it will not be because of small numbers. Rather it will be through the decision of Allah Ta'ala. Victory and help is from Him alone. However, Allah Ta'ala did not like this statement of theirs. Instead of victory, they first had to taste defeat. Allah Ta'ala says in the Qur-aan Shareef:

Chapter Twenty Three – The Battle of Hunayn

> "And on the day of Hunayn when you were proud of your large numbers, but they were of no help to you. The earth closed in upon you despite its vastness. You then turned about retreating (going back). Allah then sent down His special type of comfort to His Rasool and to the believers, and He sent down armies which you did not see, and He punished the Kuffar. Such is the punishment of the rejecters."
>
> [Surah Taubah, verses 25-26]

The Muslim army reached the valley of Hunayn on Tuesday evening. The Hawaazin and Saqeef tribes were lying in ambush (hiding and waiting). Maalik ibn 'Auf had, at the beginning, ordered them to break the covers of their swords and that when the Muslim army comes close, the entire army of 20 000 should attack the Muslims all at once. When the Muslim army started to cross that area in the darkness of the morning, 20 000 swords suddenly attacked them. This completely broke up the Muslim army. Only 10-12 loyal companions remained next to Rasulullah ﷺ. Hadhrat Abu Bakr, 'Umar, Ali, 'Abbaas, Fadl ibn 'Abbaas, Usaamah ibn Zaid رضى الله عنهم and a few others remained at his side. 'Abbaas رضى الله عنه was holding onto the reins of Rasulullah's ﷺ donkey while Abu Sufyaan ibnul Haaris رضى الله عنه was holding onto the stirrup.

Shaybah ibn 'Usmaan ibn Abi Talhah said: "Today I will take revenge for my father from Muhammad." His father was killed in the battle of Uhud. When he came towards Rasulullah ﷺ, he immediately fell unconscious and was unable to reach him. He realised that he was prevented by Allah from reaching Rasulullah ﷺ. He accepted Islam later on.

In short, when the Hawaazin and Saqeef tribes attacked from their places of hiding and began shooting arrows on the Muslims from all sides, the Muslims ran in all directions. Only the special companions of Rasulullah ﷺ remained with him. Rasulullah ﷺ announced three times: "O people! Come towards me. I am the Nabi of Allah. I am Muhammad ibn 'Abdul Muttalib."

$$\text{أَنَا النَّبِيُّ لَا كَذِبَ ۚ أَنَا ابْنُ عَبْدِ الْمُطَّلِبِ}$$

I am the true Prophet. (The promises of help, victory, my protection and defence that have been made to me are certainly true. There is no possibility of going back.) I am the son of 'Abdul Muttalib.

'Abbaas رضي الله عنه had a very loud voice. Rasulullah ﷺ ordered him to call out to the Muhaajireen and the Ansaar. He announced:

$$\text{يَا مَعْشَرَ الْأَنْصَارِ يَا أَصْحَابَ السَّمُرَةِ}$$

"O group of Ansaar! O those who had promised to obey beneath the acacia tree."

As soon as they heard this call, they all turned and rushed towards Rasulullah ﷺ and within a few minutes they all gathered around him. Rasulullah ﷺ ordered them to attack the Kuffaar. When the heavy battle started, Rasulullah ﷺ took a handful of soil and threw it towards the Kuffaar and said:

$$\text{شَاهَتِ الْوُجُوهُ}$$

"May these faces be disfigured."

Thereafter he said:

"By the oath of the Rabb of Muhammad, they are defeated."

There was no one to whom a grain of this soil did not reach. Within a moment, the enemy weakened. Many ran away from the battlefield and many were caught.

On the one hand, Rasulullah ﷺ threw the handful of soil while on the other hand, the brave soldiers of Islam placed their trust only on the help of Allah Ta'ala and attacked the enemy. Within a few moments the situation changed. Despite their strength and power, the soldiers of the

Hawaazin could no longer stand firm and fight. As a result, the Muslims began capturing them. Seventy of them were killed and many others were caught. A huge amount of booty came into Muslim hands.

Jubair ibn Mut'im ﷺ says: "Even before the defeat of the Hawaazin, I saw a black sheet coming down from the sky and falling beween us and the enemies. Black ants immediately came out from that sheet and spread throughout the valley. I had no doubt that they were angels. Soon thereafter, the enemy was defeated.

CHAPTER 24
BATTLE OF TABUK

The Christian Arabs had written to Heraclius, the king of Rome, that Muhammad (ﷺ) passed away and that the people were dying because of the drought that they were experiencing. It was therefore a very good time to attack the Muslims. Heraclius immediately began preparations. A fully equipped army of 40 000 was prepared.

The traders of Syria came often to Madinah Shareef to sell olive oil. Rasulullah ﷺ learnt from them about this army and that the front of the army had already reached Balqa', and that Heraclius had already paid the whole year's wage to the soldiers.

After hearing all of this, Rasulullah ﷺ instructed that preparations should be made immediately so that they could reach the border of the enemy lines and fight them. The border was Tabuk. The far journey, the hot weather, the drought, the poverty and the few things that they had, were such, that on hearing this order to prepare for Jihaad, the hypocrites who claimed to be Muslims, feared that they will now be exposed. In order to save themselves, they began saying among themselves and to others as well:

"Do not go out in such heat."

On the other hand, the sincere Muslims immediately followed the orders of Rasulullah ﷺ and began their preparations. Hadhrat Abu Bakr ؓ was the first person to bring all his wealth and place it before

Rasulullah ﷺ. The wealth that he brought amounted to 4000 Dirhams. Rasulullah ﷺ asked him: "Did you leave anything behind for your family?" He replied: "I left Allah and His Rasool for them." 'Hadhrat Umar رضي الله عنه brought half of his wealth. 'Hadhrat Abdur Rahmaan ibn 'Auf رضي الله عنه presented 200 ounces of silver. 'Hadhrat Aasim ibn 'Adiyy رضي الله عنه presented 70 loads of dates.

'Hadhrat Usmaan رضي الله عنه presented 300 loaded camels and 1000 Dinars. After seeing all this, Rasulullah ﷺ became very pleased with him. He continued passing his hands through the coins saying: "After this great deed, no deed can harm 'Usmaan. O Allah! I am pleased with 'Usmaan. You also be pleased with him."

Most of the Sahaabah رضي الله عنهم offered their help according to what they could afford. Despite all this, the riding animals and the provisions for the journey were not enough. A few Sahaabah رضي الله عنهم came to Rasulullah ﷺ and said to him: "O Nabi of Allah! We are totally helpless. If some arrangements for riding animals could be made, we will also be able to join you for this jihaad." Rasulullah ﷺ replied: "I have no riding animals with me." On hearing this, they went back crying.

When the Sahaabah رضي الله عنهم were ready to leave, Rasulullah ﷺ left Muhammad ibn Maslamah رضي الله عنه in charge and made him the governor of Madinah. He also left Hadhrat Ali رضي الله عنه behind in order to see to his family and take care of them. Hadhrat Ali رضي الله عنه said to Rasulullah ﷺ: "O Nabi of Allah! You are leaving me with the women and children!" Rasulullah ﷺ replied: "Are you not pleased that you are to me just as Haroon عليه السلام was to Musa عليه السلام? However, there is no Prophet after me."

Rasulullah ﷺ left from Madinah with an army of 30 000 in which there were 10 000 horses.

On the way, they had to pass that place in which the punishment of Allah Ta'ala had come to the people of Samud. When passing this place, Rasulullah ﷺ was worried so much, that he covered his face and made his camel move faster. He ordered the Sahaabah رضي الله عنهم that no one should go to this place of wrongdoers. No one should drink water from there and no one should perform wudhu with the water of that place. They should quickly pass by that place crying out to Allah Ta'ala. He ordered that those who had mistakenly taken water from there or used that water in their flour should throw that water away and feed that flour to their camels.

About a day or so before reaching Tabuk, Rasulullah ﷺ informed the Sahaabah رضي الله عنهم that they would reach the spring of Tabuk by mid-morning the following day. No person should use any water from that spring. When they reached that spring, water was dripping from it, drop by drop. After much effort, they were able to gather a container of water. Rasulullah ﷺ washed his hands and face with that water and then returned the water to the spring. Immedieately thereafter it began gushing with water. The whole army used as much as they needed. Rasulullah ﷺ told Mu'aaz ibn Jabal رضي الله عنه: "If you remain alive, you will see this land green and lush with orchards." This fountain is gushing forth till today and you can hear the gushing of the water from quite a distance. Rasulullah ﷺ remained in Tabuk for twenty days but no one came to wage war against him.

When Rasulullah ﷺ was returning to Madinah Munawwarah, his beloved followers who were waiting to see his blessed face came out to welcome him. Out of their extreme love for him, even the women came outside.

When Rasulullah ﷺ set his eyes on the houses of Madinah, he said: هذه طابة this is Taabah (another name for Madinah). When he set his eyes on Mt. Uhud, he said: "This mountain loves us and we love it." Rasulullah ﷺ entered Madinah Munawwarah towards the end of Sha'baan or the beginning of Ramadhaan. He first went to the Masjid-e-Nabawi and read Salaah. After the Salaah, he remained seated in order to meet the people. He then went to his house to rest. This was the last battle in which Rasulullah ﷺ personally took part.

Those who remained behind for the battle of Tabuk

When Rasulullah ﷺ left for Tabuk, the sincere and loyal Muslims joined him. A group of hypocrites did not join him. A few sincere Muslims also remained behind. They did not do so out of hypocrisy but because of some excuse.

Imaam Bukhaari (rahmatullahi alayh) gives the story of Hadhrat Ka'b ibn Maalik رضي الله عنه as follows. Ka'b رضي الله عنه says, "Rasulullah ﷺ left whilst I was still preparing for the journey. I thought to myself that once I have all my goods ready, I will leave in a day or two and catch up with Rasulullah ﷺ. I delayed whilst the Sahaabah رضي الله عنهم had covered quite a distance. No one remained in Madinah except a few hypocrites and a few people who were excused (due to valid reasons). When I used to look at this, I would feel saddened. When Rasulullah ﷺ returned from Tabuk, the hypocrites went and gave their false excuses to him. Rasulullah ﷺ accepted their excuses outwardly and left the condition of their hearts to Allah Ta'ala.

Ka'b ibn Maalik رضي الله عنه says: I will never speak lies to Rasulullah ﷺ. Therefore, when Rasulullah ﷺ returned, I came to him and greeted him. He turned away from me. I said: 'O Nabi of Allah! Why are you turning away from me? I take an oath by Allah that I am not a hypocrite, I am not in any doubt, nor have I turned away from Islam.' He asked: 'Why did you remain behind?' I replied: 'O Nabi of Allah! If I was sitting before some worldly leader, I could have made up some story and saved myself from his anger. However, you are the Rasool of Allah. Even if I were to lie to you, Allah Ta'ala will inform you of it. But if I speak the truth to you, you will become angry, however, I hope that Allah Ta'ala will forgive me by His grace. Really, I have no excuse. I am at fault.' Rasulullah ﷺ

said: 'This person has spoken the truth. You may wait until Allah Ta'ala decides about you.' Muraarah ibn Rabi' رضي الله عنه and Hilaal ibn Umayyah رضي الله عنه also went to Rasulullah ﷺ and admitted their mistakes. Rasulullah ﷺ ordered that no one should speak to them for 50 days.

As a result, everyone stopped speaking to us. Our friends, relatives and close ones all seemed like strangers to us. My two friends (Muraarah and Hilaal) remained in their homes because of weakness and spent their days and nights crying. On the other hand, I was young. I used to attend the Fardh Salaah. Fifty days passed in these difficult conditions. This continued so much that this earth seemed to close up on us. My greatest worry was that if I were to pass away during this period, Rasulullah ﷺ and the Muslims would not even read the Janaazah Salaah for me. After fifty days, I heard this announcement from Mt. Sila': 'O Ka'b! Good news.'

As soon as I heard this announcement, I fell into sajdah and realised that the difficulty is now over. Rasulullah ﷺ had announced that our tawbah had been accepted. People came from all directions to congratulate me and my two friends. The people were saying to me: 'May Allah's acceptance of your tawbah be blessed.' When the person who gave the good news came to me, I immediately removed my kurta and gave it to him. I then came to Rasulullah ﷺ. He was sitting in the Masjid. The moment I stepped into the Masjid, Hadhrat Talhah ibn 'Ubaydillah رضي الله عنه came running towards me, hugged me and congratulated me. No one else stood up. By Allah, I will never forget this act of Talhah. Rasulullah's ﷺ face was shining like the full moon. I greeted him and he said: 'Be happy because today is the best day that you will experience ever since your mother gave birth to you.' Without doubt, the day on which Ka'b ibn Maalik رضي الله عنه accepted Islam was the best day in his life. However, this day was even better because it was on this day that Allah Ta'ala accepted his tawbah. It was this acceptance that confirmed his Imaan and his sincerity forever.

I said to Rasulullah ﷺ: 'O Nabi of Allah! I intend giving all my wealth in charity out of thanks for the acceptance of my tawbah.' He said: 'Don't give all, keep some for yourself.' I kept the share which I received from Khaybar and gave the rest in charity. I said to Rasulullah ﷺ: 'O Nabi of Allah! It is only because of my truth that Allah Ta'ala saved me. In order to perfect my taubah, I will speak nothing but the truth for as long as I live.'"

CHAPTER 25
HAJJATUL WADAA
(THE FAREWELL HAJ)

The help of Allah Ta'ala came to the Muslims and Makkah Mukarramah was conquered. People accepted Islam in large numbers. The main power of kufr and shirk was broken. Groups and tribes from far and wide came to Rasulullah ﷺ, made tawbah from their kufr and believed in the oneness of Allah Ta'ala and the prophet-hood of Rasulullah ﷺ with ikhlaas and sincerity. The responsibilities of prophethood were carried out and the laws of Islam were taught. Rasulullah ﷺ sent Hadhrat Abu Bakr رضي الله عنه to Makkah Mukarramah in 9 A.H. in order to completely wipe out all the effects of jaahiliyyah (ignorance).

The time now came for Rasulullah ﷺ to personally perform the Haj so that the people may know forever how the Haj is to be performed, according to the method of Hadhrat Ibraaheem (alayhis salaam) and Hadhrat Ismaa'eel (alayhis salaam). Haj, from beginning to end, is about the oneness of Allah Ta'ala. There were no words of shirk and customs of the days of ignorance (jaahiliyyah). Rasulullah ﷺ used to read often the talbiyah (labbaik) so that no effects of shirk whatsoever would remain. The talbiyah that he used to recite was:

لَبَّيْكَ اَللّٰهُمَّ لَبَّيْكَ لَبَّيْكَ لَا شَرِيْكَ لَكَ لَبَّيْكَ إِنَّ الْحَمْدَ وَالنِّعْمَةَ لَكَ وَالْمُلْكُ لَا شَرِيْكَ لَكَ

"Here I am, O Allah! Here I am. You have no partner. Here I am. All praise, bounty and kingdom belongs to You. You have no partner."

Haj was made fard in 9 A.H. In that year, Rasulullah ﷺ chose Hadhrat Abu Bakr رضي الله عنه as the Ameer of the Haj and sent him to Makkah Mukarramah. The Muslims performed the Haj in that year under Abu Bakr رضي الله عنه. In Zul Qa'dah 10 A.H. Rasulullah ﷺ made an intention of personally performing the Haj. An announcement was made in the surrounding areas that Rasulullah ﷺ is going to perform Haj that year. Rasulullah ﷺ left Madinah Munawwarah on 25 Zul Qa'dah 10 A.H. on a Saturday, between the Zuhr and Asr Salaah. The Muhaajireen, the Ansaar and many other loyal Muslims joined him. It was a group of 90 000 to 114 000 or even more. Rasulullah ﷺ entered Makkah Mukarramah on the 4 Zul Hijjah on a Sunday.

Nine of Rasulullah's ﷺ wives, plus his daughter, Hadhrat Faatimah رضي الله عنها, joined him. Many other close family and friends were with him. Hadhrat Ali رضي الله عنه, whom Rasulullah ﷺ had sent in the month of Ramadhaan to Yemen, met him in Makkah Mukarramah. Rasulullah ﷺ performed the actions of Haj and gave a long bayaan at 'Arafaat. He first praised Allah Ta'ala and then said:

The Farewell Sermon (bayaan)

"O people! Listen carefully to what I have to say. It is possible that I will not meet you next year. O people! Your lives, your honour and your wealth are all holy just as this day, this month, and this city are all holy. All the things of jaahiliyyah (ignorance) are crushed beneath my feet. All the claims for murder from the days of ignorance are forgiven. I first of all forgive the Banu Huzayl for the murder of Rabi'ah ibn Haaris ibn 'Abdil Muttalib. The interest of Jaahiliyat (the time of ignorance) is cancelled. You may only keep the original wealth. I first of all cancel the interest of 'Abbaas ibn 'Abdul Muttalib."

Rasulullah ﷺ then explained the rights of the husband and the wife.

"I am leaving behind such a strong thing, that if you hold on to it, you will never go astray (off): The Book of Allah and the Sunnah of the Rasul of Allah. On the day of Qiyaamah you will be asked about me. What reply will you give?" The Sahaabah رضى الله عنهم replied: "We will confirm that you passed on Allah's message to us, that you handed over the trust of Allah and that you wished well for the Ummah." Rasulullah ﷺ pointed his index finger to the sky and said three times:

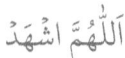

"O Allah, You be witness to this."

When Rasulullah ﷺ completed his talk, Hadhrat Bilal رضى الله عنه called out the Azaan for the Zuhr Salaah. Rasulullah ﷺ then remained busy in the zikr of Allah Ta'ala. While he was busy in this, the following aayat was revealed:

$$\text{اَلْيَوْمَ اَكْمَلْتُ لَكُمْ دِينَكُمْ وَاَتْمَمْتُ عَلَيْكُمْ نِعْمَتِيْ وَرَضِيْتُ لَكُمُ الْاِسْلَامَ دِيْنًا}$$

"Today have I perfected for you your deen and completed My favour on you, and I chose Islam as a religion for you." [Surah Maa'idah, verse 3]

When he reached Mina on the 10th of Zul Hijjah, Rasulullah ﷺ slaughtered 63 camels (as his age was 63) with his own hands. Hadhrat Ali رضى الله عنه slaughtered another 37 camels for him. Rasulullah ﷺ gave a similar bayaan in Mina like the one he gave in 'Arafaat. He eventually made the farewell Tawaaf. When he shaved his head in Mina, he distributed his blessed hair among the Sahaabah رضى الله عنهم so that they may keep it as barakah (blessings).

CHAPTER 26
PREPARATION FOR THE JOURNEY TO THE AAKHIRAT

After his return from the Farewell Haj, Rasulullah ﷺ began preparations for his journey to the Aakhirat. He was always busy in the zikr of Allah Ta'ala. The first sign of the closeness of his death was the coming down of the following Surah:

اِذَا جَآءَ نَصْرُ اللهِ وَ الْفَتْحُ ۞ وَ رَاَيْتَ النَّاسَ يَدْخُلُوْنَ فِيْ دِيْنِ اللهِ اَفْوَاجًا ۞
فَسَبِّحْ بِحَمْدِ رَبِّكَ وَ اسْتَغْفِرْهُ ۚ اِنَّهٗ كَانَ تَوَّابًا ۞

"When the help of Allah and victory came, and you see people entering the deen of Allah in large numbers, then glorify the praises of your Rabb and seek His forgiveness, surely He is forgiving."

In other words, when the help and victory which Allah had promised have come, when kufr and shirk have been smashed, when the flag of Tauheed has been raised, when the truth has crushed falsehood, when people have entered the true deen in groups, when the world has received the message of Allah, and when the deen of Allah has been completed and perfected then the reason for sending you to this world has been completed, and the responsibility that was given to you has been fulfilled. You should now prepare to return to Us. The job for which Allah Ta'ala sent you to this world has been completed. You should now prepare to return to that Being who sent you into this world. This short world is not for you to remain in. It is better for you to join the company of Allah Ta'ala

Rasulullah ﷺ would therefore read the following all the time:

$$\text{سُبْحَانَكَ اللّٰهُمَّ وَبِحَمْدِكَ اَسْتَغْفِرُكَ وَأَتُوْبُ إِلَيْكَ}$$

"Glory to You O Allah, and praise to You. I seek Your forgiveness and I turn to You in repentance."

Once Rasulullah ﷺ said to Hadhrat Faatimah ﷺ: "Jibraa'eel عَلَيْهِ السَّلَام used to come to me every Ramadhaan and complete one khatam of the Qur-aan Shareef with me. This year he came and made two khatams. I think that my time for leaving is very close." Rasulullah ﷺ used to remain in the Masjid in the month of Ramadhaan for 10 days every year. This year, he stayed for 20 days. When the aayat: "Today have I perfected your religion for you..." was revealed to Rasulullah ﷺ during the Farewell Haj, he understood the importance of it. In his bayaan during the Farewell Haj, he said to the people: "It is possible that I will not meet you next year and I may not be able to perform the Haj with you again." He also said: "I am a human, and no human has ever lived forever. It is possible that the messenger (angel) of my Rabb will soon come to take me." After returning from the Farewell Haj, he went to Jannatul Baqi (the graveyard of Madinah) and, after a period of eight years, he read the Janaazah Salaah for those who were made shaheed at Uhud and he made dua for them. This is what a person normally does when he is saying farewell. He then went into the Masjid, climbed the mimbar and gave a talk. He said: "I am going before you, so that I may prepare for you at the Haud-e-Kauthar. Our meeting place will be at the Haud-e-Kauthar. I can see it now from where I am standing. I have been given the keys to the treasures of this world. I do not have this fear that you will all go into shirk." In other words, I do not have this fear that the entire ummah will fall into shirk as was the case with previous nations. "However, I fear that you will become greedy for this world, compete with each other to get it, fight with each other for it, and finally be destroyed because of it."

Rasulullah ﷺ falls ill

In one of the last 10 nights of Safar, Rasulullah ﷺ woke up, got his slave up and said to him: "I have been ordered to ask for forgiveness for the people of Jannatul Baqi." When Rasulullah ﷺ returned from there, he suddenly fell ill and complained of a headache and flu. Rasulullah ﷺ remained ill for 13-14 days. The last week of his life was spent under the care of Hadhrat Aa'ishah رضي الله عنها.

When Jibraa'eel عليه السلام came to Rasulullah ﷺ with Surah Nasr, he said to him: "O Jibraa'eel! This Surah gives me the news of my death." Jibraa'eel عليه السلام said: "The aakhirat is far better for you than this world."

Hadhrat Aa'ishah رضي الله عنها says: "During this illness, Rasulullah ﷺ used to say that this illness was because of the poison that he had at Khaybar." It was his habit that whenever he fell ill, he would recite the following Surahs: Surah Ikhlaas, Surah Falaq, Surah Naas, and then blow onto himself and pass his hands across his whole body. Hadhrat Aa'ishah رضي الله عنها says: "During his final illness, I used to recite these Surahs and blow on him. However, I would pass my hands over his body as a source of blessing for me."

Hadhrat Faatimah رضي الله عنها Cries and Smiles

During this illness, Rasulullah ﷺ called for Hadhrat Faatimah رضي الله عنها and whispered something into her ears. She began crying. Rasulullah ﷺ again said something in her ears and she began smiling. Hadhrat Aa'ishah رضي الله عنها says: "After Rasulullah ﷺ passed away, we asked her about this." She said: "Rasulullah ﷺ said to me that Jibraa'eel عليه السلام used to recite the whole Qur-aan once every Ramadhaan, but this year he read it twice to him. He feels that he is going to pass away this year. I therefore began crying. He then said to me that from his family, I will be the first to join him. On hearing this, I smiled." Hadhrat Faatimah رضي الله عنها passed away six months after Rasulullah صلى الله عليه وسلم.

Rasulullah صلى الله عليه وسلم said to her: "You will be the leader of all the women in Jannah."

Hadhrat Aa'ishah رضي الله عنها says: "When Rasulullah صلى الله عليه وسلم returned from Jannatul Baqi', I had a headache. Because of the pain, I cried out: 'O my head!' When Rasulullah صلى الله عليه وسلم heard this, he also cried out: 'O my head! It is possible that I will pass away in this way.'" Rasulullah صلى الله عليه وسلم rested till the time of Zuhr Salaah. When he felt a bit better and the illness decreased, he asked for seven containers of water to be poured on his head and said: "Perhaps I will be more comfortable and I may give some advice to the people." This water was poured on him and he felt much more comfortable. He then took support from Hadhrat Abbaas رضي الله عنه and Hadhrat Ali رضي الله عنه on either side of him and went to the Masjid. He performed the Zuhr Salaah and then gave a talk. This was his final bayaan.

Rasulullah's صلى الله عليه وسلم Final Talk

After completing the Salaah, Rasulullah صلى الله عليه وسلم went onto the mimbar, and after praising Allah Ta'ala, he spoke about the martyrs (shuhada) of Uhud. He asked for forgiveness for them. He then spoke to the Muhaajireen saying: "You will be more while the Ansaar will be less. Look, the Ansaar gave me protection. You must be kind to those who are good from them and you must forgive those who make mistakes from them."

He then said: "O people! Allah has given a servant of His a choice between enjoying the things of this world or enjoying the gifts of the aakhirat that are with Allah. That servant has chosen to enjoy the gifts that are with Allah Ta'ala in the aakhirat." Hadhrat Abu Bakr رضي الله عنه who was the most knowledgeable from the Sahaabah رضي الله عنهم immediately understood that the servant was none other than Rasulullah ﷺ himself. He therefore began crying and said: "O Nabi of Allah! May my parents be sacrificed for you." Rasulullah ﷺ said: "Wait and be strong." He then turned towards the Masjid and asked the people to close up all the doors of the Masjid, and that only one door, the door of Abu Bakr رضي الله عنه, be left open. He then said: "With regards to his life, wealth and friendship, Abu Bakr is the one who was most kind towards me. There isn't anyone who was more kind to me than him. I repaid all those who did favours to me, except for Abu Bakr. The reward for his favours will be given by Allah Ta'ala himself on the day of Qiyaamah. If I had to make someone besides Allah Ta'ala as my best friend, I would have chosen Abu Bakr. However, he enjoys Islamic brotherhood and friendship. There is no one equal to him in this brotherhood and friendship."

In short, Rasulullah ﷺ spoke about the good qualities of Hadhrat Abu Bakr رضي الله عنه which were not shared by anyone else. He did this so that these qualities may be well known to the people and that there may be no difference of opinion about him being the khalifa after him. In order to confirm this, Rasulullah ﷺ chose him to be the imam of all the Salaahs. It was for this reason that at the time of giving Abu Bakr رضي الله عنه the promise of obeying, the Sahaabah رضي الله عنهم said: "If Rasulullah ﷺ chose him for our Deen (Imaam in Salaah) why should we not choose him for our dunya (Khilaafat and leadership)?"

In this talk, Rasulullah ﷺ also asked that the army of Usaamah رضي الله عنه be sent out quickly. He also said: "I know that some people (the hypocrites) are not happy with Usaamah as the leader (for this army) because of his young age, whereas there are so many other senior people present? Listen! Even before this, there were people who were not happy with his father's (Zaid's) leadership. By Allah! His father was qualified and so is his son. Besides, he is extremely beloved to me."

Rasulullah ﷺ then said: "Allah's curse was on the Jews and the Christians who made the graves of their Prophets into places of sajdah."

Rasulullah ﷺ wanted to warn the ummah from making his grave into a place of sajdah.

Rasulullah ﷺ said: "O people! The news has reached me that you are afraid of your Nabi passing away. Has any Nabi before me remained forever with his people that I should now remain forever with you? Allah Ta'ala says:

$$\text{وَمَا جَعَلْنَا لِبَشَرٍ مِّنْ قَبْلِكَ الْخُلْدَ}$$

"We did not allow any human before you to remain forever."

$$\text{وَمَا مُحَمَّدٌ اِلَّا رَسُوْلٌ ۚ قَدْ خَلَتْ مِنْ قَبْلِهِ الرُّسُلُ}$$

"Muhammad is only a Rasool. Prophets before him also passed away."

"Listen! I have to meet Allah and you also have to meet Allah. I advise all the Muslims to treat the early Muhaajireen with kindness, and I advise the early Muhaajireen to remain with the fear of Allah and good deeds. Allah Ta'ala says:

$$\text{وَالْعَصْرِ ۙ اِنَّ الْاِنْسَانَ لَفِيْ خُسْرٍ ۙ اِلَّا الَّذِيْنَ اٰمَنُوْا وَعَمِلُوا الصّٰلِحٰتِ وَتَوَاصَوْا بِالْحَقِّ ۙ وَتَوَاصَوْا بِالصَّبْرِ}$$

"By the qasam of time, man is certainly in loss; except those who have Imaan and did good deeds. And they advise each other with the truth and they advise each other with patience."

"O Muslims! I advise you to treat the Ansaar well and with kindness. They are the ones who protected Islam and Imaan. They made you partners in their homes, lands, orchards and fruits. They chose you over themselves although they them selves were very poor. Allah Ta'ala says about them:

$$\text{وَيُؤْثِرُونَ عَلَىٰ أَنفُسِهِمْ وَلَوْ كَانَ بِهِمْ خَصَاصَةٌ}$$

"They choose (others) over themselves even though they themselves are in a very poor condition."

"Listen! I am leaving before you. You will also meet me. Our meeting place will be Haud-e-Kausar."

Rasulullah ﷺ then got off the mimbar and went to his room.

Rasulullah's ﷺ last Salaah with Jamaat

As long as he had the strength, Rasulullah ﷺ would come to the Masjid for Salaah and continue leading the Sahaabah ؓ in Salaah. The last Salaah which he led was the Maghrib Salaah of Thursday. He passed away four days later on a Monday. When the time for the Isha Salaah came, he asked whether the people had performed their Salaah. The reply was given to him that the people were waiting for him. He tried getting up a few times but his illness would cause him to faint. He eventually said: "Instruct Abu Bakr to lead the Salaah on my behalf." Hadhrat Abu Bakr ؓ began leading the people in Salaah.

On Saturday or Sunday when he felt a little better, Rasulullah ﷺ took the support of 'Abbaas ؓ and Ali ؓ and entered the Masjid. Hadhrat Abu Bakr ؓ was leading the Zuhr Salaah at that time. Rasulullah ﷺ sat down to the right of Hadhrat Abu Bakr ؓ and led the people for the remainder of the Salaah. Rasulullah ﷺ was now the Imaam and Hadhrat Abu Bakr ؓ began following him. The remainder of the people completed their Salaah by following the Takbeers of Abu Bakr ؓ.

This Zuhr Salaah was the last Salaah which Rasulullah ﷺ led. After this, he did not come to the Masjid at all.

The day of Rasulullah's ﷺ passing away

It was a Monday when Rasulullah ﷺ left this short world for the aakhirat and met with Allah Ta'ala. On the morning of this Monday he lifted the curtain of his room and saw the Sahaabah standing in lines and reading their Fajr Salaah. On seeing the Sahaabah رضى الله عنهم, he smiled.

Hadhrat Abu Bakr رضى الله عنه wanted to go back (from the spot where he was leading the Salaah). Rasulullah ﷺ pointed to him to continue. Due to his weakness, Rasulullah ﷺ could not stand up fully. He lowered the curtain of his room and went back inside.

Rasulullah's ﷺ lifting the curtain and looking at the Sahaabah رضى الله عنهم was the last time that he came before them. It was the last chance of their seeing the beauty of Rasulullah ﷺ. A poet says:

$$\text{وَكُنْتُ أَرَى كَالْمَوْتِ مِنْ بَيْنِ سَاعَةٍ ۞ فَكَيْفَ بِبَيْنٍ كَانَ مَوْعِدَهُ الْحَشْرُ}$$

"I used to think that a single moment's separation (from him) was death. Now what can I say about this separation after which the next meeting will only be on the Day of Qiyaamah?!"

Rasulullah ﷺ in the pains of death

The people thought that Rasulullah's ﷺ health had improved and they therefore left. After a short while, he began experiencing the pains of death. He placed his head in the lap of Hadhrat Aa'ishah رضى الله عنها and lied down. Just then, her brother, Abdur Rahmaan رضى الله عنه came in with a miswaak in his hand. Rasulullah ﷺ began looking at him. Aa'ishah رضى الله عنها asked: "O Rasulullah! Should I get a miswaak for you?" Rasulullah ﷺ nodded in answer. She then asked: "Should I soften it for you?" He again nodded. She softened it by chewing on it and then gave it to him. Later on, Hadhrat Aa'ishah رضى الله عنها used to happily mention this great favour of Allah Ta'ala that He caused her saliva to mix with that of Rasulullah's ﷺ during his final hour, and that he passed away in her room, on her shoulder, when it was her turn.

The person who always uses the miswaak will automatically read the kalimah at the time of death, while this will not be the case of the one who uses opium (and other drugs).

A glass of water was kept at Rasulullah's ﷺ side. He would dip his hand in it and wipe his mubaarak face with it. While doing this, he would say: "There is none worthy of worship but Allah. Surely there are many pains at the time of death." He then looked at the ceiling, lifted his hands and said: "O Allah! I want to go to Ar-Rafiq ul-A'laa – the highest friend." This is the place which is the home of the Prophets and Ambiya.

Hadhrat Aa'ishah ﷺ says: "I had heard Rasulullah ﷺ saying many times that the life of a Rasool is not taken until he is shown his home in Jannah, and until he is given the choice to stay in this world or to leave it. When he said the above words, I immediately understood that he will not stay with us and that he has already chosen to be with Allah Ta'ala. When he said:

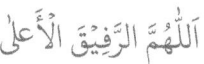

"O Allah! I wish to be in the highest friend."

His life had left this world towards the aakhirat and his hands (which had been raised) fell down.

"To Allah we belong and to Him is our return."

The confusion of the Sahaabah رَضِىَ اللّٰهُ عَنْهُمْ

As soon as the news of his death reached the Sahaabah رَضِىَ اللّٰهُ عَنْهُمْ, it was like Qiyaamat had begun. The moment they received this news, they lost their senses. The people of Madinah began to panic. Whoever heard the news began to panic. Hadhrat Usmaan رَضِىَ اللّٰهُ عَنْهُ was in a state of shock. He was sitting against a wall, and due to his extreme sadness, was unable to speak. Hadhrat Ali رَضِىَ اللّٰهُ عَنْهُ cried so much that he fell unconscious. The mountain of grief and pain that came to Hadhrat Aa'ishah رَضِىَ اللّٰهُ عَنْهَا and the other wives of Rasulullah ﷺ cannot even be described. Hadhrat Abbaas رَضِىَ اللّٰهُ عَنْهُ was also at a loss in this severe grief. Hadhrat Umar رَضِىَ اللّٰهُ عَنْهُ suffered the most grief. He took out his sword, stood up and announced in a loud voice: "The hypocrites think that Rasulullah ﷺ has passed away. He certainly has not passed away. Rather he is gone to his Rabb just as Hadhrat Musa (alayhis salaam) went to Allah Ta'ala on Mt. Sinai and then returned. By Allah, Rasulullah ﷺ will certainly come back and then completely defeat the hypocrites." Hadhrat Umar رَضِىَ اللّٰهُ عَنْهُ was in an emotional state, with his sword in his hand. No one had the courage to tell him that Rasulullah ﷺ had really passed away.

Hadhrat Abu Bakr رَضِىَ اللّٰهُ عَنْهُ was not around at the time when Rasulullah ﷺ had passed away. When he heard this terrible news, he immediately got onto his horse and came to Madinah. He got off at the entrance of Masjid-e-Nabawi and walked towards Rasulullah's ﷺ room very sadly. He asked Hadhrat Aa'ishah رَضِىَ اللّٰهُ عَنْهَا for permission and entered. Rasulullah ﷺ was on his bed with all his wives sitting around him. When Hadhrat Abu Bakr رَضِىَ اللّٰهُ عَنْهُ entered, all of them, except Hadhrat Aa'ishah رَضِىَ اللّٰهُ عَنْهَا, covered their faces. Hadhrat Abu Bakr رَضِىَ اللّٰهُ عَنْهُ removed the sheet from Rasulullah's ﷺ face, kissed his blessed forehead, and cried out saying:

وَا نَبِيَّاهُ وَاخَلِيلَاهُ وَا صَفِيَّاهُ

Chapter Twenty Six – Journey to the Aakhirat

"O the Nabi of Allah! O the friend of Allah! O the chosen one of Allah!"

Hadhrat Abu Bakr رَضِىَٰاللَّهُعَنْهُ said this three times.

He then said: "May my parents be sacrificed for you. By Allah, He will not cause you to die twice. The death that was written for you has come to you." After saying this, he came out of the room and saw that Hadhrat Umar رَضِىَٰاللَّهُعَنْهُ was very emotional. Hadhrat Abu Bakr رَضِىَٰاللَّهُعَنْهُ said: "Rasulullah صَلَّىٰاللَّهُعَلَيْهِوَسَلَّمَ has passed away. O 'Umar! Have you not heard these words of Allah Ta'ala:

$$\text{إِنَّكَ مَيِّتٌ وَإِنَّهُم مَّيِّتُونَ وَمَا جَعَلْنَا لِبَشَرٍ مِّن قَبْلِكَ الْخُلْدَ}$$

'You shall certainly die and they shall certainly die (as well). We did not allow any human to live forever since before.'"

The people then left Hadhrat Umar رَضِىَٰاللَّهُعَنْهُ and gathered around Hadhrat Abu Bakr رَضِىَٰاللَّهُعَنْهُ.

Hadhrat Abu Bakr's رَضِىَٰاللَّهُعَنْهُ bayaan

Hadhrat Abu Bakr رَضِىَٰاللَّهُعَنْهُ went towards the mimbar and announced in a loud voice that everyone should remain silent and be seated. When they were all seated, he praised Allah Ta'ala and then gave the following talk:

"Whoever from you had been worshipping Allah, then surely Allah is alive and does not die. Whoever from you had been worshipping Muhammad صَلَّىٰاللَّهُعَلَيْهِوَسَلَّمَ, then Muhammad صَلَّىٰاللَّهُعَلَيْهِوَسَلَّمَ has certainly passed away. Allah Ta'ala says: 'Muhammad is only a Rasool. Rasools before him passed away. If he dies or is killed, are you going to turn back on your heels? Whoever turns back on his heels will never harm Allah in any way. Allah shall certainly reward the grateful ones.' Allah Ta'ala had told Muhammad صَلَّىٰاللَّهُعَلَيْهِوَسَلَّمَ: 'You shall certainly die and they shall certainly die (as well).' Allah Ta'ala says: 'Everything is going to come to an end except Allah

Ta'ala. To Him belongs complete rule and it is to Him that you will be returned.' Allah Ta'ala says: 'Everything that is on earth is going to die. It is only the countenance of your Rabb, the owner of might and honour, that will remain.' Allah Ta'ala says: 'Everyone shall taste death. You shall receive your reward in full on the day of Qiyaamah.'

Surely Allah Ta'ala caused Muhammad ﷺ to live until such a time that he established the deen of Allah, clearly explained the laws of Allah, passed on the message of Allah, and went in the path of Allah. Allah Ta'ala then caused him to pass away in a way that he left you on a clear path. Now whoever goes off and is destroyed will do so after the truth had been made clear to him. He whose Rabb is Allah, let him know that Allah is alive and does not die. He who had been worshipping Muhammad ﷺ, let him know that his god has passed away. Fear Allah! O people, hold on firmly to your deen, and place your trust on your Rabb. Surely the deen of Allah shall remain and the promise of Allah will take place. Allah Ta'ala shall certainly help the one who helps Him, and He shall give honour to His deen. The Book of Allah is with us. It is a light and a cure. It was through this Book that Allah Ta'ala guided Muhammad ﷺ. It contains the halaal and haraam matters of Allah. By Allah, we are not worried about those who attack. The swords of Allah are ready; we have not put them down. We will make Jihaad against those who fight against us just as we had joined the Nabi of Allah ﷺ in Jihaad. The enemy should therefore beware and blame none but themselves."

As soon as Hadhrat Abu Bakr رضى الله عنه spoke these words, the Sahaabah رضى الله عنهم came out of their state of shock and confusion. They now realised that Rasulullah ﷺ had really passed away. It seemed as if they had never heard these aayaat of the Qur-aan Shareef before. They all began reading these aayaat.

It is also written that when Hadhrat Abu Bakr رضى الله عنه received the news of Rasulullah's ﷺ death, he immediately left his house at Sunh and left for Madinah. He came crying, gasping for breath and panting. He entered the room of Rasulullah ﷺ in that very condition while sending durood to Rasulullah ﷺ. Despite this grief and sadness, he was fully conscious and did not lose control in the least.

He opened the blessed face of Rasulullah ﷺ and kissed his forehead. He continued crying and saying: "May my parents be sacrificed for you. You remained pure both in life and in death. By your passing away, the chain of prophet-hood and wahi have both come to an end. Both of these never came to an end with the passing away of any other Prophet. You are beyond description and in no need of this crying. You are such that others can take comfort from your death. You benefited all of us so much that we all became equal before you. Were it not for the fact that your death was chosen by you (Allah had given you the choice to choose between this world and the hereafter) we would all have sacrificed our lives for your life. Were it not for the fact that you had stopped us from crying too much, we would have finished all the tears of our eyes. However, there are two things which we cannot remove and wipe out: (1) the sadness of being separated from you, (2) our bodies becoming thin because of our sadness. O Allah! Inform this condition of ours (to our Prophet). And O Muhammad ﷺ! Mention us by your Rabb. We hope that you will remember us."

"Had you not filled our hearts with peace by remaining in your company, we would never have been able to manage the loss of this separation."

Hadhrat Abu Bakr ؓ then left the room and spoke to the people.

ثُمَّ قَالَ أَيُّهَا النَّاسُ مَنْ كَانَ يَعْبُدُ مُحَمَّدًا فَإِنَّ مُحَمَّدًا قَدْ مَاتَ وَمَنْ كَانَ يَعْبُدُ اللّٰهَ فَإِنَّ اللّٰهَ حَىٌّ لَا يَمُوْتُ وَ اَنَّ اللّٰهَ قَدْ تَقَدَّمَ لَكُمْ فِىْ اَمْرِهٖ فَلَا تَدْعُوْهُ جَزَعًا وَاَنَّ اللّٰهَ تَبَارَكَ وَ تَعَالٰى قَدِ اخْتَارَ لِنَبِيِّهٖ عَلَيْهِ السَّلَامُ مَا عِنْدَهٗ عَلٰى مَا عِنْدَكُمْ وَقَبَضَهٗ اِلٰى ثَوَابِهٖ وَخَلَّفَ فِيْكُمْ كِتَابَهٗ وَسُنَّةَ نَبِيِّهٖ فَمَنْ اَخَذَبِهِمَا عَرَفَ وَمَنْ فَرَّقَ بَيْنَهُمَا اَنْكَرَ يَآ اَيُّهَا الَّذِيْنَ اٰمَنُوْا كُوْنُوْا قَوَّامِيْنَ بِالْقِسْطِ وَلَا يَشْغَلَنَّكُمُ الشَّيْطَانُ بِمَوْتِ نَبِيِّكُمْ وَلَا

$$\text{يَفْتِنَكُمْ عَنْ دِينِكُمْ وَعَاجِلُوا الشَّيْطَانَ بِالْخَيْرِ وَتُعْجِزُوهُ وَلَا تَسْتَنْظِرُوهُ فَيَلْحَقَ بِكُمْ وَيَفْتِنَكُمْ}$$

He then said: "O people! He who was worshipping Muhammad ﷺ should know that Muhammad ﷺ has passed away. He who was worshipping Allah should know that Allah is alive, He does not die. Allah Ta'ala had already informed about his (Muhammad's ﷺ) passing away. There is therefore no need to become very worried. Allah Ta'ala chose His Nabi ﷺ to be with Him than to be with you and He took him to His beautiful place. He left behind His Book and the Sunnah of His Nabi with you. He who follows both of them has truly recognised the truth. He who separates the two (e.g. by believing in one and not in the other) has not recognised the truth. O you who are believers! Bring about justice. Do not allow shaytaan to keep you busy with the death of your Nabi. Do not allow him to move you away from your deen. Rush towards good before shaytaan can mislead you. Destroy his efforts by rushing towards good. Do not give him any time to come to you and corrupt you."

The burial arrangements

The people began the burial arrangements. When they intended to do his ghusal, they became confused about whether to remove his clothes or not. Suddenly they heard an unseen voice saying that Rasulullah's ﷺ clothes should not be removed, and he should be given ghusal in his clothes. He was thus given ghusal with his clothes on and then they were removed (for the kafn).

Hadhrat Ali رضي الله عنه was doing the ghusal, 'Abbaas رضي الله عنه and his two sons, Fadl رضي الله عنه and Qasam رضي الله عنه, were changing the position of Rasulullah ﷺ, while Usaamah رضي الله عنه and Shuqraan رضي الله عنه were pouring the water.

After the ghusal, Rasulullah ﷺ was covered in three pieces of cloth which neither contained a kurta nor a turban. The clothes in which he was bathed were removed.

The people then began to wonder where he should be buried. Hadhrat Abu Bakr رضي الله عنه said: "I heard Rasulullah ﷺ saying that every Nabi is buried in the very place where he passes away."

Rasulullah's ﷺ bed was therefore moved from its spot and his grave was dug there. However, there was a difference with regard to the type of grave that should be dug. The Muhaajireen said that the type that is dug in Makkah should be dug, viz. a normal grave with a section on one side where the body is tucked in. The Ansaar said that the Madinah type of grave should be dug, viz. a normal grave with a trench at the center of the bottom of the grave. Abu 'Ubaydah رضي الله عنه was an expert in digging the makkah type of grave whilst Abu Talha was an expert in the trench type of grave. Both of them were called. It was decided that the one who reaches first will dig the type of grave that he is an expert at. Abu Talhah رضي الله عنه reached first and so a trench type of grave was dug.

The Janaazah Salaah

When they completed the burial arrangements on Monday, the blessed body of Rasulullah ﷺ was placed in front of his grave. Group after group would come into the room and read the Janaazah Salaah individually. No one was the Imaam for this Salaah. Each person came, read his Salaah and left.

The people asked Hadhrat Abu Bakr رضي الله عنه as to whether the Janaazah Salaah for Rasulullah ﷺ should be read. He replied that it should be read. They asked him the way. He said that one group at a time should go into the room, say the Takbeer (Allah is the greatest), and after sending Durood and reading the prescribed dua, he should return. Everyone should read the Salaah in this way.

Hadhrat Abu Bakr ﷺ and Hadhrat Umar ﷺ also entered the room of Rasulullah ﷺ with a group.

When Rasulullah ﷺ was on his death bed, he called his family members. They asked: "O Nabi of Allah! Who should perform your Janaazah Salaah?" He replied: "When you are over with my burial arrangements, you should all leave my room for a little while. Jibraa'eel (alayhis salaam) will be the first one to read the Janaazah Salaah. He will be followed by Mikaa'eel (alayhis salaam), Israafeel (alayhis salaam), Izraa'eel (the angel of death) and then the remaining angels. Thereafter, you should all come in groups and send durood to me."

Allah Ta'ala says the following with regard to Rasulullah ﷺ:

إِنَّ اللّٰهَ وَمَلٰٓئِكَتَهٗ يُصَلُّوْنَ عَلَى النَّبِيِّ ۚ يٰٓأَيُّهَا الَّذِيْنَ اٰمَنُوْا صَلُّوْا عَلَيْهِ وَسَلِّمُوْا تَسْلِيْمًا

"Surely Allah and His angels send greeting on the Nabi. O you who believe! Send greetings and peace on him."

This aayat commands each muslim to send his own Durood to him. Just as it was waajib to send Durood without any Imaam and without any jamaat when he was alive, so too, after his passing away, Durood is to be sent without any Imaam and without any jamaat.

30 000 people offered the Janaazah Salaah for Rasulullah ﷺ.

Burial

Hadhrat Ali ﷺ, Hadhrat Abbaas ﷺ and his two sons, Fadl ﷺ and Qasam ﷺ, lowered Rasulullah ﷺ into his grave. When they completed the burial, the grave was shaped in the shape of a camel's hump. Water was then sprinkled on it. After completing the burial, the Sahaabah

ﷺ returned to their homes, sad and heartbroken. They continued reading:

$$إِنَّا لِلَّهِ وَإِنَّا إِلَيْهِ رَاجِعُونَ$$

"To Allah we belong and to Him is our return."

CHAPTER 27
THE BEAUTIFUL FEATURES OF RASULULLAH ﷺ

Rasulullah ﷺ was neither too tall nor too short. He was of average height. He had a fairly large head which was the right size for his body. He had a thick beard. His head and beard had about 25 grey strands of hairs. His face was bright and handsome. Whoever saw his beautiful face described it to be bright like the full moon.

His perspiration had a special fragrance. When drops of his perspiration fell from his face, they looked like pearls. Hadhrat Anas ؓ says that I did not touch any silk softer than the palms of Rasulullah ﷺ, and I did not smell any musk and amber more fragrant than the fragrance that came out from the body of Rasulullah ﷺ.

The seal of prophet-hood was between his shoulders, closer to the right shoulder. There was a piece of red flesh similar to that of a pigeon's egg between Rasulullah's ﷺ two shoulders.

This seal of prophet-hood was a special sign of his prophet-hood and was mentioned in the previous Holy Books and also by the previous Ambiya of Allah Ta'ala. The Ulama of the Bani Israa'eel used to see this and recognise Rasulullah ﷺ as the last Nabi, about whom the previous Ambiya had given good news, and that the seal of prophet-hood which they had mentioned was found in Rasulullah ﷺ. This seal of prophet-hood was like a certificate from Allah Ta'ala to prove his prophet-hood.

Chapter Twenty Seven – The Blessed Features of Rasulullah ﷺ

Some Ahaadith say that this seal of prophet-hood which was on Rasulullah's ﷺ back seemed to have the words Muhammad Rasulullah naturally written on it.

Rasulullah's ﷺ hair would most of the time reach his ear lobes and sometimes go past that. He used to comb his hair and also apply surmah (antimony) to his eyes. He used surma eventhough his eyes had the natural look of having surmah.

Rasulullah's ﷺ eyes were large and wide (but the correct size for his face). They were quite black. There was a very fine line of hair from his chest to his navel. His upper arms and feet were fleshy. When he walked, it seemed that he raised his feet with force as if he was going down hill.

His blessed body and bright face were beautified by all types of beauty. Apart from smiling, Rasulullah ﷺ did not laugh with his mouth wide open. It is stated in the Hadith that he looked like Hadhrat Ibraaheem (alayhis salaam) the most, in his ways and appearance.

Rasulullah's ﷺ Blessed Beard

Rasulullah ﷺ had a thick beard. Rasulullah ﷺ did not trim it completely. However, he used to trim his moustache. He would sometimes trim those hairs of the beard that stuck out (of the normal shape of the beard) so that it does not look untidy and unkept. The beard was a Sunnah practice of all the Prophets of Allah Ta'ala.

The beard is not only a Sunnah of Nabi Muhammad ﷺ and the way of Islam, rather it is a Sunnah of all the Ambiya (who were about 124 000). A Hadith states that the beard is from among the Sunnah practices of all the Ambiya.

The Clothing of Rasulullah ﷺ

Rasulullah's ﷺ clothes used to be very simple. He led a very simple life. His clothes were a sheet, a kurtah, a cloak and a shawl – many of which used to have patches. He used to like green clothes. His clothes were usually white in colour.

The sheet that he wore was a Yemeni sheet which had green and red lines on it. He used to like this sheet a lot. He stopped men from wearing full red garments.

His hat (topi) used to stick to his head. He never wore a high hat. Rasulullah ﷺ always wore a hat under his turban. He used to say: "The difference between us and the kuffaar is that we tie our turbans on our hats."

When Rasulullah ﷺ tied his turban, one end of it would hang between his shoulders. Sometimes, he would cause it to hang to the left or to the right. Sometimes he would tie it below his chin. Rasulullah ﷺ said: "During the battles of Badr and Hunayn, Allah Ta'ala sent such angels to help me who were wearing turbans. These angels are mentioned in the Qur-aan: 'Five thousand angels on marked horses.'"

Once, Rasulullah ﷺ saw trousers being sold in the market of Mina. He liked it and said that it is more concealing (able to cover) than a lungi. Rasulullah ﷺ bought the trouser but it is not confirmed that he wore it.

Rasulullah ﷺ liked kurtahs a lot. The opening of his kurtah used to be at the chest. At times, the buttons used to be open.

Rasulullah ﷺ used to wear leather socks (moza) and make masah (passing of wet hands) on them.

Rasulullah's ﷺ pillow was made of leather. It was filled with palm leaves. Sometimes, Rasulullah ﷺ used to sleep on a straw mat.

Chapter Twenty Seven – The Blessed Features of Rasulullah ﷺ

Rasulullah ﷺ had a silver ring which he used to wear. When Rasulullah ﷺ began writing letters to the rulers of Rome, Abyssinia, etc. he made a silver ring which had the words Muhammad, Rasool, Allah written on three separate lines. The reason for making this ring was that the kings did not accept any letters that did not have a seal. This ring was used as a seal.

Rasulullah ﷺ wore flat sandals which had a layer at the bottom and two straps on the top. He would put his mubaarak toes in these straps.

Rasulullah ﷺ also had a black woollen shawl which had patches on it. A black woollen shawl with patches is also a Sunnah of the Ambiya of Allah Ta'ala. This was also worn by the Auliyaa (friends) of Allah Ta'ala and the pious.

CONCLUSION

We make dua that Allah Ta'ala accepts this humble work and make it a means of earning His pleasure and the pleasure of Rasulullah ﷺ. May Allah Ta'ala bless us with a good end for us, our children and the entire Ummah. We make dua that He allows us to enjoy the intercession of Nabi Muhammad ﷺ, to be present at his fountain of abundance (pond of kausar), and to drink from its water. Aameen.

وَآخِرُ دَعْوَانَا أَنِ الْحَمْدُ لِلّٰهِ رَبِّ الْعَالَمِيْنَ وَالصَّلَاةُ وَالسَّلَامُ عَلٰى حَبِيْبِهٖ سَيِّدِ الْأَوَّلِيْنَ وَالْآخِرِيْنَ وَعَلٰى آلِهٖ وَأَصْحَابِهٖ وَعُلَمَاۤءِ أُمَّتِهٖ وَ أَوْلِيَاۤءِ زُمْرَتِهٖ أَجْمَعِيْنَ وَ عَلَيْنَا مَعَهُمْ يَا أَرْحَمَ الرَّاحِمِيْنَ وَيَا أَكْرَمَ الْأَكْرَمِيْنَ وَأَجْوَدَ الْأَجْوَدِيْنَ وَخَيْرَ الْمَسْئُوْلِيْنَ وَيَا خَيْرَ الْمُعْطِيْنَ آمِيْنَ يَا رَبَّ الْعَالَمِيْنَ.

www.ingramcontent.com/pod-product-compliance
Lightning Source LLC
LaVergne TN
LVHW012036070526
838202LV00056B/5516